A GU

MW01031049

A GUIDE TO THE BIBLE

Antonio Fuentes

FOUR COURTS PRESS · DUBLIN

This book is published by
Four Courts Press
7 Malpas Street, Dublin 8
www.four-courts-press.ie

First printed in 1987; reprinted 1993, 1999, 2002, 2004.

© original Antonio Fuentes 1983

© translation Michael Adams 1987

Translated from
Que Dice La Biblia,
Ediciones Universidad de Navarra, S.A.,
Pamplona 1983.

Nihil obstat: Stephen J. Greene, censor deputatus.
Imprimi potest: + Joseph A. Carroll, Diocesan Administrator, 25 August 1987
(The Nihil obstat and Imprimi potest are a declaration
that a book or publication is considered
to be free from doctrinal or moral error.
This declaration does not imply approval of,
or agreement with, the contents, opinions or statements expressed.)

BRITISH LIBRARY CATALOGUING IN PUBLICATION DATA

A catalogue record for this book is available from the British Library.

ISBN 1-85182-022-1

ACKNOWLEDGMENT
With the exception of that on page 170, the
maps in the book have all been taken, with permission, from
Jewish History Atlas by Martin Gilbert,
with cartography by Arthur Banks and terry Bicknell,
3rd edition (Weidenfeld and Nicolson, London 1985).

Printed in Ireland
by Colour Books Ltd, Dublin.

Contents

Part Two: The New Testament

List of illustrations

TABLES

General introduction

Of all the books in the world the Bible must surely be the most widely distributed, the most accessible to people; but that does not mean that it is in fact read as much as it might be; and certainly it is an easy enough book to misunderstand. We often meet up with people who know nothing about Holy Scripture and the wealth of truth it contains: this is true of many Christians and many Catholics. It quite often happens that people attending classes on Sacred Scripture get all interested in reading the Bible: but their interest wanes quite quickly. Sometimes this is just because they get tired but more often it is because they do not have a good overall grasp of the Bible — of what it is and how its books fit together.

This may be the reason why some readers are shocked by the human weaknesses of key characters in the Bible story, failing to see that God used these characters with their vices and shortcomings — as well as their undeniable virtues — to demonstrate his mercy and to give man hope of future salvation. One of the encouraging things about reading the Bible is that it shows us that man is never alone and has never been forsaken by God, no matter how vicious and rebellious his behaviour.

No other book, however important from the doctrinal or spiritual point of view, can match the Bible when it comes to learning about the nature of God and his plans for us; no other book shows up so well the love God has for what he has created, or so assuages man's deep yearning for truth and happiness. Pope John Paul II asserts that Sacred Scripture "is truly divine, because it belongs to God truly and genuinely: God himself inspired it, God confirmed it, God spoke it through the sacred writers — Moses, the Prophets, the Evangelists, the Apostles — and, above all, through his Son, our only Lord, in both the Old and the New Testament; it is true that the intensity and depth of the revelation varies, but there is not the least shadow of contradiction [between one part of Scripture and another]."[1]

1 Apostolic Letter *Patres Ecclesiae*, 2 January 1980.

Indeed: God did inspire Scripture and did confirm it. This is something we learned as children and something we are reminded about by the Church. However, some people ask: How can you say this when the Bible itself makes mistakes about such things as the creation of the world, the nature of the stars, or the dating of certain events? They refuse to accept that "all that the inspired authors or sacred writers affirm should be regarded as affirmed by the Holy Spirit" and that therefore "the books of Scripture firmly, faithfully and without error teach that truth which God, for the sake of our salvation, wished to see confided to the Sacred Scriptures."[2]

Before starting to read the Bible there is one thing we should keep very much in mind: God is the principal author of Sacred Scripture. However, there is something else closely connected with that — the fact that to communicate his revelation to us God "chose certain men who, all the while he employed them in their task, made full use of their powers and faculties so that, though he acted in them and by them, it was as true authors that they consigned to writing whatever he wanted written, and no more."[3]

God made use of certain people — to whom he gave special grace — to write the various sacred books; but this did not mean that their personality or education or style changed as a result. It simply meant that God expresssly desired them to pass on his message of salvation, which forms the core of the Bible and the set of revealed truths which constitute the "deposit" of faith. These writers naturally had to use the language of their time; despite its limitations the Holy Spirit used it to get across the message of salvation with total accuracy.

In this connexion John Paul II pointed out to biblical scholars that "the language of the Bible is to some degree linked to language which changed over the course of time.... But this only reaffirms the paradox of the proclamation of revelation and, more specifically, the paradox of the Christian proclamation: people and events at particular points in history become the bearers of an absolute and transcendent message."[4]

It is therefore worth stressing three dimensions of this subject which are closely linked to one another:

1. The Bible is first and foremost a collection of *religious truths* revealed by God progressively over the centuries. These truths form the object of our faith: we must accept them unhesitatingly once the Magisterium of the Church tells us that they are in that category.

2 Vatican II, Dogm. Const. *Dei Verbum* 11.
3 Ibid.
4 Address to the Pontifical Biblical Commission, 26 April 1979.

2. These perennial and unchanging truths are connected with a series of *historical facts*, events experienced by the people who were the direct receivers of this divine message and who later became the human authors of the sacred books, in some instances, or the first links of a living oral tradition which sooner or later would be written down under the inspiration of the Holy Spirit.

3. God chose these people and gave them a message of salvation, that is, he revealed himself to them through words and actions. However — and this is important — God made use of the language and modes of speech proper to the time in question, without which it would have been practically impossible for those men to understand what God was revealing to them. If this language had not been used, it would also have been impossible to transmit this revelation or commit it to writing.

All this helps to explain two other very important matters:

a) that the *revealed truths* which the Bible contains can be *known ever more deeply*, to the degree that the human mind — with the help of grace — penetrates the essential core of the message of revelation. We should remember that God's revelation is *progressive*: it advances and deepens over the course of the centuries, reaching its apex in the New Testament. With the death of the last Apostle, St John, public revelation comes to an end: the body of faith entrusted by Jesus to the Church can grow no further in terms of its extent; but it is indeed possible for man to understand revealed truths better: this is what biblical exegesis and theology are all about.

b) the inspired writers reported events *as they saw them*, in line with the cultural and mental outlook of the period in which they lived. For example, they will say that the sun "goes down" or that it "stopped". They would be telling lies if they said otherwise. The only aspect of this which is of interest to the reader of the Bible is knowing what people mean when they express themselves in this way: if we realize what they mean then we will understand the core of revealed truth much better. It is God himself — in the case of the sun stopping for Joshua, or any other miraculous event — who intervenes in history by using natural occurrences and changing them to suit his plans, so that man thereby discovers that it is God who is addressing him, who is telling him that he is not alone but that God is his protector. At other times God intervenes in a completely supernatural way simply because he chooses to act in that way, without reference to any human *rationale*; as, for example, when Mary conceived the Son of God in her womb through the action of the Holy Spirit, without the intervention of man and with her virginity being preserved intact; and so a created being became God's Mother, through special grace.

All this shows that the Bible does not contain answers to the sort of scientific problems that man has asked over the centuries. It has nothing to tell us about the atomic structure of the universe, about molecules, about genetics and the great discovery of DNA. St Augustine said as much to his contemporaries, who were very concerned about this matter: "The sacred writers, or better the Holy Spirit who speaks through them, do not seek to teach men these things [purely scientific matters], for these things are of no avail as far as their salvation is concerned."[5]

As we can see from reading the Bible, what really concerns God, when he reveals himself to man, is man himself, his happiness; love is the only reason why he offers salvation to each individual person. If he sometimes does speak of and reveal natural things which man could grasp by reason alone — by reflecting on the things around him — the reason he does so is to show man the way to follow to avoid going astray, to make good speed, and become well-disposed to responding freely, by an act of faith, to the word which God is addressing to him personally.

God could have chosen to reveal himself in a different way; but he decided to do so in a way suited to man's rational nature. To do so he has used a language accessible to human reason; but the limits of reason are soon reached, beyond which man must take what God says on trust. The frontier of human reason is precisely the point where man enters the mystery of God One and Triune, the mystery of God's life and his relationship with the created world: there the mysteries of creation, incarnation and redemption are encountered.

What should we say, therefore, about the scientific errors which are apparently to be found in the Bible? Our answer would be that the Bible is true history — not in the modern sense of the word, but in the sense that the events it reports really did happen in time and space to certain specific people. What we have in the Bible is sacred history, a history of our salvation. This explains how "the works performed by God in the history of salvation show forth and bear out the doctrine and realities signified by the words; the words, for their part, proclaim the works, and bring to light the mystery they contain."[6] In no sense can it be said that the Bible contains error (anyone who tried to treat it as just another human book would be the one making a mistake): so much so that there is no reason for

5 *De Genesi ad litteram*, II, 9, 20.
6 Vatican II, Dogm. Const. *Dei Verbum* 2.

our celebrating when important archaeological discoveries corroborate
what the Bible says.

Over forty years ago, in *Divino afflante Spiritu*, Pius XII had this
to say about being on the alert against attacks on Sacred Scripture
— and it holds good today: "Not infrequently . . . when some persons
reproachingly charge the sacred writers with some historical error
or inaccuracy in the recording of facts, on closer examination it turns
out to be nothing else than those customary modes of expression and
narration peculiar to the ancients, which used to be employed in the
mutual dealings of social life and which in fact were sanctioned by
common usage. When then such modes of expression are met with
in the sacred text, which, being meant for men, is couched in human
language, justice demands that they be no more taxed with error than
when they occur in the ordinary intercourse of daily life. By this
knowledge and exact appreciation of the modes of speaking and
writing in use among the ancients can be solved many difficulties,
which are raised against the veracity and historical value of the divine
Scriptures."[7]

Therefore, we accept the Bible on faith and not because it is true
history (as the latest archaeological finds in ancient Babylonia,
northern Egypt and Qumran show) or because of its literary quality
or the sublimity of its teachings but because it is the revealed word
of God: "The 'obedience of faith' (Rom 16:26) must be given to God
as he reveals himself. By faith man freely commits his entire self
to God, making 'the full submission of his intellect and will to God
who reveals' and willingly assenting to the revelation given to
him."[8]

The final point I should like to make here is about the need to
avoid making the mistake of trying to understand the Bible on its
own and on one's own. "Since Sacred Scripture must be read and
interpreted with its divine authorship in mind, no less attention must
be devoted to the content and unity of the whole of Scripture, taking
into account the tradition of the entire Church and the analogy of
faith, if we are to derive their true meaning from the sacred texts"[9]

If one takes these precautions there is no reason why the Bible
should in any sense endanger our faith: on the contrary. In fact the
Church itself is forever recommending that we read Sacred Scripture:
"'Ignorance of the Scriptures is ignorance of Christ' (St Jerome).

7 Enc. *Divino afflante Spiritu*.
8 *Dei Verbum* 5.
9 Ibid. 12.

Therefore, let them go gladly to the sacred text itself, whether in the sacred liturgy, which is full of the divine words, or in devout reading, or in such suitable exercises and various other helps which, with the approval and guidance of the pastors of the Church, are happily spreading everywhere in our day. Let them remember, however, that prayer should accompany the reading of Sacred Scripture, so that a dialogue takes place between God and man. For 'we speak to him when we pray; we listen to him when we read the divine oracles' (St Ambrose)."[10]

Obviously, nothing can take the place of direct reading of the Bible. The aim of the present work is to provide short commentaries on the various books of the Bible, commentaries written for the general reader — the type of reader who is not interested in detailed exegesis but, rather, wants to know what God is saying in the Bible, and what was the social context in which each book was written. I hope this will help provide a better overview of the whole Bible and make it easier for the reader to see the gradual unfolding of the biblical message. This message has to do primarily with the promise of the Messiah, a promise made in the early pages of *Genesis* which provides the focus of the faith and deep hope harboured by the patriarchs and prophets, and of the yearnings, sufferings and joys of the people of the Old Alliance in the course of its history.

Finally, when we reach the New Testament we will see this message of salvation reaching its climax with the redemption won for us by Jesus Christ on the cross. This redemption brings us forgiveness of sins and enables us to become true children of God: that is, it enables us to savour happiness in this life and gives us the opportunity to see God face to face in heaven. Christ, the Word Incarnate, thus becomes the key to history and the true centre of mankind; for, as St Paul states, "in him all things were created, in heaven and on earth, visible and invisible, whether thrones or dominions or principalities or authorities — all things were created through him and in him. He is before all things, and in him all things hold together" (Col 1:16-17).

*　　*　　*

I should like to thank all those colleagues and friends who helped me in various ways to produce this book — particularly my colleagues at the University of Navarre. I hope this book will help to make many

10 Ibid.

people more interested in Sacred Scripture; that it will play its part in granting that wish which St Augustine expressed: "May this world estranged from God come to hear him and believe in him, and by believing hope and by hoping love."[11]

---

11 *De catechizandis rudibus*, 4, 8.

PART ONE

THE OLD TESTAMENT

Introduction to the Old Testament

The Bible consists of two quite distinct parts — the Old Testament and the New. The Old Testament, the earlier part, is a collection of inspired* books,[1] all predating Jesus Christ*, which have God as their author and are therefore accepted by the Church. By this acceptance, by being in the Church's "canon"* of Scripture, we know which books are really inspired and therefore free from error.

The books of the Old Testament are, however, open to a later, definitive revelation, the revelation contained in the New Testament, in which all the prophecies about the Messiah come true. When God reveals himself to man, it is as if he were unveiling his own intimate, personal life, showing himself as he really is. He does this because of his infinite love for man; he treats men as his friends and invites them to share in his own divine life by means of grace. Jesus Christ, in whom God's revelation shines forth,[2] leads us to discover this truth and the salvation which it contains. As Vatican II put it, "the economy of the Old Testament was deliberately so orientated that it should prepare for and declare in prophecy the coming of Christ, redeemer of all men, and of the messianic kingdom (cf. Lk 24:44; Jn 5:39; 1 Pet 1:10), and should indicate it by means of different types (cf. 1 Cor 10:11)."[3]

We should not suppose, however, that the books of the Old Testament have no value in themselves, for, as St Paul says, "whatever was written in former days was written for our instruction, that by steadfastness and by the encouragement of the scriptures we might have hope"(Rom 15:4). Thus, as we have already said, God is the author who inspired the books of both the Old and the New Testament.[4] "These books, even though they contain matters

1 See *Inspiration* in the Glossary in the Appendix to this book. Words given in the Glossary are asterisked in the text at the point where they first occur.

2 Vatican II, Dogm. Const. *Dei Verbum* 2.

3 Ibid. 15.

4 There is no room in this short book to go into the history and formation of the canon of the Bible or to explain in any detail the nature of the charism of inspiration. For further reading in this connexion see: A. Robert and A. Feuillet, *Introduction to the Old Testament*

imperfect and provisional, nevertheless show us authentic divine teaching. Christians should accept with veneration these writings which give expression to a lively sense of God, which are a storehouse of sublime teaching on God and of sound wisdom on human life, as well as a wonderful treasury of prayers; in them, too, the mystery of our salvation is present in a hidden way."[5]

Sometimes reference is made to the *Testament* and sometimes to the *Alliance** (or *Covenant*), depending on whether one is stressing the Hebrew word *berith* (= covenant, alliance), the origin of the early economy of salvation, or, instead, the death of him who brings about our salvation, whose *testament* was sealed by his redemptive death on the cross.

Probably this is the best point at which to list the books in the canon of both Testaments, which I do in the order in which they are given in the New Vulgate:

OLD TESTAMENT

PENTATEUCH

Genesis	Gen
Exodus	Ex
Leviticus	Lev
Numbers	Num
Deuteronomy	Deut

HISTORICAL BOOKS

Joshua	Josh
Judges	Jud
Ruth	Ruth
Samuel, 1 and 2	Sam
Kings, 1 and 2	Kings
Chronicles, 1 and 2	Chron
Ezra	Ezra
Nehemiah	Neh
Tobit	Tob
Judith	Jud
Esther	Esther
Maccabees, 1 and 2	Mac

WISDOM AND POETICAL BOOKS

Job	Job
Psalms	Ps
Proverbs	Prov
Ecclesiastes (Qoheleth)	Eccles
Song of Songs	Song
Wisdom	Wis
Sirach (Ecclesiasticus)	Sir

PROPHETICAL BOOKS

Isaiah	Is
Jeremiah	Jer
Lamentationes	Lam
Baruch	Bar
Ezekiel	Ezek
Daniel	Dan
Hosea	Hos
Joel	Joel
Amos	Amos
Obadiah	Obad
Jonah	Jon
Micah	Mic
Nahum	Nahum
Habakkuk	Hab
Zephaniah	Zeph
Haggai	Hag
Zechariah	Zech
Malachi	Mal

(New York 1968) and *Introduction to the New Testament* (New York 1965); Bernard Orchard and others (eds.), *A Catholic Commentary on Holy Scripture* (cited henceforth as *CCHS*) (London 1953); F. Spadafora, *Diccionario Bíblico* (Barcelona 1968); L. Arnaldich and others, *Manual Bíblico* (Madrid 1968).

5 *Dei Verbum* 5.

NEW TESTAMENT

GOSPELS

St Matthew............................. Mt
St Mark................................. Mk
St Luke................................. Lk
St John................................. Jn

ACTS OF THE
APOSTLES........................... Acts

LETTERS OF ST PAUL

Romans.................................. Rom
Corinthians, 1 and 2 Cor
Galatians............................... Gal
Ephesians.............................. Eph
Philippians............................ Phil
Colossians............................. Col

Thessalonians, 1 and 2........... Thess
Timothy, 1 and 2.................. Tim
Titus...................................... Tit
Philemon............................... Philem
Hebrews................................ Heb

LETTER OF ST JAMES   Jas

LETTERS OF ST
PETER, 1 and 2.................. Pet

LETTERS OF ST
JOHN, 1, 2 and 3.................. Jn

LETTER OF ST JUDE   Jude

REVELATION
(APOCALYPSE)................... Rev

I should also point out at this stage that in the Hebrew or Massoretic text of the Bible the books of the Old Testament are grouped in this way:

1. *Torah* (= Law). This consists of the five books of the Law, which make up the Pentateuch.
2. *Nebîîm* (= Prophets). In addition to the prophetic books properly so-called (from *Isaiah* to *Malachi*, who are called "later prophets") this group also contains the historical books of *Joshua, Judges, Samuel* and *Kings*, which are called "earlier prophets."
3. *Ketûbîm* (= Writings or Sacred Writings). This group comprises all the other books.

However, it should be borne in mind that Jews and Protestants do not include these books in their canon: *Tobit, Judith, Wisdom, Baruch, Sirach (Ecclesiasticus)* and *1 and 2 Maccabees*. Nor do they include these parts of other books: Esther 10:4-16; Dan 3:24-90 and chap. 13-14.

Some books are called "deuterocanonical" (Protestants regard them as apocryphal) because in the early period there was no unanimity among the Fathers as to their sacred origin; whereas there was never any debate about the "protocanonical" books, which were always regarded as inspired.

The Church exercised its infallibility at the Council of Trent in the sixteenth century when it identified the canon of Scripture — just at the time when the Reformers were rejecting the deuterocanonical books of the Old Testament on the grounds that they were not in the Hebrew canon. Since the Church received the Old Testament from our Lord and from the Apostles, on the Church's authority we accept each and every book in the Church's canon as inspired.

The Church has always proclaimed the unity of the two Testaments — which Vatican II described in this way: "God, the inspirer and author of the books of both Testaments, in his wisdom has so brought it about that the New should be hidden in the Old and that the Old should be made manifest in the New. For, although Christ founded the New Covenant in his blood (cf. Lk 22:20; 1 Cor 11:25), still the books of the Old Testament, all of them caught up into the Gospel message, attain and show forth their full meaning in the New Testament (cf. Mt 5:17; Lk 24:27; Rom 16:25-26; 2 Cor 3:14-16) and, in their turn, shed light on it and explain it."[6]

6 Ibid. 16.

The Pentateuch

The first five books of the Bible are called the "Pentateuch";[1] the name comes from a Greek word meaning "five boxes" — a reference to the boxes in which the scrolls of the Law were kept. The Jews referred to these books as "hat tôrah"(the Law), distinguishing them from the rest of the Old Testament — the Nebîîm (= Prophets) and the Ketûbîm (= Writings).

In the Jewish translation of the Old Testament into Greek, a version known as the Septuagint,* these five books carry the following names, which are used today — *Genesis, Exodus, Leviticus, Numbers and Deuteronomy*. The names give a rough indication of the contents of each book. Thus, we could say that *Genesis* deals with the origin of the world and of men, from creation up to the formation of Israel as a people, taking us up to just before the Jews leave Egypt. *Exodus* deals with the Jews' escape from Egypt, under Moses' leadership; the miracle of the parting of the Red Sea; and the period they spent in the wilderness of Sinai, when God gave them the Law; this was sanctioned by a Covenant or Alliance (*berith*) between God and the Jewish people, who became from that point onwards God's chosen people, specially called by him. *Leviticus* contains regulations about the way Israel should worship its God, the one true God; here pride of place is given to the tribe of Levi, which has a special priestly role. *Numbers* takes its name from the lists of people given in its early chapters, although it goes on to describe the experiences of the Jews in the wilderness. Finally, *Deuteronomy* (the word literally means "second law") summarizes the content of the Law, and earlier regulations for the benefit of those who were born after the Jews left Egypt or else were still very young at that time; this book, consisting of the last discourses of Moses, obviously has a lot of doctrinal content but it is poignant since it is Moses' farewell to his people, people

---

1 The Greek title of Pentateuch was first used by a second century Gnostic called Ptolomy; latinized later by Tertullian, it was St Isidore who gave it its final neuter form of *Pentateuchum*. For a fuller treatment of the Pentateuch, cf. E.F. Sutcliffe in *CCHS*, sections 126ff.

whom he loved so much and must leave before they start their conquest of the promised land.

The Pentateuch is a great, passionate historical record based on two main factors — God's plan for the salvation of all mankind after the sin of Adam and Eve, and the role of the people of Israel in carrying out that plan, chosen as it was to be Christ's instrument up to the time of the coming of the Messiah. Here we have a true history substantially deriving from Moses, written under God's inspiration; it is a history which can be properly understood only in the light of its purpose — God's self-revelation to man. Everything else contained in this history — the ages of the patriarchs, the long genealogies, dates, locations — are simply a backdrop which the narrator considers useful for illustrating God's saving plan.

The Pentateuch contains teachings of permanent historical and doctrinal value. Old Testament religion hinges on one unique factor — God's revelation. In making his inner self known, God takes the initiative; he tells man who he is and what he has done; he enters human history to let man see that he, God, is a person, the creator of the entire universe, man included, and that he loves man because he is holy, almighty, and merciful even though he transcends all creation. In the Pentateuch God reveals to us that mankind is descended from two people, Adam and Eve; he also reveals the existence of original sin — the ultimate cause of every kind of evil — and his promise of future redemption.

To effect redemption, he chose a people, the Jewish people, in whom all the nations of the earth would be blessed (Gen 12:28); this promise was kept in the Person and work of Jesus Christ, and all the history narrated in the Pentateuch gravitates towards Jesus, though in the obscurity typical of prophecy. Events like the sacrifice of Isaac, the passage through the Red Sea, and the Passover can, in the light of the New Testament, be seen to prefigure the redemptive sacrifice of Christ, Baptism and the Christian Pasch. This explains why the Pentateuch is the most important part of the Old Testament, from the historical as well as from the religious and theological point of view.

Before going on to look at these first books of the Bible it should be pointed out that the Church has always regarded Moses as the true human author of the Pentateuch, that is, as the man God inspired to commit to writing what he wanted to be recorded. Even so, the Church does not mean that Moses was the final redactor of these books — he may well have used scribes, for example — or that it would be erroneous to think that some parts of the Pentateuch may have been edited later or even be post-Mosaic additions by prophets or writers — who for that purpose would also have had the charism of inspiration. In its decree of 27 June 1906 the Pontifical Biblical Commission rejected the views of critics who cast doubt on the Mosaic authorship of the Pentateuch, on the grounds that their arguments were not of such weight as to justify setting aside "the cumulative evidence of many passages of both Testaments, the unbroken unanimity of the Jewish people, and furthermore the constant tradition of the Church besides the internal indications furnished by the text itself." In other words, the Commission argued that Moses was substantially the author of the Pentateuch. It stated this more explicitly in a 1948 letter to Cardinal Suhard in which it recognized that undoubtedly the Pentateuch contains written sources or oral traditions which Moses used; it even spoke of a "gradual increase of Mosaic laws due to the social and religious conditions of later times, a process manifest also in the historical narratives."[2]

Finally, I should like to recommend to new readers of the Pentateuch (and the same applies to the other sacred books of the Bible) that they focus not so much on the details of the story, on its anecdotic framework, as on the spiritual atmosphere which imbues the whole narrative and the revealed truths which underlie it. I say this because the reader may be surprised to find that many of the protagonists were far from exemplary as far as some aspects of their moral behaviour went; they should, however, remember that real history is different from fairy tales; the marvellous panorama of the Bible does contain dark patches which result from man's misuse of his freedom; but God uses the good and the bad to bring his plans into effect.

Genesis

The first book of the Pentateuch, *Genesis*, gives an account of the origin of all created things and acts, as it were, as an elaborate introduction to God's later revelation to Israel through Moses. It summarizes the early stages in the history of mankind from the creation to the death of Joseph the Patriarch. Unlike the book of *Exodus*, which follows it, and in which the history of Israel as a *people* begins, *Genesis* contains the history of Israel's ancestors, the great

2 Cf. *CCHS*, sections 47ff.

patriarchs — Abraham, Isaac, Jacob, Joseph — and therefore is the history of a *family*, Abraham's, from which the chosen people stemmed. Before concentrating on this family, in order to explain its background the first eleven chapters deal with the history of the world and of man, the history of civilization and culture, tracing the early outlines of God's plan of salvation and the role Israel is to play in it.[3]

These early chapters, written in popular language, rich in imagery, provide answers to the kind of questions every human being, in any age, is inclined to ask: Who made me? Where does the world come from? What is life all about? What is the meaning of suffering, sickness and death? What explanation is there for war and human strife? Man wants answers to these questions. He wants to know how he can re-establish peace, how and by whom can he be restored to spiritual health: he realizes his limitations and those of others and yet, in the depths of his soul he feels an infinite capacity for peace and happiness which no one and nothing on earth can satisfy.

Opening the Bible and reading these first chapters is like having a huge family album, full of colour and life, in which God shows us not only the origin of the universe but also the causes of man's unhappiness, the reason for his sense of loneliness and the origin of suffering and death. But we find more than that: we find that creation results from God's love, and that it is love which leads him to announce man's future salvation.

However, readers may be surprised to find that there is a lot left unsaid and that some of the explanations contained in these early chapters seem inadequate or farfetched. For example, what does the Bible mean by saying that God created the world in just seven days? What is this about God creating man from dust? Is it not rather childish to say that the first woman was made out of man's rib? Surely God had no hands for shaping man's body; he did not work like a surgeon to take out his rib and sew him up again. . . . Objections of this sort mean that a person does not understand biblical language, particularly not the literary genre of the first three chapters of *Genesis*: the inspired writers were using the language of their time, which was culturally backward: it was the only language available to them, and the only one their audience could understand.

We will remember that, in making himself known, it was not God's intention to give us scientific statements: he was giving us only what we needed to grasp basic religious truths. We should not expect to

3 For further reading see A. Clamer, *La Genèse* (Paris 1953); E.F. Sutcliffe, 'Genesis' in *CCHS*, sections136ff; F. Spadafora, *op. cit.*

find here a scientific explanation of the creation of the universe or the origin of man. The Bible has nothing to say about when the world was created,[4] or about various geological periods; nor, let it be said, does it provide any proof of the theory of evolution.

The teaching authority of the Church has rejected "absolute" evolutionary theory, which says that man — all of man — is descended from one of the higher animals. But, as *Humanae generis* put it, "The Magisterium of the Church leaves the doctrine of evolution an open question, as long as it confines its speculations to the development, from other living matter already in existence, of the human body. (That souls are immediately created by God is a view which the Catholic faith imposes on us.) In the present state of scientific and theological opinion, this question may be legitimately canvassed by research, and by discussion between experts on both sides. At the same time, the reasons for and against either view must be weighed and adjudged with all seriousness, fairness, and restraint; and there must be readiness on all sides to accept the arbitrament of the Church, as being entrusted by Christ with the task of interpreting the Scriptures aright, and the duty of safeguarding the doctrines of the faith. There are some who take rash advantage of this liberty of debate, by treating the subject as if the whole matter were closed — as if the discoveries hitherto made, and the arguments based on them, were sufficiently certain to prove, beyond doubt, the development of the human body from other living matter already in existence. They forget, too, that there are certain references to the subject in the source of divine revelation, which call for the greatest caution and prudence in discussing it."[5]

What the sacred text provides, therefore, is revealed doctrine about the basic principles of our faith, clothed in primitive literary language. The main principles it contains are these:

The creation of the universe In a sober style, which is quite theological and almost ritual, in a logical order and in the kind of way a teacher puts things to make it easy for his pupils to remember them, the first creation narrative (Gen 1:1-2:4a) describes the creation of the universe in ascending order, that is, working up from less perfect things (earth, sky, animals) to the most perfect (man). In describing

---

4 Geology and paleontology usually reckon that the earth is between four and five thousand million years old. *Homo erectus*, in the Stone Age, has been estimated as appearing about two million years ago, and *homo sapiens* as 120,000 years ago. All that *Genesis* says is that "in the beginning God created the heavens and the earth" and that man was created in his "image and likeness".

5 Pius XII, Enc. *Humanae generis*, EB 616.

creation as happening over a seven-day period the sacred writer has a mainly didactic purpose: he wants to show the people of Israel that it was God's express will that they should observe the sabbath rest and treat that day as especially holy and therefore he says that God himself "rested on the seventh day."

His purpose is also didactic (and in this he was inspired by God) in setting out the stages in which God went about creation after his initial act of creation, which consisted in creating out of nothing the chaotic mass described in Gen 1:2.

First he introduces order into this chaos:
 Dividing light from darkness
 Dividing the higher waters from the lower waters
 Distributing land, sea, plants

Then he ornaments creation:
 Sun, moon, stars
 Fish, birds
 Animals
 Man

A careful reading of the verses shows that it was not God's intention to give exact scientific information about the creation of each of these separate beings. His purpose was primarily one of teaching religious truths which we might summarize as follows:

1. All creation is the work of God alone. With creation time begins, as a means of measuring physical phenomena. Creation therefore occurs without there being any pre-existing matter. Hence the first effect of creation is the appearance of the chaotic mass previously mentioned.

2. This shows that only God is eternal. Everything else owes its existence to God, that is, is God's creature: which means that God is distinct from the world and prior to it; he neither proceeds from nor depends on that "initial chaos", as Babylonian or Assyrian cosmogonies make out: he transcends and is distinct from matter.

3. This creating, eternal and totally transcendent being is the only true God; he cannot be confused with the polytheistic and pantheistic gods believed in at the time *Genesis* was written and to which the Israelites themselves were very inclined. Since God was separate and distinct from the universe he created, the Israelites were shown, in this new light of revelation, that God could not be confused with the sun or the moon or with the gods of the Assyrians: anything other

than the transcendental God, the one true God, was his creation and therefore unworthy of worship.

4. Finally, God appears in this first creation account as almighty: "God said" . . . "and so it was." Creation calls for no effort on his part: full of power and majesty, he provides everything with existence; and, furthermore, he maintains in existence everything he has created, by an act of his will. In creating things he communicates to them his goodness: "God saw everything that he had made, and behold, it was very good" (Gen 1:31). It could not be otherwise, because there is only one creator, God, who is an infinite being and therefore infinitely good.

The connection between the *Genesis* **account and non-biblical cosmogonies** Archaeological excavations in the Near East have unearthed cosmogonical texts connected with mythological traditions about the origin of the world — Syro-Babylonian, Egyptian, Phoenician etc. When these are deciphered and compared with *Genesis*, we find that they contain analogies and also basic differences. For example:

Non-biblical documents

1. These are really theogonies — accounts of the origins of the gods.
2. They assign no origin to the chaotic mass, the first product of creation.
3. They have no concept of the unity of the human race: the gods created more than one human couple, and a multitude of cities.
4. They know nothing of any sabbath day of rest.

Genesis

1. This is the only cosmogony (theory of the origin of the universe) proper that is theocentric in character.
2. God the creator is one, almighty, transcendent, producing everything from nothing.
3. God formed only one human couple; the rest of the race came from them in a process of generation.
4. Genesis teaches the sabbath rest.

The analogies to be found between Sacred Scripture and non-biblical documents can be explained by reference to the existence of an initial revelation to our first parents, which was passed on and was still echoed, though in an adulterated form, in the cultures of Israel's neighbours. However, aberrations in these accounts must be attributed

to man's imagination. Whereas the people of Israel were kept free
of error, thanks to new revelations to Abraham and to Moses, other
peoples retained vestiges of primitive truth, mixed in with their various
myths.[6]

The first man and woman   One created being stands out among
all the rest as enjoying particular dignity — man. He was created
in a special way: God made him in his own image (Gen 1:27). This
creation of man is described in more detail in Gen 2:

> then the Lord God formed man of dust from the ground and breathed
> into his nostrils the breath of life; and man became a living being (Gen 2:7).

As Professor Arnaldich has pointed out, St Gregory of Nyssa noticed
the indefiniteness of the phrase used in the text, when it says that
"God created man, and by using this indeterminate phrase the text
is saying that God created mankind." However, even though the word
adam (= man, carrying no article) is indefinite, its content is then
specified: "male and female he created them", which indicates that
initially there were only two individuals in the species, man and
woman, whom God endowed with reproductive organs to enable them
to carry out the sublime task of continuing God's work, by multiplying
the individuals in the human race, generation after generation: Adam
and Eve were the first couple and therefore all other humans have
a common origin.[7]

As far as man's body is concerned, man derives from the earth;
but his soul — the breath of life — is created directly by God: to
create it God does not use any pre-existing matter. Man's soul is
completely spiritual. This means that man has certain spiritual
faculties which not only ensure his dominion over the rest of creation,
but also enable him to be gratuitously raised by God from his natural
level on to a level — the level of grace, a *super*natural level — to which
his nature gives him no right.

In addition to creating Adam, God wished him to have others of
his kind:

6   Much light has been thrown on this subject by archaeological findings since the end
of the nineteenth century. For example, cosmogonic texts have been discovered which
contain vestiges of very ancient traditions about the origin of the world — Sumerian, Assyro-
Babilonian, Egyptian etc. One of these, the Babylonian poem *Enuma Elisch*, found inscribed
on seven cuneiform tablets, is extraordinarily similar to the biblical account. This was
found in the library of Asurbanipal in 1875 and it is estimated that it goes back to the
twelfth century B.C. Cf. E. Wallis Budge, *Babylonian Legends of the Creation* (1931); R.
Labat, *Le poème-babylonien de la Creation* (1935).

7   Cf. L. Arnaldich, *El origen del mundo y del hombre según la Biblia* (Madrid 1957);
F.Ceuppens, *Origini dell'Universo e dell'Uomo secondo la Biblia* (Turin 1953).

> Then the Lord God said: "It is not good that the man should be alone;
> I will make him a helper fit for him." So out of the ground the Lord
> God formed every beast of the field and every bird of the air, and brought
> them to the man to see what he would call them; ... but for the man
> there was not found a helper fit for him. So the Lord God caused a deep
> sleep to fall upon the man, and while he slept took one of his ribs and
> closed up its place with flesh; and the rib which the Lord God had taken
> from the man he made into a woman and brought her to the man. Then
> the man said, "This at last is bone of my bones and flesh of my flesh;
> she shall be called Woman, because she was taken out of Man" (Gen
> 2:18-23).

It is interesting to note that the sacred text points up the difference
between woman and the animals. Once she is formed out of the man's
"rib"and man is awakened from his deep sleep he remembers that
he is different from all the animals. But now he has the being he
has dreamed about, who is completely like him: he exclaims
enthusiastically and gratefully: "This at last is bone of my bones
and flesh of my flesh" (2:23). That is, he recognizes the woman as
a human being, identical in nature to himself. The sacred writer
simply reports this; as in the case of man nothing specific is said
about the matter which God used in shaping woman. The only thing
which is made clear is that God worked in a direct and special way
in creating both our first parents.

The main points in this teaching about the creation of man are:

1. Man was created in a special way. God took a pre-existing piece
of matter (in this respect the creation of man was done in the same
way as that of animals) but *he infused a soul into it* — the breath of
life — which meant that man was enabled to share in God's own
life by means of grace.

2. Created in this way, man is *higher than all the animals*, whose
Lord he is, as he is over all other creatures; but man himself is
subordinate to God, his creator.

3. The dignity of woman, also created by God, stems from her
being like man, exactly the same in nature as he, created to
complement man, but in no sense to be his slave. The image of the
rib in fact confirms that God has given man and woman the same
nature and the same purpose.

4. In addition to telling us about the creation of man and woman,
the sacred text also asserts the *divine origin of the institution of marriage*;
marriage is one and indissoluble. The text specifically states that:
"Therefore a man leaves his father and his mother and cleaves to
his wife, and they become one flesh" (Gen 2:24).

Later on, in the New Testament, Jesus Christ authoritatively adds,

"So they are no longer two but one" (Mt 19:6).

5. God specifically states that the primary purpose of marriage is its fruitfulness, the generation of children: he blesses the couple and says, 'Be fruitful and multiply, and fill the earth and subdue it" (1:28). He thereby makes them cooperators in the tremendous task of generating each single, unrepeatable human being.

6. The second chapter of *Genesis* also states that there was no concupiscence of the flesh, due to the state of innocence in which our first parents were created: it tells us that after man and woman were married they "were both naked, and were not ashamed" (2:25). Their reason had perfect control over their external and internal senses and all their faculties were perfectly synchronized.

7. Man's original happiness and his elevation to the supernatural order are indicated by the images, so meaningful to orientals, of the peaceful garden and the rivers watering it; and by the ease with which Adam and Eve related to God, speaking to him face to face; they were truly God's friends.

Temptation and fall   God laid one commandment on man: "You may freely eat of every tree of the garden; but of the tree of knowledge of good and evil you shall not eat, for in the day that you eat of it you shall die" (Gen 2:16-17). This was a reasonable commandment, and man at first accepted it without raising any objection.

However, the devil,* who appears in the third chapter of Genesis in the form of a serpent, tempted the woman: "Did God say, 'You shall not eat of any tree of the garden'?" (3:1). He, who had already fallen, seeks to seduce the woman to imitate him by also disobeying God. He begins by exaggerating God's commandment; he questions God's justice and honesty and tries to undermine our first parents' trust in God.

The woman falls into his trap and begins to dialogue with the devil. At first she defends God, but she soon becomes less sure of herself as she listens to what the devil has to say. As soon as she begins to think about the forbidden tree her sensuality is awakened and it rapidly becomes more intense. At last she reaches the point where she feels herself totally attracted to the apple and mistakenly sees it as the key to contentment.

The woman's disobedience and then that of her husband constitute the first sin in the history of mankind — what we, their descendants, call the "original sin", a sin which affects all of us — the basic cause of the breakdown of man's friendship with God.

By abusing their freedom in this way, our first parents suffered death with respect to the life of grace to which God had gratuitously raised them, and they also lost what are termed their "praeternatural" gifts. God had created them to be immortal but one sin was enough to deprive them of this gift — as he had warned them (2:17). Through their sin death entered the world and, as St Paul affirms (Rom 5:12), it spread to all men because all are descended from Adam and Eve and all of us sinned in them. Physical death brought with it a whole cumulation of evils — diseases, effort demanded by work, pains, anxieties, unrestrained concupiscence, as far as the body is concerned. In the spiritual sphere, in addition to the loss of sanctifying grace, it brought disorder in man's higher faculties, resulting in pride, sloth, ambition, envy and self-assertion: in other words, estrangement from God, man's creator.

Paul VI sums up this teaching in these words: "We believe that in Adam all have sinned. From this it follows that on account of the original offence committed by him, human nature, which is common to all men, is reduced to that condition in which it must suffer the consequences of that fall. This condition is not the same as that of our first parents, for they were constituted in holiness and justice, and man had no experience of either evil or death. Consequently, fallen human nature is deprived of the economy of grace which it formerly enjoyed. It is wounded in its natural powers and subjected to the dominion of death which is transmitted to all men. It is in this sense that every man is born in sin. We hold, therefore, in accordance with the Council of Trent, that original sin is transmitted along with human nature, *not by imitation but by propagation,* and is, therefore, incurred by each individually."[8]

In spite of Adam and Eve's disobedience God still acts as a true Father to them. He knows what they have done but he still seeks them out, as *Genesis* describes in this way: "They heard the sound of the Lord God walking in the garden in the cool of the day, and the man and his wife hid themselves from the presence of the Lord God among the trees of the garden. But the Lord God called to the man and said to him, 'Where are you'?" (3:8-9).

Man's first reaction after committing sin is to feel totally ashamed and afraid of God's presence. He finds it difficult to recognize his sin. But, even so, God comes to his aid; he wants man to be happy; which is why he wants him to admit the truth. But man makes excuses; he does not want to take responsibility for his own free act and at last he resorts to putting the blame on his wife. She, in turn,

8 *Creed of the People of God,* 16.

is also reluctant to recognize that she has offended God and she blames the serpent, who "beguiled me and I ate." Eventually man loses the state of happiness in which he was created and there is nothing he can do to recover it.

The first announcement of salvation (the proto-evangelium) Just when Satan thought that he had totally defeated man — which he saw as a victory over God himself — a great light shines out, the promise of a future Messiah*: "I will put enmity between you and the woman", God tells Satan, "and between your seed and her seed; he shall bruise your head, and you shall bruise his heel" (Gen 3:15).

From this point onwards, when our first parents are still in paradise, God's infinite mercy shines out on man. After punishing Satan in the serpent (3:14), God announces a relentless struggle between the devil and the woman's offspring. The final outcome of this struggle will be the victory of man over Satan: it will be one of Adam and Eve's descendants who will crush the head of the serpent.

The message of salvation which God gives us in Sacred Scripture is the working-out in history of this promise made in paradise. It starts in the Old Testament and reaches its climax in the New with the coming of the Messiah, Jesus Christ, our Saviour. All the events recounted in the Bible symbolize or foreshadow the Saviour to be born to the Blessed Virgin in Bethlehem.

However, Genesis has nothing to say about the long period between Noah and his family, the survivors of the great flood, and the appearance of the quite outstanding figure of Abraham, who marks the beginning of the unfolding of God's plans of salvation: we know nothing until we come up to around the year 2,000 B.C., the historically dated period in which Abraham lived. This silence is easy to understand if we remember, as St Augustine points out, as quoted earlier, that Sacred Scripture is not a scientific treatise: the Holy Spirit — who speaks through the inspired writers — did not wish to tell men things which had no part to play in the attainment of eternal salvation.[9]

God's covenant with Abraham After the fall of our first parents, God announced that a Saviour would redeem man from the power of Satan. The first step towards the fulfilment of this promise was God's choice of Abraham, whose faith would make him the father of a great people.[10] God tells Abraham, "Go from your country and

9 Cf. *De Genesi ad litteram*, II, 9, 20.   10 On all this period see P. de Surgy, *The Mystery of salvation: step by step through the Bible* (London 1966).

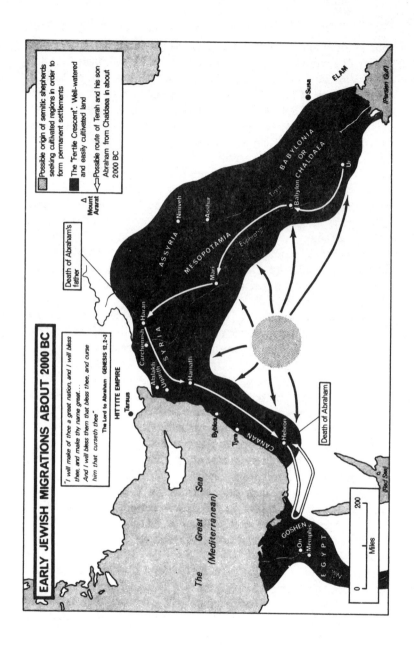

EARLY JEWISH MIGRATIONS ABOUT 2000 BC

Possible origin of semitic shepherds seeking cultivated regions in order to form permanent settlements

The "Fertile Crescent". Well-watered and easily cultivated land

Possible route of Terah and his son Abraham from Chaldaea in about 2000 BC

"I will make of thee a great nation, and I will bless thee, and make thy name great, . . .
And I will bless them that bless thee, and curse him that curseth thee"
The Lord to Abraham GENESIS 12, 2-3

Death of Abraham's father

Death of Abraham

ELAM

Susa

PERSIAN GULF

Mount Ararat

BABYLONIA OR CHALDAEA

Ur

ASSYRIA

Nineveh

Asshur

MESOPOTAMIA

Mari

Tigris

Euphrates

Babylon

HITTITE EMPIRE

Tarsus

Carchemish

Haran

SYRIA

Ahlakh

Ugarit

Hamath

Byblos

Tyre

CANAAN

Hebron

The Great Sea (Mediterranean)

GOSHEN

On

Memphis

EGYPT

Red Sea

0   200
Miles

Map 1

your kindred and your father's house to the land that I will show you. And I will make you a great nation, and I will bless you, and make your name great, so that you will be a blessing" (Gen 12:1-2).

From this text and from non-biblical documents we learn that around the year 1850 B.C. a man by the name of Abraham, the son of polytheist parents, a shepherd living in Ur of the Chaldees, moved with his family to go to a new land, Canaan. He did so because of his unconditional faith in a calling he received from God, a calling which had nothing to do with any merit on his part. The same thing happens when God chooses Isaac rather than Ishmael, and Jacob rather than Esau. He calls whomever he wants to use as an instrument of his grace. Being chosen by God in this way is an honour but it is also something very demanding.

In contrast to Adam's disobedience, Abraham responds to God's call in total obedience. His faith is the cause of the very existence of the chosen people: just as Mary's act of faith marks the start of the New Testament.

In response to Abraham's faith God makes further promises. He promises him an innumerable posterity, despite the fact that he has no children and his wife is barren and past childbearing age: "'Look towards heaven, and number the stars, if you are able to number them.' Then he said to him, 'So shall your descendants be'" (Gen 15:5). He further promises to give the land of Canaan to his posterity: "To your descendants I will give this land from the river of Egypt to the great River, the river Euphrates" (Gen 15:18).

In return for this God asks Abraham and all his offspring to believe in him, the one God. This monotheistic faith will now grow vigorously in the midst of the reigning polytheism. Circumcision* will act as the mark to show that one belongs to God and obeys his commandments. From now on Abraham belongs completely to God, who changes his name from Abram to Abraham (= father of a multitude) (17:5), and God describes himself as "El Shaddai"* (17:1), God Almighty.

This build-up of relations between God and Abraham is concluded by a covenant, which seals their promises to one another. This alliance or pact is made in the manner typical of the culture: the contracting parties immolate animals which have previously been divided into two sets of pieces; they face one another and then pass between the bloody pieces of the sacrificed animals; this shows that they are tying themselves to contractual obligations and that if they break them they accept that they will suffer the same fate. However, in Abraham's case, to show God's transcendence there is a variation from the normal procedure: God shows his presence in the form of fire: "When the sun had gone down and it was dark, behold, a smoking fire pot and a flaming torch passed between these pieces... 'As for you, you shall keep my covenant, you and your descendants after you through their generations'." (Gen 15:17; 17:9). It is only God who passes between the pieces, because only he commits himself totally, since man cannot provide anything to balance what God promises.

The covenant made here with Abraham is personal and individual; later on God will make it again with the people of Israel on Mount Sinai, with Moses acting as their representative. All these covenants, sealed with the blood of animals, symbolize the definitive covenant which Jesus Christ, the Son of God, will seal with his own blood, when he gives himself up on the cross to redeem mankind eternally (cf. Heb 9:12).

God's pact with Abraham is the first stage in this definitive Covenant. Hence the extraordinary importance of Abraham in the history of our salvation. The Gospel proclaims this at the beginning of the messianic era in the *Benedictus*, the canticle of Zechariah (Lk 1:72-73) and in Mary's *Magnificat* (Lk 1:54-55). The Church's liturgy invokes Abraham in the first canon of the Mass, in the ceremony of adult baptism, in the Mass for marriage and the Mass for the dead.

A little further on God will renew the same covenant with Abraham's son Isaac (Gen 26) and with his grandson Jacob (Gen 28:12).

Exodus: the establishment of Israel as the people of God

Like his forebears, Abraham and Isaac, Jacob led a semi-nomadic existence in Canaan. He was forced by a severe famine to emigrate with his entire family to Egypt, where they settled around the beginning of the eighteenth century before Christ.

Over the next four hundred years the sacred text tells us nothing about the stay of the Jews in Egypt. God makes no revelation during this period. All we know is that by the end of it the Hebrews had become a numerous, strong, hardworking people; so much so that the Egyptians, growing afraid of them, forced them into slavery; their lives "became bitter with hard service...; in all their work they made them serve with vigour" (Ex 1:13-14).

The book of *Exodus* (= "leaving") is a continuation of *Genesis*; the fact that it takes its name from the Israelites' going out of Egypt shows the importance of this episode in the life of Israel: now, after many long years of apparent silence on God's part, he keeps faith with his promises to their forebears, the patriarchs, and comes to their rescue to free them from the slavery,[11] imposed on them by Pharaoh. As he explains to Moses: "I have seen the affliction of my people who are in Egypt, and have heard their cry because of their taskmasters; I know their suffering, and I have come to deliver them out of the hand of the Egyptians" (Ex 3:7-8).

The calling of Moses   Humanly speaking, the Jews can see no way out of their oppression; they are deeply depressed. God is going to come to their rescue in a very overt way. First he chooses a man — Moses. The episode of the basket in which his sister Mary puts the baby Moses is a clear sign of God's special providence. Saved from the waters of the Nile[12] by Pharaoh's daughter and nursed by his own mother, Moses is brought up and educated in Pharaoh's own palace and becomes one of the most prominent people of his time. However — and this is very important — he retains the faith of his forefathers and is ready to profess that faith and defend his people even at the cost of his life if necessary. One example of this is his killing of the Egyptian whom he found beating a Hebrew (Ex 2:11-12); in doing so he was not acting out of anger but in accordance with the *lex talionis* which laid down that justice must be done either by the authorities or by whoever suffered the injustice: since recourse to Pharaoh was impossible Moses applied the law even though this meant putting his own life at risk.

The mission God gave Moses was a very demanding one, involving his whole life. From the moment that he received his definitive vocation with the vision of the burning bush his faith was often put to the test: "He looked, and lo, the bush was burning, and yet it was not consumed. And Moses said, 'I will turn aside and see this great sight, why the bush is not burnt'. When the Lord saw that he turned aside to see, God called to him out of the bush, 'Moses, Moses!' And he said, 'Here I am.' Then he said, 'Do not come near,

11   On the enslavement and liberation of the people of Israel see G. Anzou, *De la servidumbre al servicio* (Madrid 1966).

12   The etymology of the name Moses (= saved from the water) was suggested by Flavius Josephus and Philon of Alexandria and is Egyptian not Hebraic. Some western Egyptologists think that it has a more specific meaning, "child of the Nile". Cf. F. Spadafora, *Diccionario bíblico*, op. cit.

put off your shoes from your feet, for the place in which you are standing is holy ground'" (Ex 3:2-5). From this text and Moses' conversation with God, the following important points emerge:

1. In his dialogue with Moses, God's transcendence is evident. The very ground on which Moses stands is sacred, but God allows him to stand there because he wants to give a special mission to this man in whom he has complete confidence.

2. To fulfil this mission Moses should not rely on his own resources alone, even though he is highly educated and talented. When he learns what God wants him to do he exclaims, "Who am I . . .?" (Ex 3:11), but the Lord immediately sets his mind at rest: "I will be with you" (v. 12).

3. However, before he accepts God's charge, Moses asks him what he should say when the children of Israel ask who sent him. This is the point at which God reveals his name, Yahweh*, which has such importance for our faith:

> God said to Moses, "I am who am". And he said, "Say this to the people of Israel, I am has sent me to you'" (Ex 3:14).

4. Moses' faith is always in evidence and at all stages he accepts what God tells him. He is a humble man, who does not overestimate his virtues and knows his limitations. For example, he was not a good speaker — in fact he had a stutter[13] — and he could see it would be difficult for him to pass God's word on to his people or to inform Pharaoh as God required him. At first he tries to decline God's calling and offers all kinds of excuses, to which God listens patiently, and then says, "Who has made man's mouth? Who makes him dumb, or deaf, or seeing, or blind? Is it not I, the Lord? Now therefore go, and I will be your mouth and teach you what you shall speak" (Ex 4:11-12).

5. Like his ancestor Abraham, Moses puts his trust entirely in God. He immediately leaves the peace and security of his home in Midian, where he had taken refuge, and returns to Egypt with the special mission of taking his suffering people away from that country and leading them into Canaan. The covenant which will be made on Sinai will make Israel God's own people.

The Israelites leave Egypt   So, since making his promise to save

---

13 In spite of being chosen to set his people free, Moses, according to the sacred text, was "slow of speech and of tongue" (Ex 4:10; 6:12). God desires to make it plain that it is he really who makes things happen and that the man he calls is always an instrument quite unequal to the role he is given.

man, God has taken two important steps — by choosing first Abraham and then Moses. The first he makes the father of a numerous people and now, with Moses, he will turn that people into a special people of his own, by a singular choice.

Before the Hebrews leave Egypt, Moses has a series of meetings with Pharoah, as God had instructed him. In order to show Pharaoh that Yahweh is the only true God, much more powerful than Pharaoh, Moses warns him of a series of plagues which will befall Egypt if the Hebrews are not allowed to leave: but Pharaoh will not listen, despite the evidence.

Coinciding with the announcement of the tenth and last plague, that of the death of the firstborn, Moses instituted on God's instruction the feast of the Passover* as a permanent commemoration of the Jews' liberation from slavery in Egypt:

> This month shall be for you the beginning of months; it shall be the first month of the year for you. Tell all the congregation of Israel that on the tenth day of this month they shall take every man a lamb according to their fathers' houses, a lamb for a household. . . . Your lamb shall be without blemish, a male a year old . . . and you shall keep it until the fourteenth day of this month. . . . This day shall be for you a memorial day, and you shall keep it as a feast to the Lord; throughout your generation you shall observe it as an ordinance for ever (Ex 12:2-14).

After the Passover meal, with the permission previously given by Pharaoh — who had seen his own son die — the Israelites begin their journey into Sinai. Before reaching Sinai, indeed immediately after leaving Egypt, God works a most spectacular miracle, to enable his people to cross the Red Sea.[14] In terror, the Egyptians cry out, "Let us flee from before Israel; for the Lord fights for them against the Egyptians" (Ex 14:25).

The Red Sea can become passable through natural causes but in this case God enables Moses to orchestrate natural phenomena in order to save the Israelites. The crossing of the Red Sea has always been seen by the Church as symbolizing Christian Baptism.

The history of Israel as a people really begins with their departure from Egypt. God moulds the clans together to lead them towards their final destination — possession of the land of Canaan. The Israelites become his chosen instrument to effect his plan of salvation.

The Covenant at Sinai In line with what he promised in *Genesis*, God now tells Moses: "This you shall say to the house of Jacob., . .

14 Cf. F. Spadafora, op. cit.

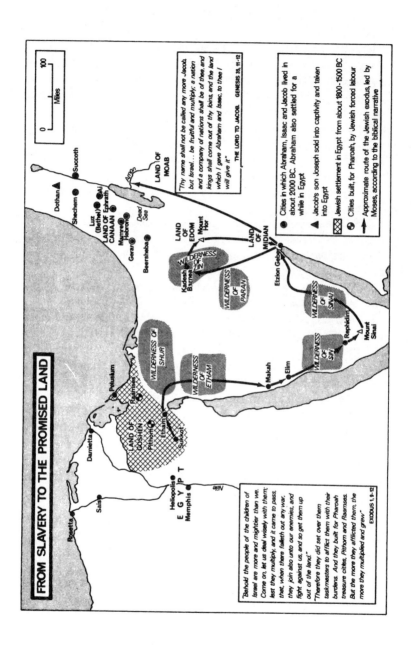

FROM SLAVERY TO THE PROMISED LAND

"Behold the people of the children of Israel are more and mightier than we. Come on, let us deal wisely with them; lest they multiply, and it came to pass, that, when there falleth out any war, they join also unto our enemies, and fight against us, and so get them up out of the land."

"Therefore they did set over them taskmasters to afflict them with their burdens. And they built for Pharoah treasure cities, Pithom and Raamses. But the more they afflicted them, the more they multiplied and grow." EXODUS 1, 9-12

"Thy name shall not be called any more Jacob, but Israel... be fruitful and multiply; a nation and a company of nations shall be of thee, and kings shall come out of thy loins, and the land which I gave Abraham and Isaac, to thee I will give it."
THE LORD TO JACOB   GENESIS 35, 11-12

● Cities in which Abraham, Isaac and Jacob lived in about 2000 BC. Abraham also settled for a while in Egypt

▲ Jacob's son Joseph sold into captivity and taken into Egypt

⬚ Jewish settlement in Egypt from about 1800-1500 BC

◉ Cities built, for Pharoah, by Jewish forced labour

→ Approximate route of the Jewish exodus, led by Moses, according to the biblical narrative

Map 2

If you will obey my voice and keep my covenant, you shall be my own possession among all peoples" (Ex 19:3-5). God's choice of Israel, as that of Abraham, stems from his love and not from Israel's merits.

The narrative begins by describing the impressive theophany which happens on Mount Sinai: "And Mount Sinai was wrapped in smoke, because the Lord descended upon it in fire; and the smoke of it went up like the smoke of a kiln, and the whole mountain quaked greatly" (Ex 19:18). Here we can see God's infinite majesty and also his total transcendence. He is the Lord of all creation. He is all-holy and therefore the people cannot approach the mountain because they are as yet unpurified.

The Covenant of Sinai seems to have three purposes:

1. It makes Israel the people of God, and Yahweh the God of Israel — as *Leviticus* later reminds them: "I will be your God, and you shall be my people" (Lev 26:12).

2. God promises to give special help and protection to Israel against other nations, and to give it a land of its own — Canaan.

3. Finally, God gives Israel a Law to regulate its religious and moral life. The Decalogue* will henceforth determine the relations of each individual and of Israel as a whole with God. This commitment to Israel is made more explicit in the "Book of the Covenant" which contains a whole series of laws and precepts which are to govern the religious and civil life of the chosen people.

The Covenant is ratified or signed by means of a sacrifice, and then the people — represented by the twelve tribes of Israel — and the altar — representing God — are twice sprinkled with the blood of the sacrifice. "Then he [Moses] took the book of the covenant, and read it in the hearing of the people; and they said, 'All that the Lord has spoken we will do, and we will be obedient'" (Ex 24:7).

The teaching contained in Exodus Although this book takes the form of a popular narrative, easy for a primitive people to understand, it also contains important religious teachings. The episodes in this history obviously involve special divine intervention: there is no other explanation for the liberation of Israel or the crossing of the Red Sea or its survival for so long in the wilderness.

God chooses Moses as his faithful intermediary with his people, and Moses' response to his vocation and to the mission God gives him is a clear example of how people should make themselves available to God. A man of great humility and patience, Moses is put to the test on innumerable occasions. When Israel bemoans its plight, Moses always responds faithfully to Yahweh and stays completely loyal to the Covenant of Sinai. Yet he did not live to see the day when Israel entered the promised land, because on one occasion he doubted God's patience, thinking that God could not tolerate the Israelite's insolence and distrust. As the book of *Numbers* (20:1-12) reports, when Israel was in the middle of the desert at Meribah, they had no water. The people complained against Moses and Aaron and God commanded them to give them water by striking a rock with Moses' rod. Because they had to strike the rock twice God punished Moses and Aaron for doubting his mercy, which is infinite despite his people's incredulity and disloyalty. And so the episode ends: "These are the waters of Meribah, where the people of Israel contended with the Lord, and he showed himself holy amongst them" (Num 20:13).

Another piece of explicit teaching in this book is its revelation of the name of Yahweh, the only God, absolute Lord and master of the universe and of history. God's Alliance with the people of Israel, chosen without merit from all other peoples to be a holy people, a priestly nation, marks the beginning of salvation for the rest of mankind as well. In a shadowy and symbolic way, everything said in this book points to its full development centuries later, in the New Testament, where it becomes flooded with light when the Messiah arrives.

Seen from this angle, we can glimpse in *Exodus*, Jesus Christ, the ultimate goal of the Law and of all history. The passage of the Red Sea is seen as prefiguring Baptism; the manna, the Eucharist; the bronze serpent lifted up on the pole (Num 21:8-9), which cures the Israelites if they just look at it, becomes the cross of Jesus Christ, which has the power to heal or redeem man from all his sins; the rock which produces water in the desert is Jesus Christ, who nourishes Christians as they make their way through life; the blood of the victims which is used to seal the Old Alliance is the blood of Jesus, who is immolated on the cross as an offering for our sins (Heb 9:12): with his blood he seals the New and definitive Alliance.

All of this means that *Exodus* is one of the most important books in the Old Testament; without meditating and appraising it, it is difficult to understand God's later revelation to men in his Son Jesus Christ.

Leviticus: the sacrifices of the Old Testament

This book, breaking the historical narrative which is taken up again in *Numbers*, focuses mainly on one of the tribes of Israel, Levi, and particularly on its priests and their duties in regard to divine worship.

The Hebrews called this book, like the others in the Pentateuch, after its opening word, *wayyiqra* (= and he called). The Church recognizes it as an inspired book, part of the Old Testament canon.

Although Catholic exegetes admit the Mosaic authorship of this book, they usually say — and in this also follow the Magisterium of the Church — that some details in the book may have been later modified, or indeed may be additions, without this in any way affecting the book's substantial Mosaic authenticity or its inspiration. For example, Vaccari asserts that "Moses found the use of sacrifices to be something firmly rooted in the customs of all peoples. In the tablets discovered in Rãs Shamra (ancient Ugarit) there is reference to the same kinds of sacrifices as in the Pentateuch, even with the same names, given the affinity of the languages. In making his laws," Vaccari says, "Moses simply regulated and consecrated to the worship of the true God rites already in use."[15]

It should be remembered that because of its geographical position Israel was open to all sorts of Canaanite, Assyrian, Babylonian and Egyptian influences, and that additionally the Israelites retained very ancient cultural practices inherited from their ancestors. This entire tradition was raised, purified and enriched over the centuries by the revelation of Sinai.

The *Leviticus* account begins with the second year of the Exodus, when the Hebrews are already in the middle of the wilderness. In the previous book the Tent already figured with its altars and regulations about the worship to be given to Yahweh. Now Moses develops these forms of worship in much more detail: Leviticus is really a manual for that liturgy.

To understand the book properly one must bear in mind two basic reference points: the first being that Yahweh, the God of Israel, is infinitely holy, inaccessible to man (Ex 19:21), and therefore completely transcendent; the second, that despite this he dwells in the midst of his people (Lev 23:32;26:12). Therefore he asks of them, not only reverence, love and adoration, but a holiness of life which enables them to live as his true children forever in his presence (Lev

---

15 A Vaccari, *La S. Biblia*, I (Florence 1943).

11:44; 19:2; etc). Worship and holiness of life are the two main concerns of Leviticus.

Worship and sacrifices Israel gave great importance to external public worship of Yahweh, the only God and Lord of the universe, and in this worship sacrifices of different kinds were very much in evidence. Another aspect of these sacrifices, also very relevant, was their role in atoning for personal sins, in order to restore friendship with God, which sin shattered. Despite their imperfections all the Israelite sacrifices had a clear objective — to engrave on the people's minds the notion of God's sublime holiness and man's unworthiness to enter his presence. To him alone were sacrifices to be offered, by the ministry of priests. The sacrificial victims had to be perfect, unblemished, and who shared in sacrificial meals had to be free from legal uncleaniness, that is, they had to be as holy as possible.

In its first chapters *Leviticus* tells us about the five forms of sacrifice under the Old Covenant — constituting a code of sacrifice.[16]

a) *The holocaust.* This is a word of Greek origin meaning "offering". It is the main sacrifice, where the victim is wholly burnt. The victim is considered as going up in the flames of the altar, reaching up to God (the corresponding Hebrew word comes from the verb *alah* = to go up). This kind of sacrifice certainly goes back to the time of Noah (Gen 8:20); it symbolizes man's recognition of God's universal sovereignty; it was performed only by priests, who had a special role in Levitical liturgy. In addition to the daily morning and evening holocaust (Ex 29:38-42), others were offered on festive days and other specified occasions.

b) *The peace-offering.* This was a type of sacrificial meal. The Hebrew word *selamin* (Lev 3:1-17) refers to the sacrifice offered to God for favours bestowed, although it may be connected with *shalôm* (= peace), hence peaceful, friendly relations with God. This latter sense fits in better with all forms of peace-offering, the distinguishing feature of which is the sacrificial meal in which the offerer had the right to partake. Part of the victim was given to and consumed by offerers and priests as a sign of peace, and the blood and the fat, being the more vital part, was reserved to God. Peace-offerings were prescribed on the fulfilment of a Nazarite vow (Num 6:14) and on the Feast of Weeks (Lev 23:19). All peace-offerings had to do either with asking or thanking God for favours.

c) *Sin-offering and trespass offering.* The difference between these

16 For a fuller treatment of this, cf. P.P. Saydon in *CCHS*, sections 182ff.

is unclear. They both had to do with restoring relations with God, which had been broken by sin. A "sin" was an ordinary offence committed through human frailty or passion. A "trespass" denoted fundamentally a state of culpability, imputability and indebtedness. Sin also involved culpability, but in not so obvious a way when committed through ignorance or inadvertence (4:2-3; 13:22ff). These unintentional sins constituted a real, though involuntary, transgression, and therefore had to be expiated when the offender became conscious of his offence. Trespass was a formal sin involving material damage to one's neighbour. Sin-offerings therefore expiated ritual faults against Yahweh, whereas trespass-offerings also looked to actions involving injustice to one's neighbour.

d) *Bloodless sacrifices*. These usually took the form of offerings of cereals. They consisted of finest flour which could be presented as uncooked flour, unleavened bread (leaven and honey could not be burned in honour of Yahweh because they fermented and fermentation was associated with corruption) (2:11), or parched grain. Leavened bread and honey could be presented to God only as offerings of first fruits but were never burnt on the altars.

Election and holiness of priests Prior to Israel's establishment as a people, the priesthood was not reserved to any particular social group; any prominent person could represent the community as its priest — a father his family, a chief his tribe or clan etc. After the Covenant, however, a special corps of priests had to be established, to be totally dedicated to the service of Yahweh. All this is covered in *Leviticus* 8-10. The priests had to come from the tribe of Levi, the tribe which would be given no share in the later division of Canaan. They were required to be detached from material possessions in order to spend more time in God's service; this called for more holiness on their part, and they had already been put to the test successfully at Massah and Meribah (Deut 33:8-11). Lev 21:6 expressly states that "they shall be holy to their God, and not profane the name of their God; for they offer the offerings by fire to the Lord, the bread of their God; therefore they shall be holy."

All the ceremonial to do with their consecration was a vivid reminder of the importance given to their function. They had to be holy because God, whom they served, was holy (11:14; 19:2; 20:26). In the New Testament this principle will be applied to everyone: at the end of the Sermon on the Mount Jesus says, "You, therefore, must be perfect, as your heavenly father is perfect" (Mt 5:48).

Laws of purification Because Israel was God's chosen people, it had an obligation to follow a more spiritual way of life than that of other nations. Hence the rules laid down by God and specified by Moses to protect the people from being contaminated by pagan influences. A whole series of rules about uncleanness and purification rites is contained in *Leviticus* 11-16, ending with a description of the ritual of the Day of Atonement* (the day when Israel was cleansed from its sins in an as yet merely external way, for this did not approach the kind of interior justification to which Christ's redemption would give all mankind access).

The law of holiness *Leviticus* 17-26 spells out the way in which members of the people of God should relate to each other. If they keep the rules contained therein, they are promised peace even in this life (26:3-13), which will take various forms — God's sending rain at the right time; abundant harvests; peace and security; punishment of one's enemies; having many children; being on good terms with God; etc.

It also specifies a number of scourges (26:14-39) to be visited on transgressors of the Law — disease, famine, sterility, wars, deportation etc.

The message of Leviticus To understand Leviticus properly the reader must be familiar with the notion of sacrifice, which lies at the core of genuine religion. If man had not sinned, the only sacrifice he would have needed to offer God would have been that of doing his work well and looking after his family. But by sinning man became unworthy and led all his descendants into a state of alienation from God. He could not offer himself as a pure victim: he was not acceptable.

This meant that he needed someone to purify him and reconcile him with his creator, someone whose merit at least balanced out the blame he had earned through sinning. Out of compassion for man God designated his Son to be the victim who would effect this reconciliation. And so Christ became man and out of love for us offered himself as a sacrifice for our sins.

However, until that moment arrived, until the expected Messiah (Gen 3:15) came, God wanted man to offer him worship as his infinite majesty demanded; by doing so, man would be publicly recognizing his dependence on his creator. God therefore accepted the symbol of the blood of the animals sacrificed to him, and the other bloodless sacrifices. Although these sacrifices had their significance they were incapable of justifying or redeeming man; that is, they could not restore lost happiness to him. They were of use as a way of honouring God and of keeping Israel away from idolatry, as practised by its neighbours, and of showing those neighbouring peoples the Israelites' faith in the one true God.

Clearly the sacrifices offered by the patriarchs up to the time of the Law of Sinai and from then up to the Messiah, were only symbols of Jesus Christ's own sacrifice as a spotless victim acceptable to God. Because he was both God and Man, only Christ could offer himself to God and restore man to righteousness and to friendship with God. What is said in *Leviticus* is a figure of the sacrifice of Jesus Christ, because as St Paul says, "Christ is the end [purpose] of the law" (Rom 10:4). Christian sacrifice will have all the elements of Levitical sacrifice, with this essential difference: Christ himself is at the centre of it. St Augustine goes as far as to say that "in the victims of those animals which the Jews offered to God lies the prophecy of that victim still to come, which Christ offered to the Father in the great sacrifice of the cross."

Christians should always be thankful to God for the one, true sacrifice, that offered by Jesus Christ on Calvary in expiation for our sins (cf. Heb 7:27). This very sacrifice is renewed in a bloodless way in the sacrifice of the Christian altar — the same victim, the same priest — when the bread and wine are changed through transubstantiation into the body and blood of our Lord, who has chosen in this way to give himself to us as spiritual nourishment and to build us into his mystical body.[17]

Numbers: from Sinai to Canaan

This book is a narrative running from the second year after the Israelites leave Egypt up to almost the end of Moses' life — a total of about thirty nine years' wandering in the wilderness. It takes its name in the Hebrew Bible from *bammidbar* (= in the wilderness). The Greek translation of the Septuagint, however, prefers to call it "Numbers", and the Latin follows suit. As a title this is less than satisfactory, because the counting of the people does not take up much of the book, which really is a history of the main events of the wanderings in the desert.

17 Cf. Paul VI, *Creed of the People of God*, 24-25.

The book begins with God's express command to Moses to make a census of the people, the effect of which will be to show that God indeed has kept his promise to Abraham: "I will indeed bless you, and I will multiply your descendants as the stars of heaven and as the sand which is on the seashore. And your descendants shall possess the gate of their enemies" (Gen 22:17). The seventy-member family of Jacob which entered Egypt, now, some 450 years later, numbered around 600,000. Even if this statistic is not mathematically exact (that is not the purpose of the Bible) there is no doubt about the Jews being a very numerous people.

The structure of the book The book can be divided into three parts:

a) *In Sinai*. This part, which goes up to chapter 10, presents Israel as a holy people, in line with its vocation: its holiness comes from God, not from its own merits. It is divided into twelve tribes, according to Israel's twelve sons, taken in groups of three. They all gather round the tent of meeting*, with the Levites in the place of honour. The Israelites closeness to the tabernacle, with which they journeyed, meant that they had to have a high degree of legal purity; the regulations contained in chapters 5ff were aimed at ensuring this.

b) *The journey through the wilderness*. This is described in chapters 10-21. Moses maintains order while they are encamped in the Sinai. Then the entire people starts out again on its journey, conscious that they travel under the protection of Yahweh, who appears to them in the form of a cloud. They reach Cades, where they stop. Moses uses this respite to reconnoitre the land of Canaan and to promulgate a series of laws aimed at clarifying the basis of Moses' and Aaron's authority. Then, because of the opposition of the king of Edom they have to backtrack. Their entry into Canaan is delayed for thirty eight years. If they had been docile to the Lord's commandments, they would not have had to undergo all these privations. As it was, most of those who set out from Egypt did not live to enter Canaan.

c) *On the plains of Moab*. The third and last part of the book, up to chapter 36, describes events just prior to the entry into the promised land. Almost at its gates, Israel meets its last obstacle, Balac, King of Moab. Balac had tried to get Balaam, a seer, to put a curse on the chosen people, but providentially not only does Balaam not cooperate: he extols the privileges and promises God has given his people.

After this, when the Israelites cavort with the daughters of Moab and turn from Yahweh, a second census is held and towards the end

of the book Moses establishes new laws to govern the life of Israel
— laws more suited to a settled than a nomadic people, which will
apply as soon as the Israelites take possession of Canaan.

The religious teaching of Numbers   The events narrated in
Numbers do bring out into the open the infidelities and rebellious
nature of the people of Israel. However, we would be mistaken if
we thought that the lessons and punishments contained in the book
applied only to these people. We are guilty of the same faults as they.
We may be surprised at their hardness of heart, given all the miracles
God worked for them, but the truth is that the same thing happens
among Christians. If we carefully examine our own attitudes, we will
be even more surprised: the Son of God dies for us to reconcile us
to God and redeem us from sin and from the power of the devil;
he gives us the great gift of divine sonship, and we respond not just
ungratefully but with daily signs of infidelity, even to the point of
insulting God's majesty.

Israel's pilgrimage through the wilderness has a deep religious
meaning for Christians. We are "a chosen race, a royal priesthood,
a holy nation, God's own people, that you may declare the wonderful
deeds of him who called you out of darkness into his marvellous light"
(1 Pet 2:9). God lives in our midst, in each of us personally, provided
we stay faithful to his grace. But just as the people of Israel fall foul
of temptation by dreaming about advantages of life in Egypt, so too
Christians are easily deflected from the search for holiness and union
with God by being attached to material possessions, ambition,
sensuality or the easy life. The history of the chosen people as they
make their way through the desert is often reflected in each Christian's
own story.

Deuteronomy: a new promulgation of the Law

On the plains of Moab, God charges Moses — now close to death
— once more to proclaim the Law which he received through the
revelation on Mount Sinai. This proclamation is contained in the
fifth and last book of the Pentateuch, called in Hebrew *had-debharim*
(= the words) and by the Septuagint *deuteronomion* (= second law).
Moses is addressing a new generation of Israelites, all those who would

have been under twenty when the Exodus began. By having the Law read again Yahweh is saying that his Covenant with Israel is made with all generations (29:13), both present and future: it is an everlasting Covenant.

Life for Moses means serving God and leading his people to the promised land. Here, with characteristic humility and patience, he repeats the precepts and directives given him by God. He wants to engrave them on the minds and hearts of his people, to keep them loyal to the commitment their parents made to the Alliance. The kings and judges who will rule over them (17:18), must, like other members of the people, stay true to the law if they want to attain salvation (27:1). As a permanent reminder for future generations, when they cross the Jordan they must write the Law on stone (27:2-3), to symbolize their fidelity to Yahweh. And from then on the Law is to be read out to the people every seven years to ensure that they obey it. These commandments of God can be understood and kept, St Augustine says, when man is aided by grace. The Law of Moses was unable itself to cause grace: it could do so only by virtue of the merits of Jesus Christ, to which it pointed in an obscure way; in the New Law the Lord enables us to have a deep understanding of the mysteries of God and his commandments, which in turn leads us to love them and practise them.

Exhortations *Deuteronomy* is structured in the form of three discourses or exhortations, the second of which, particularly, contains the laws proper.

The first discourse (1-4:43) acts as a kind of introduction to the book. It stresses what the book — and the entire Bible — are all about: it is telling us that God in his providence is constantly watching over his people — over every single man and woman — as can be seen from the prodigies he worked during the long years the Jews spent in the wilderness. But it also emphasizes another basic fact: Yahweh requires of Israel strict fidelity to the Alliance: that was what Israel committed itself to in Sinai, to adore the one true God.

The second discourse takes up the centre of the book (4:44-28:69). From chapter 5 to chapter 11 Moses promulgates the Decalogue and spells out what the first commandment of the Law entails:

> Hear, O Israel: The Lord our God is one Lord; and you shall love the Lord your God with all your heart, and with all your soul, and with all your might. And these words which I command you this day shall be upon your heart; and you shall teach them diligently to your children, and shall talk of them when you sit in your house, and when you walk

by the way, and when you lie down, and when you rise. And you shall
bind them as a sign upon your hand, and they shall be as frontlets between
your eyes. And you shall write them on the doorposts of your house and
on your gates (6:4-9).

In this text we can see the two basic principles in *Deuteronomy* —
1) monotheism: Israel has to believe in the one true God; and 2) it
must love him above all else. This prayer, called the *Shema*, is a
summary of true religion. No other book in the Old Testament puts
such stress on the love man gives God. Jesus Christ quotes this text
when he promulgates the law of love of God (Mt 22:37). Because
God is the only origin of all creation, he is to be adored and loved
above all things.

God's choice of Israel, a grace which must imbue its lifestyle forever
more, is a pure act of love on his part. Chapters 12 to 28 give a whole
series of liturgical, civil and criminal laws all deriving from the fact
that Israel is the people chosen by God to carry out his promises.

The third discourse, which is by way of epilogue, is a vigorous
exhortation to obedience to Yahweh. What God hid from their parents
is now being revealed to them and their descendants (29:28) — to
all their decendants, which includes us. Their love of God should
be inspired not by fear of punishment but by appreciation for all
the gifts he has given. True wisdom consists in this — not in exploring
the hidden mysteries of God out of curiosity, but in knowing his
commandments and practising them faithfully (4:6). The book ends
with an account of the last days of Moses' life and of his death,
mourned for thirty days by the children of Israel on the Plains of
Moab.

The message of Deuteronomy *Deuteronomy* marks the high point
of Old Testament religion. The whole history of Israel, from Egypt
to Canaan, is described in terms of Yahweh's love for his people and
of the love they owe him in return. No other Old Testament book,
says Driver, breathes forth an atmosphere of such generous devotion
to God and of such magnanimous divine benevolence towards men;
nowhere else are man's duties so tenderly, so eloquently and so
persuasively expressed, or the principles to do with service of
neighbour given with such wealth of detail.

Deuteronomy can be said to be the last will and testament of Moses.
It is imbued with his feelings of affection and understanding for his
people and also with sincere recognition of God's goodness and mercy.
Chosen as he is to guide his people Moses is not content with simply
dictating laws: he acts like a true father, seeking the salvation of all

Israel. He tirelessly exhorts them and encourages them not be deflected by any obstacles they meet on their way to the promised land. But he also warns them of the serious consequences that will follow if they allow themselves to stray into the idolatry practised by their new neighbours.

Deuteronomy contains many prophecies about the New Covenant of the future, of which the following is the most outstanding:

> The Lord your God will raise up for you a prophet like me from among you, from your brethren — him you shall heed — just as you desired of the Lord your God at Horeb on the day of the assembly, when you said, "Let me not hear again the voice of the Lord my God, or see this great fire any more, lest I die." And the Lord said to me, "They have rightly said all that they have spoken. I will raise up for them a prophet like you from among their brethren; and I will put my words in his mouth, and he shall speak to them all that I command him. . . " (Deut 18:15-18).

This is, among other things, a prophecy concerning Jesus Christ, *the* Prophet. Just as Moses was the legislator of the Old Law, St Augustine says, Jesus Christ will be that of the New, for which all the Old Testament prophets are preparing the way. From this point onwards, the people of Israel will live in hope of this prophet, the Messiah announced from the beginning (Gen 3:15).

Deuteronomy also contains passages of great doctrinal depth, especially those to do with love of one's neighbour, which is inseparable from love of God; passages speaking about mercy and compassion towards people who are suffering deprivation of any kind; passages defending the family, women and public and private morality. *Deuteronomy* is one of the Old Testament books which comes closest to the teaching of the Gospel and in fact it can be best understood in the light of the Gospel.

When we read this book we should remember that its blessings are addressed to us as well — when we do what Jesus Christ, the Messiah, has commanded us; and that its threats also apply to us if we act in a way which conflicts with his teaching. The Israelites' hardness of heart prefigures our own blindness, our own rebellion against God's goodness and mercy: today, as then, he "desires all men to be saved and to come to the knowledge of the truth" (1 Tim 2:4).

Other historical books of the Old Testament

We will now look at a series of inspired books covering the religious history of Israel from the time of Moses' death (towards the end of the twelfth century B.C.) and the succession of Joshua, up to John Hyrcanus (135-104 B.C.) — that is from the entry into Canaan to the time of the Maccabees. The history contained in these books is sketchy and selective but it does give a true account of events and since it is inspired writing everything it contains which God wanted to communicate to us is free from error.

Like all the books in the Bible these historical books are sacred because their content is sacred: they recount God's relationships with his people. It is a religious history that they are reporting; that was God's express purpose in inspiring them. They stem, however, from faith in Yahweh's gratuitous choice of Israel and from the Covenant which bound Israel to God for ever. To understand them properly we must see them in the context of a theological view of history — which will show all these events as leading up to the last, definitive event, the coming of the Messiah, whom God promised at the beginning and whom Israel awaited as its true saviour.

This means, as the Second Vatican Council put it, that:

> The economy of the Old Testament was deliberately so orientated that it should prepare for and declare in prophecy the coming of Christ, redeemer of all men, and of the messianic kingdom (cf. Lk 24:44; Jn 5:29; 1 Pet 1:10), and should indicate it by means of different types (cf. 1 Cor 10:11). For in the context of the human situation before the era of salvation established by Christ, the books of the Old Testament provide an understanding of God and man and make clear to all men how a just and merciful God deals with mankind. These books, even though they contain matters imperfect and provisional, nevertheless show us authentic divine teaching. Christians should accept with veneration these writings which give expression to a lively sense of God, which are a storehouse of sublime teaching on God and on sound wisdom on human life, as well as a wonderful treasury of prayers; in them, too, the mystery of our salvation is present in a hidden way.[1]

---

1 Vatican II, Dogm. Const. *Dei Verbum* 15.

It is true that these books contain genuine sacred history, written by men inspired by God; but it is also true that God wanted each writer to keep his own personality and style. It is easy to see this; we can identify the kind of environment — religious, political and social — in which each particular writer lived and the kind of literary genre he was using — historical, prophetic, poetic, didactic, midrashic or even popular.

Although Israel's continuous infidelity to the grace of God is evidenced in these books, the door is always left open to hope of forgiveness. Even though God chastises his people for their apostasy, he still shows them abundant mercy: the punishment he inflicts on them is paternal and medicinal rather than heartless edicts of a distant God. The Lord does not want the death of the sinner but rather his repentance; and once he is converted he sets out again enthusiastically on the road of true love of God.

Also, these books are really the "prehistory" of the Church, given the many figurative references to the future Church which they contain.

Invasions suffered by the kingdoms of Israel and Judah   Before looking at these books more closely, we will try to situate the history of Israel and Judah in this period into that of its near neighbours — with whom it had to fight or enter into treaties.

Egypt (950-525 B.C.)   From the end of the New Empire (c. 1087 B.C.) Egypt entered a decline. It became divided into two parts — the Delta, the true seat of power, and the South, the traditional seat of power, ruled by the priests of Thebes.

Shesonq I, the founder of the XXIInd dynasty, re-united the country and made his third son the high priest of Thebes. He also took an active interest in Palestine. He gave asylum to Jeroboam, who later became king of Israel, and in 927 B.C. he invaded Palestine, reaching as far as Samaria. The XXIInd dynasty remained in power for another two hundred years, but in the eighth century the Delta cities became independent principalities such as those ruled by the XXIIIrd dynasty in Tanis and by the short-lived XXIVth dynasty in Sais.

In 730 B.C. the Ethiopian warrior-king Pianki invaded Egypt, penetrating as far as Heliopolis, north of Cairo. Fifteen years later his brother Shabako conquered the rest of the Delta. The XXVth, an Ethiopian dynasty, came from Napata, a city in the Sudan near the Fourth Cataract which had been the principal capital in the XVIIIth dynasty. In 671 B.C. the Assyrian king Sargon defeated the Ethiopian pharaoh Tahzarqa putting to an end Ethiopian control of the Delta and, for a while, of the northern part of the Nile valley. The Delta broke up into small states whose rulers theoretically owed allegiance to Assyria. One of these petty kings was Psemmitichus I (664-610 B.C.), who threw off the Assyrian yoke and established himself over the rest of the Delta princes. The XXVIth dynasty brought great prosperity to Egypt. After the fall of Assyria, the Egyptians regained control of the territory west of the Euphrates and in this exercise Neco killed King Josiah at Megiddo in 609 B.C. But in 506 the Egyptians were defeated by the Babylonians at Carchemish and lost control of the Levant. In 525 Egypt became part of the Persian empire as a result of Cambyses' invasion.

The Assyrian empire   The Assyrian state was military and religious in character. Its king was head of the army and chief priest of the God Asshur. The country's wealth was dependent on the military campaigns the king undertook every spring in which he looted, exacted tribute from and generally weakened his enemies or potential enemies. Assyria's rise to power began at the beginning of the ninth century. Shalmaneser III (858-824 B.C.) conquered Babylon, Urartu (the great kingdom centred on Armenia) and the Syrian states as far as Damascus. In 853 he was confronted at Qarqar by a coalition of twelve kings, including Ahab of Israel. The outcome of the battle was indecisive, but Ahab was badly shaken and ten years later Shalmaneser was in receipt of tribute from Jehu, king of Israel. During the following century Assyria decreased in power due to internal difficulties. Tiglat-pileser III (745-727 B.C.) reorganized the army and changed foreign policy, conquered territories were incorporated into the empire, their princes replaced by Assyrian governors or officials and large sectors of population were deported. The empire regained control of Syria and went on to annex half of Israel but its capital, Samaria, was not occupied until 721 when the emperor deported its inhabitants and did away with Israel as a kingdom. When Sennacherib (704-681 B.C.) ascended the throne, Babylon and the Mediterranean provinces rebelled; Sennacherib eventually laid siege to Jerusalem and forced Hezekiah to pay tribute. The Assyrians went on to conquer Egypt. Under his son Ashurbanipal (668-631) the empire reached its maximum extent, but it had overstretched itself and within twenty years of Ashurbanipal's death it fell to combined forces of Babylonians and Medes. A small pocket of resistance held out in the north of Syria but in 609 the empire ceased to exist.

Neo-Babylonian empire (626-539 B.C.) Nabopollasar (626-605), a Chaldean chief, led a successful rebellion against Assyria in 626 and over the next decade freed southern Mesopotamia from Assyrian control. The Babylonians and Medes formed a coalition and took Ashur in 614. In 612 they destroyed Nineveh and in 610 Harran. The Egyptians occupied the Levant for a short while at this point but their territorial ambitions were brought to an end by their defeat by Nebuchadnezzar II (605-562) at Carchemish in 605.

Babylon's prosperity depended on taxes it levied on its provinces and on its control of the trade routes of Mesopotamia. Because of these taxes, and with the encouragement of the Egyptians the provinces of Syria and Palestine rebelled and Nebuchadnezzar had to send troops to put down the rebellion. Judah withdrew its tribute and in 587 Nebuchadnezzar occupied Jerusalem and installed Zedekiah as king in place of his uncle Jehoiachin who rebelled in 589 B.C. After eighteen months' siege Jerusalem was taken in July 587, the city was razed and many of its inhabitants executed or deported to Babylon.

When Nebuchadnezzar died, Babylon fell into chaos, until after six years Nabunaid attained power. To weld his empire together and improve its economy, Nabunaid fostered the cult of the moon-god Sin and moved his capital to Tema, in northeast Arabia, from where he could control the Arab trade routes of the South. He left the government of Babylon in the charge of his son, Belshazzar, but his neglect of Babylon and its gods alienated many of its citizens. In 539 Cyrus of Persia invaded Babylon and brought to an end the independence Mesopotamia had enjoyed for over one thousand years.

The Persian empire (559-330 B.C.) During the last period of the Assyrian empire, the Indo-European tribes of Medes and Persians harassed the eastern frontiers of Assyria. After the collapse of the empire, the Medes, who governed the Persians at that time, consolidated their position and extended their empire into Anatolia and central Persia. Cyrus the Great ascended the Persian throne in 559 B.C. He immediately proclaimed the independence of Persia and within a decade had conquered the Medes. He expanded his empire still further after defeating the Lydians in 547 and extended his rule into India, Afghanistan and Turkistan and, in 539, Babylon. Cyrus treated conquered peoples generously, helping them to rebuild their temples and restore their traditional forms of worship. An edict of Cyrus permitted the Jews return to Palestine and rebuild their Temple. Cyrus died while fighting the tribes of Central Asia and was succeeded by his son Cambyses (529-522 B.C.), who conquered Egypt in a fierce battle in 525.

Darius I (522-486) usurped the throne and expanded and reorganized the empire, specifying the limits of the satrapies and fixing levels of tribute. He unified the Medes and the Persians, introduced his own coinage and devised a legal code for the whole empire. Although Darius was an adherent of the god Ahuru-Mazda, he pursued a policy of religious tolerance and permitted the Jews to finish the building of the Second Temple. Both Darius and his son Xerxes (486-465) failed to conquer Greece: the Persian army was defeated first at Marathon (490), then at Salamis (480) and at Plataea (479). During the fifth century B.C., there was a colony of Jewish mercenaries in Elephantine, in southern Egypt, and its dealings with the local population are described in Aramaic papyri found there. In 330 B.C. Alexander of Macedonia defeated the last Achaemenid king, Darius II, and annexed a vast empire.

Joshua: the successor of Moses

Joshua was the person designated by Moses to succeed him in the governing of Israel: "Be strong and of good courage", Moses told him, "for you shall go with this people into the land which the Lord has sworn to their fathers to give them" (Deut 31:7). Moses passed all his authority on to Joshua, with the exception of his priestly powers, which went to Eleazar (cf. Num 27:18-23; Deut 31:14-23; 34:9). Joshua had been Moses' closest collaborator during the period of the pilgrimage in the wilderness.

It was Joshua who led the Hebrews to victory over the Amalekites while Moses remained in prayer (Ex 17:8-16). He was elected as Ephraim's representative in the group of twelve sent to reconnoitre the land of Canaan (Num 13:8). He and Caleb were the only people over the age of twenty when the Jews left Egypt who lived to enter the promised land: all the rest died in punishment for their infidelity (Num 14:30-38; 26:65; 32:13).

Biblical tradition is unanimous in extolling Joshua as a great warrior, a man of unshakeable faith, ever-obedient to God's commands. The book of *Sirach* says of him that Joshua the son of Nun was mighty in war and the successor of Moses in prophesying. In accordance with his name, which means salvation, he became a great saviour of God's elect, the avenger of their enemies, and their leader into

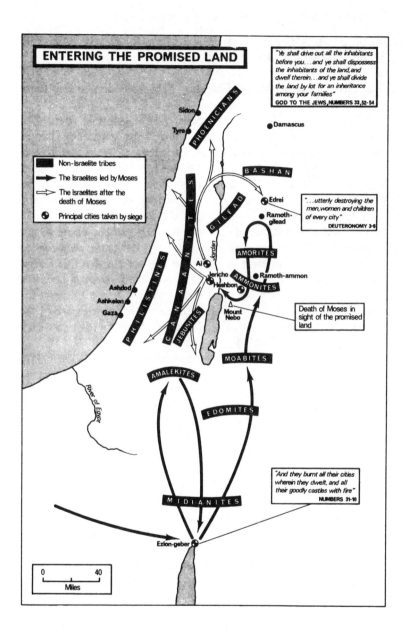

ENTERING THE PROMISED LAND

"Ye shall drive out all the inhabitants before you... and ye shall dispossess the inhabitants of the land, and dwell therein... and ye shall divide the land by lot for an inheritance among your families"
GOD TO THE JEWS, NUMBERS 33, 52-54

PHOENICIANS

Sidon

Tyre

Damascus

Legend:
- Non-Israelite tribes
- The Israelites led by Moses
- The Israelites after the death of Moses
- Principal cities taken by siege

BASHAN

GILEAD

Edrei

"...utterly destroying the men, women and children of every city"
DEUTERONOMY 3-6

Ramoth-gilead

AMORITES

Jordan

Ai

Jericho

AMMONITES

Ramoth-ammon

Heshbon

Mount Nebo

Death of Moses in sight of the promised land

PHILISTINES

Ashdod

Ashkelon

Gaza

CANAANITES

JEBUSITES

MOABITES

River of Egypt

AMALEKITES

EDOMITES

"And they burnt all their cities wherein they dwelt, and all their goodly castles with fire"
NUMBERS 31-10

MIDIANITES

Ezion-geber

0   40
Miles

Map 3

the promised land. No one could resist him, for he waged the wars of the Lord (cf. Sir 46:1-10).

Stages in the conquest of Canaan The book divides into these three sections:

a) Preparations and conquest (chap. 1-12). Joshua is charged to conquer the land which Yahweh promised the patriarchs. Before crossing the Jordan he reminds all the tribes of Israel about their commitments to Yahweh and then chooses spies who manage to enter Jericho with the aid of Rahab and report back to Joshua, "Truly the Lord has given all the land into our hands; and moreover all the inhabitants of the land are fainthearted because of us" (Josh 2:24).

By a special providence of God they cross the Jordan whose waters open to let them pass, and they erect twelve stone columns to commemorate this miracle. The Jordan in is full flood at this season — springtime — and often overflows its banks: the snows of Lebanon melt just around the time of the first harvest. Some Fathers (for example, St Gregory and St Augustine) see this turning back of the waters as symbolizing the effects of Baptism, whereby man goes back to the origin from which he deviated.

After they cross the Jordan, everyone is circumcised at Gilgal (5:2ff). This is highly significant. St Augustine says it is "not the person but the people" who revive the practice of circumcision, which was interrupted when they left Egypt. Circumcision was unnecessary when they were living in the wilderness: it was a sign of belonging to Israel and therefore served no useful purpose while they were moving around uninhabited territory. Also, St Jerome says, God dispensed them from circumcision in the desert because it would have been difficult or dangerous to carry out properly in that situation.

They then move on and conquer Jericho after a seven day siege, putting all to the sword except Rahab and her family (6:17-25). How did they manage to do this? "By faith the walls of Jericho fell down after they had been encircled for seven days" (Heb 11:30). What could have been more ridiculous than silently circling a strong, well-defended city? Clearly the methods the Israelites used were completely disproportionate to what they achieved — an example of how God confounds human reason by apparent foolishness (cf. 1 Cor 1:19-25).

After this comes a first, unsuccessful, attack on Ai. Joshua discovers in prayer the reason for the failure: an Israelite had taken booty — which God had explicitly forbidden should be done. Achan confesses his crime and is punished and then the Israelites succeed in taking the city (chap. 8). At the end of this chapter the covenant is renewed

at Mouth Ebal, to the east of the plain of Shechem.   The first part
of the book ends with the account of two more conquests: that of
southern Palestine (chap. 9-10) with the episode of the Gibeonites
who shrewdly make a treaty with Joshua and obtain his aid in their
struggle with the Amorites: this is when Joshua "stops" the sun to
give himself an advantage;[2] and that of southern Palestine, with the
account of his victories (chap. 11) and the list of conquered kings
(chap. 12).

b) Distribution of lands. Chapters 13-19 give details of the division
of territory among the tribes and the establishment of cities of refuge
(chap. 20) and of cities allocated to the Levites (chap. 21). Chapter
22 finishes with the return of the Tranjordanian tribes and the erection
of an altar beside the Jordan.

c) Last dispositions (chap. 23-24). The book closes with a kind of
appendix in which Joshua states his mind about the as yet
unconquered territory and which reports his great address to the
people assembled at Shechem on the subject of the fidelity to God's
Law. And finally we are told where Joshua and Eleazar and Joseph
are buried.

The religious scope of this book   The book of *Joshua* does report
on key events in the history of the people of Israel. But we should
remember that it is both a history book and a doctrinal book: in
reporting history — and doing so accurately — it is also teaching
religious and moral lessons. Although the conquest of Canaan comes
across as a great achievement, it is one which could not have happened
without Yahweh's continuous support. Over this period of almost
thirty years Joshua is conscious that God is at his side in all his
difficulties: sometimes he actually sees this help — at the pushing
back of the Jordan, his vision as he approaches Jericho, the staying
of the sun, etc.

The whole book speaks eloquently of God's fidelity to his promise,
which makes it a source of encouragement to Israel to remain faithful
to him.

Throughout the book of Joshua we can see that it prefigures the
New Alliance, which will come about centuries later in the person

2 Joshua helped the Gibeonites in their war against their enemies. "The sun stood still,
and the moon stayed". God listened to Joshua's prayer and worked a miracle, suspending
the laws of nature — his laws. Joshua does not explain how this happened. He simply
reports what he saw with his own eyes: he could not explain the event scientifically, which,
besides, would have been quite out of context. The episode demonstrates God's protection
of his people. Cf. S Garafola, *La S. Biblia (Joshua)* (Turin 1952); A. Vaccari, *La S. Biblia*
(Florence 1961).

of Jesus Christ, the promised Messiah. Even Joshua's name (= Yahweh saves) is a symbol of Jesus, for only in him can we find true salvation, which neither the Law nor the priesthood nor the sacrifices of the Old Testament can bring about. Faith in Jesus Christ, when accompanied by works, has power to bring a person into the new and final land — Jerusalem which comes down out of heaven from God (Rev 21:1-2).

Even the division of Canaan by drawing lots is a figure of the gratuitous nature of the calling which Christians receive in Jesus Christ; "even as he chose us in him", St Paul says, "before the foundation of the world, that we should be holy and blameless before him ... he destined us in love to be his sons through Jesus Christ, according to the purpose of his will" (Eph 1:4-5).

Finally, it may seem strange for a leader like Joshua, charged with leading his people to conquer a series of enemies much more powerful than themselves, to be given the express instruction from God to apply himself night and day to the meditation of his Law, to have it forever on his lips and in his actions. However, we must remember that God has assured us that the source of true prudence lies in faithfulness to the divine Law, and the only way to achieve success in our undertakings is to keep in line with God's will. Hence we should frequently check on our actions and motives to make sure they are in line with our beliefs. Unfortunately some people do not take God's law into account when shaping the structures of society and support the introduction or maintenance of laws which are in conflict with the natural law and therefore with the common good (for example, divorce laws); in cases like these people's minds and wills are bent out of their true pattern and they have come a long way from the model conduct of Joshua.

Judges: liberators and leaders of Israel

This book, which is the continuation of *Joshua*, takes its name from the men whom God raised up to govern Israel for almost two centuries, from the death of Joshua to the birth of Samuel. The biblical concept of "judge" is not the same as ours;[4] "judges" (liberators,

---

3 There is no mention in Scripture or in the Fathers of children of Joshua. The Fathers' general opinion is that Joshua remained celibate all his life. See the eulogy of him in Sir 46.

4 Cf. Robert and Feuillet, op cit.

saviours) were people (they included one woman, Deborah) who were seasoned warriors, sometimes chosen directly by God, sometimes by the people, who were given the mission to protect Israel from attacks by its enemies and to take possession (not without a struggle) of the territory earmarked for them in the division; then, once peace reigned, their role was to administer justice. In most cases their authority did not extend to all Israel but only to one tribe or a group of tribes. This explains why there is no chronological succession in the Judges: sometimes you find a number of Judges contemporary with each other.

Israel's unfaithfulness Before going into the narrative proper, the first chapter gives a summary of the political and religious situation at the time. After Joshua's death, now that each tribe had been assigned a particular territory, each began to take possession of its lot, by force. However, they soon realized that the territories allocated were not large enough to accommodate each tribe. In some cases the tribe only managed to win part of the territory or it had to share it with others: in other words, because Israel failed to keep its part of the Covenant (it was supposed to destroy altars erected to the Baals*, the gods of the conquered lands), God would not give it total victory.

Everything began to go badly, yet God had pity on them and sent them the Judges; but, as soon as a Judge died the people again began to revert to idolatry. The net result was that God did not wipe out, as they had expected, all the inhabitants of the country (Sidonians, Philistines etc).

The central part of the book (chap. 3, 6-16ff) deals with the vicissitudes experienced by the various Judges, all of which are on the same lines: infidelity leads to defeat, repentance to liberation; just as sin leads to punishment, and confession to forgiveness. All this is contained in six long narratives, interspersed with shorter accounts of the great deeds of the Judges. The number of Judges is given as twelve, which may be taken as symbolizing the perfect Israel: it is at least possible that there were other Judges, of lesser importance, of whom no record remains.

The chronology of the book; deeds of the Judges The chronology of the book is somewhat artificial. Clearly the many references to the figure 40 — 40 years = a generation — or its multiple (80) or half (20) — indicate that these numbers are symbolic. Nor was all Israel affected by the oppression or liberation described.

During this difficult period of settlement the Israelites had to fight the Canaanites, the previous occupiers of the territory, whom Deborah and Barak defeated on the plains of Esdraelon. Deborah was a prophetess, that is, a person who spoke in God's name and also acted as an administration of justice, resolving all kinds of litigious complaints, thanks to special divine inspiration. She also ruled the people, led the army into battle, appointed generals, declared war and won victory. Scripture also praises Barak, a humble man, full of faith, who, recognizing that the spirit of Yahweh inspired Deborah, worked in support of her (Judg 4:8).

The Judges also had to fight against other neighbouring people — Moabites (Ehud), Ammonites (Jephthah), Midianites (Gideon) and the Philistines, recently settled on the coast (Samson).

The sacred text says of Samson that he would be dedicated to God from birth (Judg 13:5). God endowed him with enormous strength. His long hair was connected with his being a Nazarite, consecrated to God. However, Samson was not a Judge; he never led an army into battle against the enemies of Israel; his deeds of prowess were isolated, some to defend himself, other indirectly to help his people fend off their enemies.[5]

The book closes with two appendixes (chap. 17-21), which briefly describe the dire straits of an Israel which has strayed from Yahweh on the path of idolatry. Each of these two narratives ends in the same words: "In those days there was no king in Israel" (18:1; 21-25) — apparently reflecting the general attitudes of the Israelites at the time: they saw the establishment of a monarchy as the only way out, and soon it came to be.

Doctrinal content   The inspired writer of this book prophesies that each of the Judges adores Yahweh and is determined to be faithful to the Covenant. They all invoke God and implore his protection before and after battles, for this purpose going to the sanctuary of Shiloh, the centre of worship of Yahweh at this period. The struggles into which they are drawn to gain complete control of Canann also have the effect of binding the tribes of Israel together, since all make common cause.

The book of *Judges* shows how the Alliance made at Sinai worked out in practice: Yahweh is protective of Israel as long as it stays faithful to its commitments, and punishes it whenever it violates them. God wishes to show the Israelites that oppression is a punishment for impiety, and victory a reward for faithfulness. This is why *Sirach*

5 Cf. E. Power in *CCHS*, sections 244ff.

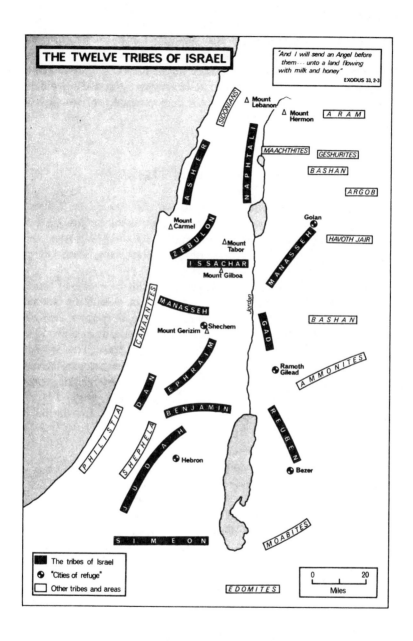

THE TWELVE TRIBES OF ISRAEL

"And I will send an Angel before them ... unto a land flowing with milk and honey"
EXODUS 33, 2-3

SIDONIANS

△ Mount Lebanon

△ Mount Hermon

A R A M

MAACHTHITES

GESHURITES

BASHAN

ARGOB

ASHER

NAPHTALI

Mount △ Carmel

ZEBULON

△ Mount Tabor

Golan ⊕

MANASSEH

HAVOTH JAIR

I S S A C H A R
△
Mount Gilboa

CANAANITES

MANASSEH

Mount Gerizim ⊕ Shechem
△

Jordan

EPHRAIM

GAD

BASHAN

DAN

Ramoth ⊕ Gilead

AMMONITES

PHILISTIA

BENJAMIN

SHEPHELA

J U D A H

REUBEN

⊕ Hebron

⊕ Bezer

S I M E O N

MOABITES

The tribes of Israel
⊕ "Cities of refuge"
Other tribes and areas

0   20
Miles

EDOMITES

Map 4

(46:11-12) praises the Judges and why the Letter to the *Hebrews* (11:32-34) stresses that their exploits were the reward for their faith and a lesson for us: "Therefore, since we are surrounded by so great a cloud of witnesses, let us also lay aside every weight, and sin which clings so closely, and let us run with perseverance the race that is set before us" (Heb 12:1).

Ruth: her place in the line of David

This short book deals with a family during the time of the Judges. The Septuagint and the Vulgate both locate it immediately after *Judges*, whereas the Jews put in among the *Ketubim* (Writings), as one of the five *mequillot* used on the main feast days, Ruth being read on the day of Pentecost.

We do not exactly know the precise year when the events of Ruth took place; possibly during the time of Deborah, in view of the famine which forces Elimelech and his family to leave Bethlehem and go into Moab. The author must have written the book during David's reign, given the reference to it at the end of the book. This would not be surprising in view of the many archaic words it contains, which are indicative of a very early date. Also the serene tone of the narrative would seen incompatible with the calamities which marked later periods. However, some scholars argue for a later date, after the exile to Babylon.[6]

Elimelech emigrates from Bethlehem during a period of acute famine, with his wife Naomi and their two sons, Mahlon and Chilon. They go to Moab[7] where the sons marry two local women, Orpah and Ruth. In due course Elimelech dies, and ten years later his sons die. Circumstances have improved in Israel and Naomi decides to return to Bethlehem. Ruth offers to go with her, as if she were her own daughter.

Once they get to Bethlehem Ruth has to work to support her mother-in-law. While she is gleaning she meets Boaz, a rich relative

---

6 A. Robert, op. cit., is one who is of this opinion.

7 The region of Moab, in Arabia, had as its capital Petra, from where it is thought Ruth came. On the basis of this St Jerome applies to Ruth these words of Isaiah: "They have sent lambs to the ruler of the land, from Sela, by way of the desert, to the mount of the daughter of Zion" (Is 16:1). Since Obed was born of Ruth, and David of Obed, and Jesus of David, this interpretation could not be more messianic.

of Elimelech, who, attracted by her virtues, decides to take her as his wife, thereby fulfilling the custom of Levirate* marriage. A son of this marriage is Obed, the father of Jesse and the grandfather of David.

Although the primary purpose of the book is to show the genealogy of David, this is done in the context of a moral tale. The writer emphasizes that trust in God is always rewarded: his mercy has no limits and extends to all who sincerely seek his help. In this instance it extends to a foreigner, Ruth,[8] and the result is that she becomes the great-grandmother of King David and a direct forebear of the Messiah. The very fact that Ruth figures in the genealogy of Jesus Christ, as do other foreign women (Mt 1:3-5), points up the universal scope of the salvation which Christ will bring to all men (1 Tim 2:4), Gentiles as well as Jews (Heb 10:34-35; 11:18).

This is a doctrinally rich book which the Church often uses in its liturgy. The names of Ruth and Boaz are read three times at Mass — where the liturgy of the word uses the genealogy given in Matthew. Boaz' greeting, "The Lord be with you" (Ruth 2:4) is used often in the Mass and elsewhere. Naomi's lament (1:20) is applied to the sorrows of the Blessed Virgin (feast of 15 September); and Ruth's words (2:13) are also used to express Mary's sentiments in the Liturgy of the Hours on the feast of her Immaculate Heart.

The book also contains interesting information about the rite of Levirate marriage, the ceremony for the assigning of property and agricultural customs of the time to do with sowing and reaping.

1 and 2 Samuel

The two books under Samuel's name in the Greek version of the Septuagint correspond to one book in the Hebrew Bible located among the "later prophets". The Vulgate — following the Greek — puts *1 and 2 Samuel* and *1 and 2 Kings* under the same heading — *1-4 Kings*. The New Vulgate shows *1 and 2 Samuel* and *1 and 2 Kings* as separate.

In line with Hebrew tradition, we can say that the inspired writer

---

8 The very blessing which the whole people gave Ruth is interpreted by St Ambrose as a kind of prophecy: from her numerous descendants Jesus, the Messiah, will be born — precisely in Bethlehem, surnamed Ephrathah, as mentioned in Ruth 4:11.

of the first book was the prophet Samuel himself, at least up to chapter 25 where his death is described. The rest of that book and all the second book are attributed to two other prophets, Gad and Nathan. However, some scholars question the attribution of the first part of the first book to Samuel on the grounds that the events it recounts refer to a period other than that in which Samuel lived. Some think that Ezra wrote chapters 1-25, using an early original of Samuel's and various writings from the time of David to produce a survey of the period from the start of the monarchy up to the end of David's reign, a period of some one hundred and fifty years.[9]

Towards the unification of Israel   The main purpose of *1 and 2 Samuel* is to provide a history of the foundation of the kingdom of Israel and the settlement of the throne on David and his line. It will be remembered that at the end of *Judges* the people saw a monarchy as the only way out of a situation of internal strife and anarchy. Outside enemies had been reduced to one — the Philistines, who were established along the Mediterranean coast; but the Philistines were so formidable and expansionist that the very survival of Israel seemed to be at stake and the tribes really needed to combine forces.

Samuel, who is regarded as the last of the Judges, was the man chosen to bring about this unification. God used him to make Saul the first king of Israel. Everything connected with this choice of Saul, as with later events resulting from it, shows that God is still with his people; he is going to bring them to new political and military heights. The Philistines are defeated, though not brought under total control. Like the Ammonites, Moabites, Edomites, and Aramites, they become tributaries of Israel. This whole campaign was brought to a conclusion during the reign of David, whose vassal even the king of Tyre became. The effect of all this is that all Transjordania came to be dominated by David.

Despite these impressive victories the unity of the tribes of Israel under one king was still somewhat artificial. It was very much dependent on the military and political genius of David, who managed to get the twelve tribes to pull together: but differences among them ran deep; their underlying causes were not removed and later led to permanent divisions. David was shrewd enough to unite the two previously separated kingdoms (north and south) but the distinction

---

9 Whichever theory is proposed about the early redactions, generally critics now agree that the *Samuel* text we now possess existed as a book before the Deuteronomy division.

between them still remained and a final schism took place after David's death, accelerated by the unfortunate policy of his son Solomon, who started well and finished badly.

The sequence of events *1 and 2 Samuel* are structured in four parts, with an appendix. The first part covers the miraculous birth of Samuel and his upbringing in the Temple. Here we should note especially the canticle of his mother Hannah, after Samuel is consecrated in the temple of Shiloh; it is one of the most beautiful hymns in the Old Testament (1 Sam 2:1-10) and is regarded as an anticipation of the *Magnificat*, echoing as it does the messianic hopes of the *anawim* (= the poor, the humble). God will enrich the poor and bring down the proud. The nations will fear the Anointed (the Christ*) who will reign over them so that his name will be honoured to the ends of the earth.

The narrative then goes on to describe the first war against the Philistines: the Israelites lose and the ark falls into the hands of their worst enemies. In the second part (1 Sam 8-15) the establishment of the monarchy is described and the consecration of Saul as king. The people ask for a king and Samuel at first refuses, but then God tells him to do what they want and in fact nominates Saul. Samuel proclaims Saul king, after anointing him with oil to show that he is a sacred person. In 1 Sam 9:16 God's providence shines out; he fills Saul with the insight and courage necessary to give his people good government.

After Saul's coronation his divine election is confirmed by his great victories over the Amalekites. Once Samuel retires from his position as judge, the book goes on to describe more of Saul's victories. However, despite all these victories, God rejects Saul because he transgresses his commandments.

We noted that during the period of the Judges, Israel very often failed to stay loyal to God. The same thing happens under the monarchy. Saul himself is rejected — which again shows that God chooses people irrespective of their merits and then expects them to remain true to the grace received.

The third section (1 Sam 16 — 2 Sam 1) deals with the relationship between Saul and David. At God's express wish, David is secretly anointed and Saul, in his jealousy, does everything to kill him. David has to flee and he remains a fugitive until Saul and his son Jonathan are killed in battle against the Philistines. David with his usual magnanimity composes a funeral eulogy in their honour. In the fourth part (2 Sam 2-20) the narrative centres on David: the civil war, ending with the deaths of Abner and Ish-Bosheth, the pretender to the throne of Judah; the transfer of the ark to Jerusalem, which David makes his capital; the messianic promise that an eternal throne will be given to one of David's lineage (2 Sam 7:12ff). However, the exceptional peace which ensued was disturbed by King David's double sin, followed by Absolam's conspiracy and death.

2 Sam 11:4ff deals with these sins of David — his adultery with Bathsheba and his arrangement of her husband's death in battle. God condemns David's sin — and punishes him for it — but hope of pardon is present throughout the narrative. God allowed David, whose life had been so upright, to sin in this serious way in order to show his mercy and forgiveness — the final expression of this being the messiahship of his descendant. After this episode David changes completely and remains contrite until his death.

In an appendix (2 Sam 21-24) two great calamities are reported — a famine which lasts for three years, ending when David makes satisfaction to the Gibeonites for a wrong done them; then the three days of pestilence which ravages the entire country from Dan to Beersheba. The end of the book also contains an account of David's deeds against the Philistines; his song of deliverance and the prophetic messianic oracle about David's lineage.

Nathan's messianic prediction *Samuel* makes more explicit God's promise of salvation given to our first parents and developed in the sacred books which we have been describing. Many centuries of chequered history must pass before this promise finds its fulfilment and the kingdom of God is established on earth. David's reign is one of relative peace, preceded by the fall of Saul and following the infidelities of Solomon. When least expected, God sends a message of hope, in the form of a prophecy by Nathan to the effect that God will establish his offspring on his throne forever:

> When your days are fulfilled and you lie down with your fathers, I will raise up your offspring after you, who shall come forth from your body, and I will establish his kingdom. . . . And your house and your kingdom shall be made sure for ever before me; your throne shall be established for ever (2 Sam 7:12-16).

The New Testament repeatedly refers to this prophecy (cf. Lk 1:32-33; Acts 2:30; 2 Cor 6:18; Heb 1:5) and the Fathers see it as referring to Jesus Christ, the promised Messiah: chosen to bring salvation to all, he was persecuted by those of his own house; although he was humiliated he pardoned and atoned for the behaviour of those who ill-treated him; in his meekness he did not rebel but rather acted with infinite patience.

David, who originates the dynasty which will eventually lead to the fulfilment of God's promise of salvation, was one of the most humble and devout personalities in the Old Testament. He was the first man since Moses to unite the various Israelite tribes, spiritually as well as politically. He led them to victory over their enemies, but, what was more important, he renewed their faith in their Alliance with Yahweh and taught them an all-important lesson — never to embark on any enterprise without first consulting Yahweh their God.

His sense of devotion led him to take particular care of everything to do with the worship of God. Even in his old age his piety never faltered; and it stood to him when he fell into sin, leading him to repentance and atonement.

He was a humble man. He admitted his sins and was not ashamed to weep before God, whom weakness caused him to offend. As a prophet he composed songs extolling the future Messiah who will be his descendant — the "son of David", whom later prophets will call "King David" (Jer 30:9; Hos 3:5), "My servant David" (Ezek 34:23; 37:24) — the best praise God could give this faithful and pious king.

1 and 2 Kings

In the Hebrew Bible the two books of *Samuel* and the two books of *Kings* all make up one book. The division into two stems from the Greek Septuagint, which the Vulgate and later editions followed and which was in fact adopted by the Hebrew Bible from 1517 forward. The Septuagint and the Vulgate called them *3 and 4 Kings* (because they called Samuel *1 and 2 Kings*). The title of *Kings* is very appropriate: the text covers the history of the kingdoms of Judah and Israel from the death of David (c. 970 B.C.) to the Babylonian exile.

The books appear to have been written in various stages. The earliest form offers us an outline of the history of the various kings which the inspired writer took from the "Book of the Acts of Solomon" (1 Kings 11:41), the "Books of the Chronicles of the King of Israel" (1 Kings 14:19) and the "Book of the Chronicles of the

Kings of Judah" (1 Kings 14:29), often citing his source.[10] These were public documents accessible to everyone, not private papers in the royal archives.

Moreover, since the kings are assessed here against the yardstick of idolatry in the "high places"* (cf. 1 Kings 15:14; 22:44), this indicates that these books were written after Josiah's reform (621) and probably after his death. The text says of him: "Before him there was no king like him, who turned to the Lord with all his heart and with all his soul and with all his might, according to the law of Moses; nor did any like him arise after him" (2 Kings 23:25)

This would suggest that the passage just quoted, with the exception of its final words, may very well have marked the end of the work and that the books therefore originate from before the exile to Babylon in 587, when the Temple was still in operation and the ark of the covenant was still in position in the *Debir* or most holy place: "The priests brought the ark of the covenant of the Lord to its place, in the inner sanctuary of the house, in the most holy place, underneath the wings of the cherubim" (1 Kings 8:6).

However, the first draft must have been followed by a second in the reign of Jehoiachin (609-598), given that the former makes no reference to the prophet Jeremiah. The third and final redaction would date from after 562, during the Babylonian captivity (2 Kings 25:22-30).

The content of these books *1 and 2 Kings* follow directly on *1 and 2 Samuel* and are perhaps easier to understand if divided into three parts:

1. *The story of Solomon* (1 Kings 1-11). After a short introduction dealing with the last days of David and the succession of his son, the author centres his attention on Solomon, who becomes a king renowned for his wisdom (the neighbouring kings acknowledge this), magnificence (witness his building programme) and wealth: chapters 3-10. The weaknesses in the king's character do, however, cast their shadow. Foreign wives influence him to worship their gods, Molech and Ashtoreth (1 Kings 11:5). Israel will pay dearly for his infidelity.[11]

Solomon's initial drive and his undoubted intelligence and valour fade into the background due to his neglect of the worship of Yahweh. As St Augustine comments, external worship is not pleasing to God

10 Cf. A Robert, op. cit.
11 Cf. S. Garofalo, *Il libro dei Re* (Turin, 1951), pp. 28-205.

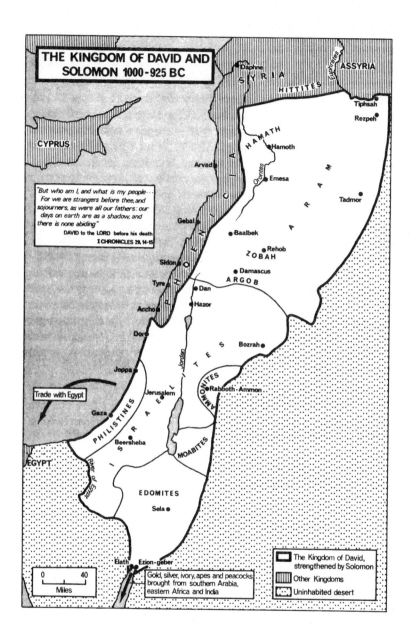

THE KINGDOM OF DAVID AND SOLOMON 1000-925 BC

ASSYRIA

SYRIA

Daphne

Tiphsah

Rezpeh

HITTITES

CYPRUS

HAMATH

Hamoth

Arvad

Emesa

Orontes

Tadmor

A R A M

"But who am I, and what is my people...
For we are strangers before thee, and
sojourners, as were all our fathers: our
days on earth are as a shadow, and
there is none abiding"
DAVID to the LORD before his death
I CHRONICLES 29, 14-15

Gebal

Baalbek

Rehob

Z O B A H

Sidon

Damascus

Tyre

A R G O B

Dan

Hazor

Accho

Bozrah

Dor

J
O
R
D
A
N
I
T
E
S

Joppa

Jordan

Jerusalem

A
M
M
O
N
I
T
E
S

Rabboth-Ammon

Trade with Egypt

I
S
R
A
E
L

Gaza

PHILISTINES

Beersheba

MOABITES

EGYPT

River of Egypt

E D O M I T E S

Sela

Elath Ezion-geber

0   40
Miles

Gold, silver, ivory, apes and peacocks
brought from southern Arabia,
eastern Africa and India

The Kingdom of David,
strengthened by Solomon

Other Kingdoms

Uninhabited desert

Map 5

however splendidly and richly it is done, unless it is inspired by the interior worship of faith, hope and charity and is accompanied by good works, that is, faithfulness to God's commandments.

2. *The kingdom is split in two: Judah and Israel* (1 Kings 12:22). The differences between the northern and western tribes, latent during David's reign, lead to a permanent split — religious as well as political — after Solomon's death (chap. 12-13). From this point onwards parallel histories are given for the two kingdoms (chap. 14-22).

In chapter 17 Elijah the prophet appears out of nowhere to preach a message of strict fidelity to Yahweh and to defend worship of Yahweh against that of Phoenician idols. His name, which means "My God is Yahweh", describes his whole life-programme. He is the greatest of the non-writer prophets.[12] In addition to the passage which describes his challenge to the prophets of Baal (1 Kings 18:24ff), his experience on Mount Horeb is well worth meditation: earlier symbols of God's presence — the hurricane, earthquake, fire — give way to the "still small voice" of a gentle breeze, which symbolizes that God is pure spirit: his goodness and mercy, which invite man but never force him, are a veiled reference to the God-Child who will be born at Bethlehem, who has no need of noisy show to win man's attention.

3. *The history of Judah and Israel up to the time of the exile* (2 Kings 1-25). These chapters deal mainly with the wars between the two kingdoms and the attacks on them from outside. The situation became even more criticial when the Assyrians invaded, first in the ninth century and more vigorously in the eighth. Samaria, the capital of the northern kingdom, fell in 721, and later Judah became an Assyrian vassal. From this point onwards biblical history centres on Judah and continues to do so up to the fall of Jerusalem in 587.

After the apotheosis of Elijah on Mount Carmel (chap. 2) Elisha the prophet takes over the role of promoting the Covenant.

The message of Kings   To understand God's message in *Kings* we need to keep in mind the teaching of *Deuteronomy*. The basic teaching of *Deuteronomy* had to do with there being only one God and only one valid Temple for his worship. This centralization of priesthood and liturgy is first legislated for in Deuteronomy 12.

The kings are condemned in these books because instead of concentrating on the Temple in Jerusalem they establish rival shrines

---

12 Cf. Profesores de Salamanca, *Biblia commentada*, I; C. Tresmontant, *La doctrina moral de los profetas de Israel* (Madrid 1958), pp. 63-212.

at Bethel and Dan in the north in opposition to the Temple; furthermore, they are neglectful of their duty to suppress the "high places" all over Palestine where sacrifice is offered to Baal in contravention of the Covenant.

This and none other is the reason for the collapse first of Samaria and later of Judah. Yahweh is not at fault: he kept his word; it is Israel who has been faithless. God's judgment is accepted submissively because he is justified in his sentence and blameless in his judgment (cf. Ps 51). Everything recounted in *Kings* is a canticle in praise of divine justice; any punishment meted out simply means that unfaithfulness to the covenant is being dealt with as promised (cf. Deut 28:15ff).

In spite of the sadness felt by the survivors of the catastrophe, there is still that ray of hope coming from Nathan's prophecy of an everlasting Davidic kingdom (2 Sam 7). This is underlined when after years in prison Jehoiachin, king of Judah, is pardoned by the king of Babylon (2 Kings 25:27-30). The people who stay faithful to Yahweh do realize that the keeping of his law "is no trifle, but it is your life" (Deut 32:47), for God always keeps his word (1 Kings 2:4; 2 Kings 10:10).

Kings contains a lot of important theological material but it is also historically very accurate as recent archaeology shows. For example, the list of cities conquered by Pharaoh Sheshonq (Shishak) I is carried on a wall in a temple in Karnak, and Jerusalem is included (cf. 1 Kings 14:25-28); the monolith of Shalmaneser III commemorates that king's victory at the battle of Qarqar over an alliance of Syrian and Palestinian kings; the black obelisk which shows Jehu or his representative prostrated before Shalmaneser and lists the various objects given as tribute by the son of Omri; the Taylor prism and the bas-reliefs of Sennarcherib's palace in Nineveh which refer to Sennacherib's campaigns against Judah (cf. 2 Kings 18:13-19:37). Within Palestine itself we have the stele of Mesha, the Siloe inscription, the "obstraca" of Lakish and Samaria and many other cities which have been excavated and whose findings corroborate what the sacred text says.[13]

---

13 Cf. L. Arnaldich, *La Santa Biblia*, p. 373.

1 and 2 Chronicles

The Old Testament contains a second set of historical books which repeat and expand on the sacred history covered in the earlier books. These are *1 and 2 Chronicles, Ezra* and *Nehemiah*. As in the case of *Samuel* and *Kings* the two books of *Chronicles* began as one book but they appear as two in the Greek version of the Septuagint and this division is maintained in the Vulgate and in later editions, including the Hebrew Bible.

St Jerome gave them the name of "Chronicles": he called them the "Chronicle of Chronicles". The Jews continued to call them *Dibre hayyamïm* (= the events of the days) and the Greek version *Paralipomenon*, because they fill in for what was omitted or only treated in passing in *Samuel* and *Kings*.

The inspired writer was probably a Levite from Jerusalem, given his respectful attention to the Temple and its institutions; he probably edited the text — if one accepts Ezra and Nehemiah as authors — after the death of those prophets, and before the second century, since *Sirach* takes it as read in the year 180 B.C. This suggests a date for the final edition of some time in the second half of the third century B.C.[14]

The main stages   In its early chapters *Chronicles* gives a summary of salvation history over a long period from the start of mankind up to the Babylonian exile. The sacred writer, who is also referred to as the "Chronicler", deals with this history in four stages:

1. *Up to David* (chap. 1-9). These chapters summarize sacred history from Adam to David. They give long genealogical lists for each of the tribes, paying special attention to Judah and to David's descendants, and to the Levites and the inhabitants of Jerusalem.

2. *The history of David* (chap. 10-29). These chapters cover the choice of David as king; the conquest, and the selection of Jerusalem as capital; the installation of the ark in the holy city and arrangements for worship, as also preparations for the building of the Temple. However, there is no mention of discord between David and Saul or of David's relations with Bathsheba, but particular emphasis is given to Nathan's prophecy, which is expressed in these words:

> When your days are fulfilled to go to be with your fathers, I will raise

---

14 A. Robert is of this opinion.

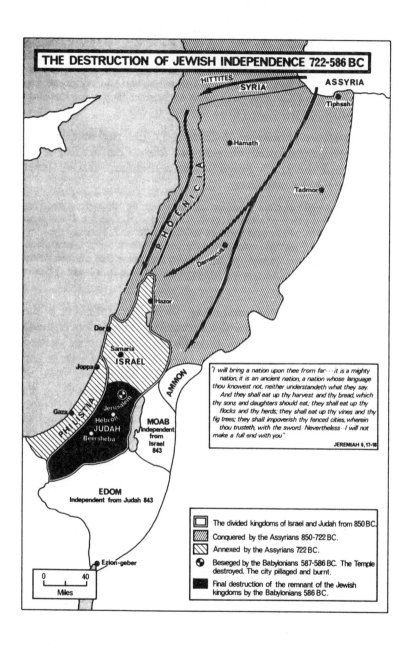

THE DESTRUCTION OF JEWISH INDEPENDENCE 722-586 BC

HITTITES
SYRIA
ASSYRIA

Tiphsah

Hamath

Tadmor

P H O E N I C I A

Damascus

Hazor

Dor

Samaria
ISRAEL

Joppa

AMMON

Gaza

Jerusalem
Hebron
JUDAH
Beersheba

MOAB
Independent
from
Israel
843

PHILISTINA

EDOM
Independent from Judah 843

Ezion-geber

0   40
Miles

"I will bring a nation upon thee from far···it is a mighty
nation, it is an ancient nation, a nation whose language
thou knowest not, neither understandeth what they say.
  And they shall eat up thy harvest and thy bread, which
thy sons and daughters should eat; they shall eat up thy
  flocks and thy herds; they shall eat up thy vines and thy
fig trees; they shall impoverish thy fenced cities, wherein
  thou trustest, with the sword. Nevertheless···I will not
make a full end with you"

JEREMIAH 6, 17-18

☐ The divided kingdoms of Israel and Judah from 850 BC.

▨ Conquered by the Assyrians 850-722 BC.

◹ Annexed by the Assyrians 722 BC.

⊕ Besieged by the Babylonians 587-586 BC. The Temple
destroyed. The city pillaged and burnt.

■ Final destruction of the remnant of the Jewish
kingdoms by the Babylonians 586 BC.

Map 6

up your offspring after you, one of your own sons, and I will establish his kingdom. He shall build a house for me, and I will establish his throne for ever. I will be his father, and he shall be my son; I will not take my steadfast love from him, as I took it from him who was before you, but I will confirm him in my house and in my kingdom for ever and his throne shall be established for ever (1 Chron 17:11-14).

3. *The history of Solomon* (2 Chron 1-9). The next section deals with Solomon, particularly the start and finish of the building of the Temple and the king's prayer at the dedication, with all Israel assembled for the ceremony:

If my people who are called by my name humble themselves, and pray and seek my face, and turn from their wicked ways, then I will hear from heaven, and will forgive their sin and heal their land. Now my eyes will be open and my ears attentive to the prayer that is made in this place. For now I have chosen and consecrated this house that my name may be there for ever; my eyes and my heart will be there for all time (2 Chron 7:14-16).

4. *Religious reforms and exile* (chap. 10-36). From the time of the break with Samaria,* the text concentrates on the kingdom of Judah and its kings, who are all of the line of David. These kings are assessed in terms of adherence — or not — to the Covenant. Disorder and anarchy are countered by religious reforms, particularly those of Hezekiah and Josiah.[15] Josiah's example was not followed by his successors, who took Judah in a direction leading inexorably to ruin. The book finishes with an account of the fall of Jerusalem, exile to Babylon and the edict of Cyrus, king of Persia, allowing the Jews to return to Israel.

Supernatural religious teaching   To understand the teaching contained in these books we must remember that they are not a complete account of salvation history or even a supplement to one (such as the Greek name suggests). The sacred writer, who is more concerned with theology than history, has two purposes in mind. The first is to show that on their return from exile each tribe should by right get its own lands back, those given it in the time of Joshua; this is why the writer gives the detailed genealogies of the patriarchs and why he is at pains to point out which cities they lived in and which territories belonged to each family.

His second and principal purpose concerns the reestablishment of worship after the exile. Although the tribe of Levi is given a place

15 There is a very close connexion between Josiah's reform and the appearance of the Deuteronomic movement in its time.

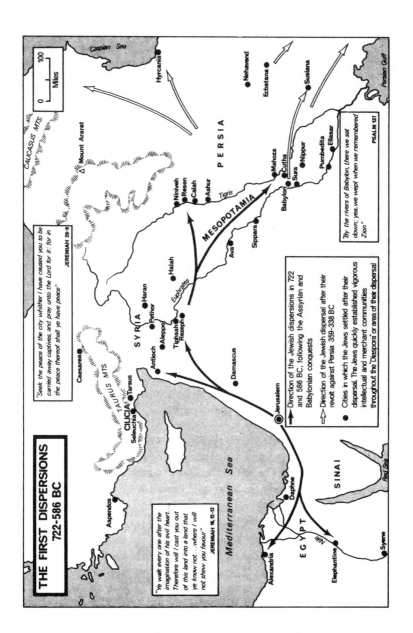

THE FIRST DISPERSIONS
722-586 BC

"Seek the peace of the city whither I have caused you to be carried away captives, and pray unto the Lord for it: for in the peace thereof shall ye have peace"

JEREMIAH 29:9

"Ye walk every one after the imagination of his evil heart... Therefore will I cast you out of this land into a land that ye know not... where I will not shew you favour"

JEREMIAH 16:12-13

→ Direction of the Jewish dispersions in 722 and 586 BC, following the Assyrian and Babylonian conquests

⇨ Direction of the Jewish dispersal after their revolt against Persia 359-338 BC

● Cities in which the Jews settled after their dispersal. The Jews quickly established vigorous intellectual and merchant communities throughout the 'Diaspora' or area of their dispersal

"By the rivers of Babylon, there we sat down; yea, we wept when we remembered Zion."

PSALM 137

Miles
0   100

Caspian Sea
CAUCASUS MTS.
Mount Ararat
Hyrcania
Nehavend
Echatana
Susiana
Persian Gulf

PERSIA

Nineveh
Resen
Calah
Ashur
Tigris
MESOPOTAMIA
Mahoza
Cutha
Babylon
Sura
Nippur
Pumbedita
Ellasar

Sippara
Ava
Halah
Euphrates
Haran
Pethor
SYRIA
Aleppo
Tiphsah
Rezeph
Antioch
Damascus

Caesarea
TAURUS MTS.
Tarsus
CILICIA
Seleucia

Jerusalem

Aspendos

Mediterranean Sea

Daphne
EGYPT
Nile
SINAI
Red Sea
Alexandria
Elephantine
Syene

Map 7

of special honour the main message of the book as far as worship is concerned is that God requires holiness not only of the ministers who are dedicated to his service, but also of the people at large, through their participation in sacrifices; this means that Temple sacrifices regain their original value.

In line with these objectives *Chronicles* also reflects a very important fact: the new holy community of Israel will consist of the "remnant"* who remained faithful during the Babylonian exile. But this remnant is not a small religious or ethnic sect: it transcends the kingdom of Judah and even the apostate kingdom of Samaria; all the twelve tribes will be reunited to form the "new Israel" and even pagans will obtain access to it by being invited to pray in the Temple of Jerusalem.

The Chronicler, working for his contemporaries, reminds them of the moral of the exile: the existence of Israel as a people depends on the people's faithfulness to the Covenant. This faithfulness means keeping the commandments and seeing that the worship of God is attended to meticulously. He puts spiritual things first and always has his eye out for even the slightest sign of God's intervention in history.

A person with faith can see the hand of God in events. Although God did say that "he would dwell in thick darkness" (2 Chron 6:1) he does give us physical signs of his presence, to help us rely on him; but as long as we are on earth he leaves us to some extent in darkness, to have us practise virtue, especially faith and hope, which must be inspired by charity.[16]

These books are well worth reading, even if the earlier chapters are rather heavy and sometimes obscure; the meaning becomes clearer if read in the light of the key to the Old Testament — God's promise of a Saviour, the Messiah, who will establish the House of David for ever (cf.Lk 1:32-33).

Ezra and Nehemiah

These two books cover a fifty-year period after the Babylonian captivity. As we have seen, Cyrus, the king of Persia, in 538 B.C. issued an edict allowing the Jews* to go back to Jerusalem. These two books are named after their main protagonists — Ezra, a priest, and Nehemiah, the king's governor. The two books really form one,

---

16 Vatican II, Dogm Const. *Lumen gentium* 11.

and the old Hebrew Bible grouped them both under the title of "The Book of Ezra". The Vulgate established the division and Daniel Bomberg's Hebrew edition of 1517 went along with this.

Although they are attributed to Ezra and Nehemiah, the final edition — that is, the edition we have, which is the canonical version — is of a later date. It may date from the time of Greek domination around the end of the fourth century B.C.: the reason for saying this is that the list of high priests given in *Nehemiah* (12:11) ends with Joiada, who according to Flavius Josephus was contemporary with Darius II Codomannus (336-330).[17]

Historical background These books cover the main historical events subsequent to Cyrus' decree and Nehemiah's second mission, particularly the religious restoration in Israel after the exile.

Cyrus had authorized the return to Jerusalem and the rebuilding of the Temple, which was in ruins after Nebuchadnezzar's invasion. Flavius Josephus recounts how the Jews showed Cyrus the text of the prophecy of Isaiah (44:28; 45:1) where Cyrus' name appeared and the king was so impressed that he immediately decreed the return of the exiles. In the last analysis the Jews owed their liberation to the special intervention of God, who guides all human events; but he certainly availed of the Persians' preference for "the gods of heaven"; in fact, even official Persian documents identified Yahweh with the supreme God, the God of heaven, whom the Persian kings adored and regarded as their own.

Although the Jews returned immediately after the king's decree and started to rebuild the Temple, the building works were soon stopped due to fierce opposition from the Samaritans. What particularly rankled with the Samaritans was that they were not allowed to join in the building. The work was not re-started until 520, under Darius I, and it was completed four years later thanks to the intervention of Zerubbabel and the prophesying of Haggai and Zechariah (Ezra 6:14). However, although the Temple was finished, forty years passed without the walls of Jerusalem being rebuilt — again due to Samaritan opposition.

Meanwhile, Ezra, a scribe★ skilled in the Law, who was in charge of Jewish affairs at the Persian court, was authorized in 458 to undertake a journey to Jerusalem. He arrived there in the same year in a Jewish caravan. King Artaxerxes had empowered him to reestablish the Law of Moses in the new community at Jerusalem;

17 Cf. A. Gelin, *Le livre d'Esdras et Nehemie* (Paris 1960).

from then on the Mosaic Law is the King's Law. When they reached the river Ahava (which has not been positively identified) they decided to celebrate a feast to implore God's help and protection. On entering Jerusalem Ezra visited the Jews but in applying the Mosaic Law he had to adopt severe measures to deal with marriages of Jews with foreign women.[18] The erring Jews repented and promised to repudiate their wives.[19] Judges were appointed to apply Ezra's decree; the transgressors' names are listed in the book.

Seven months after this arrival Ezra solemnly promulgated the Law to the people. They celebrated the feast of Tabernacles and a few days later did public penance and confessed their sins (8:1-9, 37). Finally Ezra established a covenant to which all the people subscribed (chap. 10).

Some years after these events — in 445 — Nehemiah, King Artaxerxes' governor, was aided by God to obtain royal permission to rebuild the walls of Jerusalem and the city itself. This was done despite the Samaritans' opposition and the city was repopulated.

The king appointed Nehemiah governor of Jerusalem. Nehemiah took his role very seriously; he administered the city very well and maintained a high level of religious observance. Some years later, Nehemiah, on a second mission to Jerusalem, tried to get the Levites to agree to an equitable distribution of tithes and to ensure that the Jews kept the sabbath properly; he also upbraided those who had foreign wives. *Nehemiah* ends with this invitation: "Remember me, O my God, for good" (13:31).

When he comes to the end of his labours Nehemiah does not seek his own glory or any human reward; instead he lifts his gaze to heaven and entreats God to remember him and all he has done to promote the glory of God, in whom he places all his trust.

Religious restoration Ezra and Nehemiah played a key part in the religious restoration of the Jewish people after the exile. The land in which they lived was no longer politically dependent; it was part of the Persian empire. The chosen people, the remnant, could no longer say that they owned their country: the only property which

18 Such marriages were forbidden in order to ward off the possible worship of false gods by the Israelites (cf. Ex 34:16; Deut 7:3-4). After the return from exile there was more risk of the returnees — mainly men — marrying women of another religion.

19 According to the Law, these marriages were invalid or null because they were not in keeping with the Law (cf. Ex 34:16; Deut 7:3). When the man dismissed the woman the children shared her lot; but possibly the mother and children were still supported by the father.

was absolutely their own is the Law of Yahweh, their God. Prayer had taught them that they were the "faithful remnant", called upon to bring about the religious restoration so vigorously fostered by the prophets. Haggai and Zechariah managed to overcome the sloth of some and the human respect of others and got them to take up the task again, but it was Ezra who most energetically reminded them of their Alliance with Yahweh and exhorted them to be totally faithful to it.

Thus, the people gradually began to adopt a new, more religious lifestyle. Even daily life became imbued with greater optimism and hope, through meditation on the Law, which Ezra recommended. They came to realize better what God's election of them meant — holiness, an upright life, constant recourse to God; national sovereignty no longer seemed to be a priority.

Certain institutions developed in this spiritual climate, institutions which may have originated during the exile. The more important of these were the Synagogue,* where the Law was read out and commented on and where the scribes typically studied; and the Sanhedrin,* which originally had a religious function but which soon took over civil affairs, such as the administration of justice, for which it became exclusively responsible.

Ezra and Nehemiah were the two men chosen by God to spearhead this religious restoration. Ezra, in his eagerness for holiness, infected those around him with his own optimism and brought the "remnant" of Israel to really commit itself to its religion.

Nehemiah had the same kind of zeal, also directed towards getting the returned exiles to aim at religious and moral purity. He put his trust fully in God and yet showed understanding towards the weaknesses of people. He spared no effort to improve the economic position of the Jews, who were very poor indeed in the period immediately after their repatriation — as *Sirach* describes: "The memory of Nehemiah also is lasting; he raised for us the walls that had fallen, and set up the gates and rebuilt our ruined homes" (49:13).

Tobit

The book of *Tobit* together with *Judith* and *Esther* form a little group which Latin and Greek editions place among the historical books after *Ezra* and *Nehemiah*. It takes its name from its two main characters, father and son; the Septuagint, to distinguish them, calls the father Tobit and the son Tobias, the name being an abbreviation of the Hebrew title *tobhiyyahu* (= God is good).

The book which we have derives from a lost Semitic original. St Jerome used a Chaldean (Aramaic) text, which also is no longer extant, to produce the Latin translation included in the Vulgate. The Qumran discoveries[20] include a few Hebrew and Aramaic fragments of this book, but our main source for the text is the Greek Septuagint of which we have four separate recensions, which are divided into two groups — the Vatican and Alexandrian manuscripts on the one hand, and the Sinaitic Codex and the *Vetus latina* on the other.

Jews and Protestants regard the book of *Tobit* as deuterocanonical although they read it with respect and regard it as containing true history. The Catholic Church recognized it as an inspired book very early on, in the patristic period, placing it among the canonical books in the West from the 382 Roman synod forward, and in the East from the council of Constantinople in 692.

We do not have the name of the human author but he could well have been a Jew in the Diaspora* and could have written it in Egypt, in Aramaic perhaps, in the third or fourth century B.C. The words of the angel at the end of his assignment (12:20) — "Write in a book everything that has happened" — or the fact that the first three chapters are written in the first person, are probably a literary device often found in narratives (cf. *Wisdom*), used by someone writing in a later period, but still writing under divine inspiration.

The story given in *Tobit* is an episode of family history. All the indications are that the sacred writer is reporting something that really happened: he gives the family tree of the main people involved and is very precise about details of geography and historical chronology; however, we cannot exclude the possibility of some passages being fictitious — the writer's purpose being one of spiritual and moral teaching rather than history proper.

Tobit, a Jew of the tribe of Naphtali who had been deported to Nineveh, was a man of exceptional piety and charity. He soon gained the trust of King Shalmaneser but he later got into trouble because he buried some Jews executed by the king. Everything goes wrong

---

20 These important documents were found between 1947 and 1953 in the caves of Khirbeth Qumran and Wadi Murabbat, the first being discovered by a group of Bedouin in a cave about twelve km from Jericho, to the west of the Dead Sea and four km. from the springs of Ain el-Feshka. The main finds included the complete scroll of *Isaiah*, a commentary on *Habakkuk* and a Manual of Discipline, all from around the second to first centuries B.C., and other fragments from the same period, including that of *Tobit*.

for him: his property is confiscated, he loses his sight, his friends and even his wife taunt him.[21] In a moment of severe tribulation he begs God to let him die because life holds no more for him.[22]

At around the same time a relative of his, in Ecbatana, Raguel, is saddened to see his daughter Sarah reproached by her maids because her seven husbands have each died on their wedding-night, slain they think by the evil demon Asmodeus. Like Tobit, Sarah also prays to God to end her life. But God listens to both their prayers and comes to their rescue, to turn their sorrow into joy.

He sends his angel* Raphael, under the name of Azarias, to accompany and guide Tobit's son Tobias to the house of Raguel. This would be a stage on his journey because he was headed for Rages to collect money his father lent to a man called Gabriel. After being blessed by Tobit they start out, the angel saves Tobias from a dangerous fish and suggests that he marry Sarah. He also gives him the means to cure his father's blindness. Everything the angel predicts happens: Tobias marries Sarah, who is freed from demonic influence; the angel collects the money in Rages and returns with the young married couple to Nineveh, where Tobit miraculously recovers his sight.

The story told in *Tobit* contains a whole series of teachings which are useful for the education of conscience and also encourage people to practise virtue, especially virtues to do with the works of mercy. Parents feel urged to educate their children in the love of God and in the practice of prudence, generosity etc — and themselves to imitate Tobit's patience when they encounter unforeseen difficulties in their family life, even to the point of their own relatives turning their backs on them.

The book also shows that things which we normally regard as difficulties or misfortunes can become blessings if accepted and appreciated as coming from God's hands. God is the Father who never abandons us; he is in fact watching over us night and day because he desires only our good.

Additionally, the book shows us that angels are the protectors of men. Raphael reveals this when he says:

21 In spite of this Tobit did not become depressed; he told his relatives, "Do not speak thus, for we are children of saints, and we look forward to that life which God must give to those who never cease to have faith in him."

22 Tobit desired death not because he despaired but because he desired to go to his "eternal abode"; the book shows Tobit's submissiveness to the will of God, who knows what best suits him (cf. Tob 3:6).

> I will not conceal anything from you. . . . God sent me to heal you and your daughter-in-law Sarah. I am Raphael, one of the seven holy angels who present the prayers of the saints and enter into the presence of the glory of the Holy One. . . . Do not be afraid; you will be safe. But praise God for ever. For I did not come as a favour on my part, but by the will of our God. Therefore praise him for ever. All these days I merely appeared to you and did not eat or drink, but you were seeing a vision. And now give thanks to God, for I am ascending to him who sent me (Tob 12:11-20).

Tobit's conversation with his son contains important teaching on marriage (4:12ff), stressing the purity of mind and heart with which a couple should approach marriage. Marriage, we know, is a lifelong union of one man and one woman; they become one (Mt 19:15;1 Cor 6:16). Jesus will raise the marriage contract to the status of a sacrament (cf. Prov 2:17; Mal 2:14), thereby giving the true interpretation of what marriage was at the beginning of the human race (Mt 19:4-8).

Tobit also stresses the importance of love of one's neighbour, which should lead us to act justly — "what you hate, do not do to any one" (4:15);[23]; to accept the advice of prudent people; and to praise God always and ask him to keep us on the right road. It also emphasizes the essential need for works of mercy, especially alms giving.[24]

Tobias learned from his father to lead a life of service and to be appreciative to God for everything. He is an example to Christian families, especially those concerned about the religious or spiritual education of their children.

Judith

Like the book of *Tobit*, that of *Judith* was also written in a Semitic language — probably Hebrew — but the original text was lost early on. There are now a number of Latin and Greek texts which can be used as controls on one another. St Jerome made a free translation of an Aramaic text — cutting it down to appoximately a fifth of its size — and this is the Latin version in the Vulgate, which the New Vulgate has corrected and expanded.

23 Jesus couched the commandment of love of one's neighbour in positive terms: "As you wish that men would do to you, do so to them" (Lk 6:31).

24 In the Vulgate it says that almsgiving delivers from death (Tob 4:10; see RSVCE note). Alms given to God and one's neighbour are a source of supernatural grace by which a person lives in friendship with God and can gain heaven.

It is not known who the author was but he very likely was a post-exilic Jew who probably lived around the third century. The text presupposes the repatriation of the Jews from Babylon; Palestine is depicted having a sizeable population and the Temple being fully operational.

The book of *Judith* was excluded from the Jewish canon by Pharisees around the first century A.D. on very arbitrary grounds. Nor is it accepted by Protestants (who describe these deuterocanonical books as "apocryphal"). The Catholic Church has always regarded them as inspired; they are often quoted by the Fathers; the Councils of Nicea (325), Hippo (393) and Carthage (397) included them among the Sacred Scriptures; since Trent they have been listed in the Church's canon.

It is important to bear in mind, however, that this is a free narrative of an historical event, written with a teaching, moralising purpose in mind (cf. comments of Miller, Sonbignon and Vaccari). This explains, for example, why Nebuchadnezzar (604-562 B.C.), is described as king of Nineveh, whereas Nineveh is known to have been destroyed in 612. According to the narrative itself we are in the post-exilic period, after the rebuilding of the Temple (4:3-13; 5:18). There are no signs of idolatry (8:18) and the Law is being rigorously observed (12:2-9). All this suggests, Vaccari says, that the sacred writer, for some reason of symbolism, wanted to give fictitious names to people and places . His contemporaries would have had no difficulty in working out what the characters' real names were, whereas we have the greatest difficulty.[25]

What can be said, however, is that here is a book built on a nucleus of historical fact but developed without paying much attention to historical detail: it was written in order to get across a message: that faithfulness to Yahweh saves Israel from every danger (8:11-27; 16:1-7).

Danger appears on the horizon when Holofernes reaches the plains of Esdraelon, after crushing the cities of the Phoenician and Jewish coast, bent on destroying all forms of worship incompatible with the quasi-divine aspirations of Nebuchadnezzar. When they hear the news, the Jews get ready to fight him, even though they have very limited resources — which both surprises and annoys Holofernes. The leader of the Ammonites, Achior, advises him to act prudently because whenever Israel is faithful to its God, he tells him, it has no reason to be afraid of anyone (5:1-21).

25 Cf. A Vaccari, op. cit., pp. 303-343.

The Jews are based in Bethulia.[26] The Assyrians manage to cut off their water supply and their situation becomes so desperate that they eventually decide that they will surrender in five days time unless God comes to their rescue (chap. 7) — a sensible decision, given their plight.

Just at this point Judith, a young widow, comes in — beautiful,[27] prudent, devout. "Who are you", she asks the rulers, "that have put God to the test?" They give their approval to the daring plan she proposes. After doing penance (chap. 9) she dresses in her finery and jewellery and, accompanied by her maid, she leaves the city and goes to Holofernes, whom she captivates with her beauty and intelligence. Holofernes invites her to attend a banquet, in the course of which he drinks too much. Judith is left alone with him and grasps her opportunity (chap. 13); she calls on God to strengthen her and cuts off his head with two blows. As soon as she gets back to Bethulia she displays the head; all the people praise God for the great miracle. The Assyrians flee in panic and the Jews sack their camp (chap. 14 and 15).

Judith spends the rest of her long life in peace and honour. She declines all offers of marriage. Before she dies she distributes her property to her relatives and when she dies she is buried with her husband and mourned for seven days by a grateful people.

The book of *Judith* is a very well told story in a literary form reminiscent of apocalyptic writing. Holofernes is shown as epitome of the power of evil. Judith, whose name means "the Jewish woman", represents God's cause and symbolizes the Jewish people which wishes to stay faithful to their Alliance with Yahweh. Just when everything seems lost, God, who is ever faithful to his promises, causes the very weakness of his people to produce strength, in the form of a woman, who in this instance will be the instrument of his justice. Judith's victory represents the just reward of her trusting prayer and exemplary life of penance.

The deception which Judith uses was of a type regarded as licit in a war against an invader. Judith, according to Vaccari, did not

---

26 Nowhere in the Old Testament is there mention of Bethulia, the centre of events in *Judith*. Here it is seen as a bastion strategically placed to protect Judah.

27 The Vulgate says: "The Lord endowed her with beauty, for beauty was born not of sensuality but of virtue: he gave her an increase in beauty so that in the eyes of all there would be none to compare with her" (Jud 10:4). Judith's beauty was an important factor in God's plans to liberate his people; Holofernes was entranced by her and gave her every facility.

seek or even fear Holofernes' lust. God led her to act in the way she did (13:16-19). By beheading him without her honour being damaged in any way, she achieves a double victory, moral and patriotic. This is why Catholic piety sees in Judith a symbol of Mary Immaculate who, without being affected by the promptings of the tempter, crushes the head of the infernal serpent.

On the plain of Esdraelon, near that other plain of Armageddon, where St John places the battle at the end of the world on the great day of God the Almighty (cf. Rev 16:15-16), the book of *Judith* exhorts us to be vigilant, through prayer and good works, so as not to lose faith or hope. The story is a simple one, told with a certain naivety, but it carries a message for all individuals and all nations. St Jerome in fact in his preface to *Zephaniah* proposes Judith as a figure of the Church of Jesus Christ: her personal qualities — of beauty, wealth, good repute, and public spirit — seem to reflect the Spouse of Christ, all beauty, without stain or wrinkle, adorned with the finest of gifts and prerogatives. She it is who defends us, despite our weaknesses, from the attacks of God's enemies in this world.

Esther

Together with *Tobit* and *Judith*, the book of *Esther* forms a special grouping within the historical books of the Old Testament. The Jews include it as the eighth book of the *Ketûbim* (= writings) — and the fifth in the *meghillôth* (= scrolls), which were used in the liturgy. Her earlier name was Hadassah, the daughter of Abigail, of the tribe of Benjamin, of the house of Kish. Her family had been deported to Babylon in 597 B.C. Her kinsman Mordecai was born when his parents were already in captivity, which was why he was given a Babylonian name, derived from the name of the god Marduk.

To the Hebrew text, which is fairly complete, the Greek version adds seven chapters which are regarded as deuterocanonical; in the New Vulgate these are inserted into the text and their verses listed alphabetically.

The name of the author is not known. As far as the Greek text is concerned, it seems to have been written by a Jew who was familar with Persian history and customs. He had access to Persian chronicles (2:23; 10:2) and the writings of Mordecai (9:20). He must have written the book in Persia between 300 and 250 B.C. The Jews in Palestine were already celebrating in 160 "Mordecai's day" (2 Mac 15:36), which implies that they not only knew of the story of Esther but also were very probably familiar with the book of *Esther*.[28]

The book of *Esther*, as we saw in connexion with the book of *Judith* on which it is dependent from the literary point of view, recounts an historical event which modern Catholic scholars classify as belonging to the literary genre of free narrative, that is, "an historical account freely embellished" (Spadafora). This does not mean that free narrative is the same as fiction, for the historical veracity of the book is confirmed by its precise knowledge of Persian customs, its detailed description of the royal palace at Susa, which recent excavations have made better known to us, and the narrative is fresh and full of detail, with no anachronism of any kind (Vaccari).

The whole story is quite dramatic. Mordecai has a dream in which he sees in a somewhat symbolic way the danger that lies ahead of his people, and how they will escape it. In the third year of his reign Ahasuerus gives a magnificent banquet which his queen, Vashti, refuses to attend. The king is so incensed that he repudiates her and chooses Esther to take her place.

Relations between Mordecai and Haman, the king's first minister, become strained because Mordecai refuses to do obeisance to him (it was quite customary for oriental courts to require people to prostrate themselves as a sign of subservience, but Mordecai refused to conform, on religious grounds: adoration of a man he regarded as being in conflict with the worship he owed God). His conduct puts the Jewish people at risk.

Through Esther Mordecai appraises the king of a plot to kill him. However, he is not rewarded as he expected: Haman in fact is so furious that he devises a sinister plan to exterminate Mordecai and his fellow Jews. He obtains a royal decree to this end, but Mordecai asks Esther to intercede with the king and beg for clemency for the Jews. The prayer first of Mordecai and then of Esther prepare the way for the king's final decision: God inspires him to change his mind and the scaffold which Haman has prepared for Mordecai is used for Haman himself.

After Haman's death Mordecai's honour and loyalty is immediately recognized and he becomes the king's first minister. He obtains a royal decree permitting Jews to use arms in self-defence. The Jews are not long in taking their revenge and, with Ahasuerus' approval,

28 Robert and Feuillet, op. cit.

many Persians are put to the sword. To commemorate this victory the Jews establish the feast of *Purim*, more a secular rather than a religious celebration.

This book is reminiscent of the story of Daniel and even of that of Joseph, who, after being sold by his brothers, is victimized and then rehabilitated; promoted by Pharaoh, he later saves his people (cf. Gen 37:2ff). In *Esther* direct intervention by God is not exactly mentioned but although the Hebrew version avoids mentioning God's name the whole book is impregnated with a sense of divine providence: the protagonists always place their reliance on him who controls all human events, beseeching his help and doing penance (4:3-17).

The Liturgy prefers to use the Greek fragments of the text which makes explicit what the inspired writer only hints at. Here again God's great mercy is evident; he never abandons his people, even though sometimes it seems that humanly speaking there is no way out for them. In this instance he uses a woman, Esther, to change a course of events which seem to be working against the people of Israel. St Jerome sees Esther as a figure of the Church: unknown at first, she grows like a little stream to become a deep river which irrigates and brings fruitfulness to all the land. Even the persecutions which Esther suffers point up her exceptional qualities and virtues and her love of her people. This explains why the Church in its liturgy applies to Mary (on the feast of our Lady of Lourdes) some quotations from the book of *Esther*, though obviously Esther cannot be compared with the Blessed Virgin, the humble maid of Nazareth chosen to become the Mother of God.

Maccabees

The title of 1 and 2 Maccabees is taken from the surname of Judas (1 Mac 2:4), the third son of Mattathias, the hero of the war of Jewish independence against Syria. The origin of the word "maccabee" is unclear; it may derive from the Hebrew word *maqqabi* (= hammer) — a reference to Judas' physical strength and exploits. As a surname it was also applied to his brothers, and, by extension, to the seven martyred brothers who appear in 2 Mac 7.

The books had separate authors. Given its exactness of dates, places and documents, and its enthusiasm for the Jewish cause, *1 Maccabees* must have been written by a Palestinian Jew who eye-witnessed the events he describes; the author of *2 Maccabees* was more likely an Alexandrian Jew, and a Pharisee given what he has to say about resurrection. The first book was written in Hebrew, although what we have is only a Greek translation; the second, in Greek, shows that the author had a good grasp of Greek rhetoric and the Greek language, which suggests he may have been from Alexandria.

As far as the date of composition is concerned, this can be taken as approximately 100 B.C. for the first and 124 B.C. for the second, on the basis of the information given in the first letter they refer to (2 Mac 1:9).

Both these books, which Protestants regard as deuterocanonical, were recognized by the Fathers as inspired and were later defined as canonical by the Council of Trent (1546).

Historical background   After the death of Alexander the Great (323 B.C.) two main dynasties established themselves in the territories of his huge empire — the Ptolemies, who controlled Egypt, and also Palestine up to 200 B.C.; and the Seleucids, who took over large parts of the Middle East, and moved in to Palestine in 200 B.C.

The Ptolemy kingdom was founded by Ptolemy I, the son of a Macedonian nobleman. Ptolemy, a loyal general of Alexander's, was made satrap of Egypt in 323 when Alexander died and in 304 he assumed the title of king, annexing Cyprus, Palestine and the Lebanon. In 285 he abdicated in favour of his son Ptolemy II, who became involved in a struggle with the Seleucid kings. Ptolemy II's court at Alexandria was famed for its learning. His son, Ptolemy III Euergetes, extended his empire into Persia.

The kingdom began to decline under Ptolemy IV Philopator, who was a bad administrator and led a dissolute life. From the time of Alexander onwards Greek culture spread throughout the Middle East. The early Seleucid rulers were tolerant of the political and religious cultures of the territories they controlled, but things changed when Antiochus IV Epiphanes (= the illustrious) came to power, and the scene in Palestine became one of persecution and war. Antiochus was determined to impose hellenic religion and civilization in Palestine as elsewhere and naturally this was anathema to the Jews, who at this time were quite faithful to the Covenant with Yahweh.

The sequence of events   *1 Maccabees* gives a detailed account of the struggle in Palestine over a period of fifty years, from the time

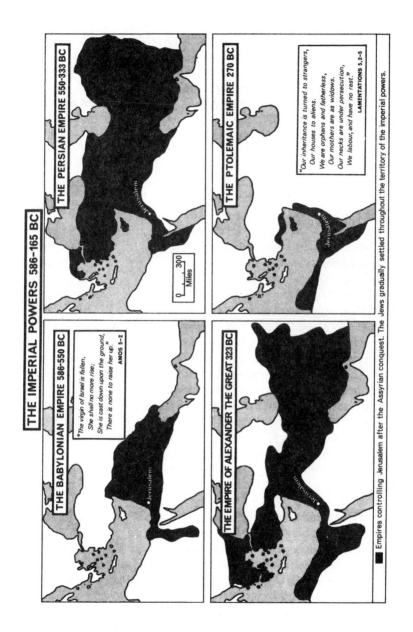

THE IMPERIAL POWERS 586-165 BC

THE PERSIAN EMPIRE 550-333 BC

Jerusalem

0 ___ 300
Miles

THE PTOLEMAIC EMPIRE 270 BC

Jerusalem

"*Our inheritance is turned to strangers,*
Our houses to aliens.
We are orphans and fatherless,
Our mothers are as widows.
Our necks are under persecution,
We labour, and have no rest."
LAMENTATIONS 5.2-5

THE BABYLONIAN EMPIRE 586-550 BC

Jerusalem

"*The virgin of Israel is fallen,*
She shall no more rise;
She is cast down upon the ground,
There is none to raise her up."
AMOS 5-2

THE EMPIRE OF ALEXANDER THE GREAT 323 BC

Jerusalem

Empires controlling Jerusalem after the Assyrian conquest. The Jews gradually settled throughout the territory of the imperial powers.

Map 8

Antiochus IV Epiphanes came to the throne up to the death of Simon, the last of the Maccabee brothers (134 B.C.).

After a short introduction the book describes the Jewish uprising against Antiochus, whose persecution led to the desecration of the Temple. Mattathias proclaimed a holy war; Jewish armed resistance operated from the wilderness with great success under the successive leadership of three of Mattathias' sons — Judas Maccabeus, the undisputed leader of the Jews (3:1-9); Jonathan (9:28 — 12:53), and Simon (chap. 13-16). When Simon died he was succeeded by his son John Hyrcanus, who became the founder of the Hasmonean dynasty.[29] At this point the book ends.

The second book overlaps with the first, starting earlier. It runs from the end of the reign of Seleucus IV, the predecessor of Antiochus IV Epiphanes, up to the defeat of Nicanor, shortly before the death of Judas Maccabeus — that is, a period of fifteen years (176-161), which are covered in chapters 1-7 of the first book.

The sacred writer's purpose is to build up the morale of the Jews. Naturally any account of the war of liberation led by Judas Maccabeus would have this effect and would show that victory was due to God's powerful aid (2:19-22). But he also wants to show that God's purpose in permitting persecution is to discipline the Jews "in order that he may not take vengeance on us afterwards when our sins have reached their height" (6:12-17). After the episode of Heliodorus (3:1-40), the writer lays great emphasis on the inviolate sanctity of the Temple and implies that Antiochus suffers the terrible death he does suffer because of his profanation of it. The same fate overtakes another persecutor, Nicanor, who dies because he threatened to destroy the Temple. Judas' victory over Nicanor ensures the liberation of the Jewish people and guarantees the proper worship of the true God.

Teaching contained in Maccabees   Although the author of the first book devotes a lot of space to wars and political intrigues extending over a period of forty years, his primary purpose is a religious one. He reports the calamities the Jewish people experience on account of their sins, while also stressing the role played by God in his providence, who watches over them as he promised he would

29   The meaning of "Hasmonean" is unclear. Flavius Josephus calls Mattathias the son of Hasmoneus, a name which he also applies to Simon. It may have been another surname of Judas or else the name of some ancestor of Mattathias or even of a people or a region. In any event the name is important because it was used to describe the dynasty from John Hyrcanus onwards (cf. Flavius Josephus, *Jewish Antiquities*, XII, 265; J.M. Lagrange, *Le Judaisme avant Jesus-Christ*: Paris 1931).

(cf. Ps 119:89-90). The success of the Jewish campaigns he attributes to God's protection, but he makes it clear that faithfulness to the Covenant is, as was the case with their forebears, the ground on which Israel must totally rely. From this it follows that, for the just man, supreme glory consists in being ready to give one's life, if necessary, to defend God's interests — the Law, which every Jew must strictly obey.

The second book is even more important from the doctrinal point of view. It aims at bringing out even more strongly the religious lessons of the time, and the story is written more like a sermon than a history. It includes such fundamental texts as that which states that God created all things *ex nihilo*, out of nothing, not out of things which existed (7:28), and those which make it clear that the sacrifice of martyrs is a voluntary form of atonement which placates God's anger (7:36; 8:5).

In this connexion it gives a very moving account of the martyrdom of seven brothers, whose names are unknown but who are popularly called "the Maccabees" (2 Mac 7:1ff). Their faith in the resurrection, which they explicitly assert (v. 11), gives them the courage to undergo terrible sufferings to keep the holy Law of God, sufferings in which they are also supported by their mother's faith. She, having offered God the lives of her sons, then offers herself in sacrifice, giving an example of fortitude and also of that faith in which she had reared her children. Christian tradition venerates these seven brothers as martyrs and churches were dedicated to them in Antioch, Rome, Lyons and Vienne.

Other texts lay stress on the *intercession of the saints*, and the value of *prayers for the dead* (12:43-46), which are the basis of the dogma of the *communion of saints*. As we know, those who have left this world and enjoy the beatific vision, in the same act of charity in which they love God are also praying for their brothers, who are members of the Church like themselves. After Jesus redeemed mankind by dying on the cross, the just of the Old Testament were enabled to enter heaven and thus the ancient people of God became the new Israel, which is the Church.

This book also tells us more about *atonement beyond the grave* by asserting the existence of *purgatory* (12:38ff). It also asserts the *resurrection of the just* and tells us what we need to know about the fate of the unjust (7:9, 14, 23, 29; 14:46). Thus, for example, in 2 Mac 12:43 there is Judas' act of faith in the resurrection and salvation of his fallen soldiers; but he realizes that they must atone for their sins in the next life and he wishes to help them in this and asks for prayers from the living. This text explicitly states that there is an interim stage where souls are purified and that they can be helped by suffrages offered by the living.

All this shows that these inspired books are well worth prayerful reading, particularly the second, which provides us with many edifying examples — especially the humility which leads its protagonists to trust in God; their fortitude in defending their faith; their patience in dealing with obstacles to observance of the Law; and their deep piety, as shown in their prayer for their dead comrades.

1 and 2 Maccabees help us to realize that God always watches over his own, and they show that Israel always wins victory over its enemies when it stays true to the Covenant.

The history of the Maccabee family given in these books ends with the death of Simon and the succession of his son, John Hyrcanus. Flavius Josephus, the first century Jewish historian, carries the story forward; only he gives the surname Hasmoneus, which applies to the successors of the early Maccabees up to Aristobulus II.

Aristobulus I, the son of John Hyrcanus, was the first to add the title of king to that of chief priest. When he died his widow Alexandra married his elder brother, Alexander Janneus, and after the death she remained on the throne while her son Hyrcanus II was high priest. She was succeeded by another son Aristobulus II. When war broke out between these two brothers the Romans intervened, took Jerusalem and brought the monarthy to an end.

THE GENEALOGY OF THE MACCABEES

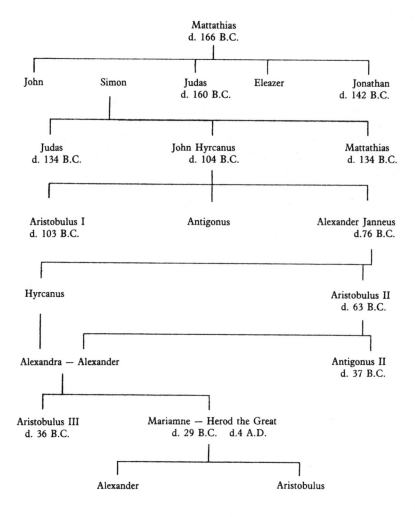

The prophetic books of the Old Testament

God's promise to Abraham that he would be the father of a great people was obviously fulfilled by the time the people of Israel took possession of the land of Canaan. They had been made into a people and had become God's special property through the Covenant made at Sinai. Israel became the depository of the word of God and the instrument of the plan of salvation which would be emerging over the centuries until the coming of the Saviour, whom Israel would provide, the Messiah prophesied by Nathan to King David (2 Sam 7:13), who would reign forever.

From this point onwards all Jewish religious teaching would be based on expectation of the Messiah and on strict fidelity to the Covenant through faith in the one, transcendent and personal God and practice of the Law promulgated on Sinai.[1]

The people charged with this religious instruction were primarily the prophets of Israel, particularly from the ninth century on. Although prophecy was not a religious phenomenon exclusive to the people of Israel (remember, for example, Elijah's challenge to the 450 prophets of Baal at Mount Carmel: 1 Kings 18:19-40). they are to be found throughout Jewish history and unlike other prophets they do have a God-given mission. All of the Old Testament shows the importance of the prophets and how much Israel had need of their teaching as well as their often stern warnings and threats. The prophet was so important to Israel that when there was no prophet the people saw this as a punishment from God: "Behold, the days are coming," says the Lord God, "when I will send a famine on the land; not a famine of bread, nor a thirst for water, but of hearing the words of the Lord. They shall wander from sea to sea, and north to east; they shall run to and fro, to seek the word of the Lord, but they shall not find it" (Amos 8:11-12).

Types of prophet The prophets who appear in the Bible can be divided into three main groups:

1 Cf. P. de Surgy, op. cit; F. Spadafora, op. cit., pp. 489-496.

1. *The sons of the prophets* These were people who, without being expressly called by God, chose this form of life. They carried out their duties in connexion with the main holy places of the time — Bethal, Gilgal etc. — from the time of Judges onwards. They usually lived together in small groups fostering divine worship and all types of public religious ceremonies, almost always involving song and dance: cf. this reference in 1 Samuel 19:20: "Then Saul sent messengers to take David; and when they saw the company of the prophets prophesying, and Samuel standing as head over them, the Spirit of God came upon the messengers of Saul, and they also prophesied" (1 Sam 19:20) — that is, they began to sing inspired by the spirit of the Lord.

These men did much to foster popular fervour and defend the Covenant in all its purity. They stayed faithful to Yahweh even at the cost of their lives, as can be seen from the persecution they suffered in the time of Queen Jezebel, who put them to death because they opposed the cult of Baal (1 Kings 18:22).

2. *False prophets* Possibly most of the prophets in the Bible were people who claimed to prophesy in the name of Yahweh but were not in fact called by him and had not received any message from him. Jeremiah denounced them in these terms: "The prophets are prophesying lies in my name; I did not send them, nor did I command them or speak to them. They are prophesying to you a lying vision, worthless divination, and the deceit of their own minds" (Jer 14:14).

They were only too ready to take issue with Yahweh's true prophets and not only accepted but actually sought adulation from simple folk. They tailored their message to suit the people, never warning them of the punishment they earned through breaking the Law of God. They were so deceptive in what they said and in their behaviour that many people regarded them as sincere and upright men. As early as *Deuteronomy*, the people were given pointers to help them identify false prophets:

> And if you say in your heart, "How may we know the word which the Lord has now spoken?" — when a prophet speaks in the name of the Lord, if the word does not come to pass or come true, that is a word which the Lord has not spoken; the prophet has spoken it presumptuously, you need not be afraid of him (Deut 18:21-22).

3. *Prophets called by God* The true prophet (the name in Hebrew comes from *nab*, one who is called or one who announces) is a man called by God to proclaim a message communicated to him by God. This calling is the key to the prophet's life; he is convinced of his mission and the people in turn trust what he says. He is God's

spokesman. He lends God his mouth to transmit God's message in an unadulterated form. He does not appropiate the teaching which he proclaims; it belongs to God.

Hence, these are the characteristic features of the true prophet:

a) His *vocation* confirms that God wants to use him as his instrument. God freely chooses him to fulfil this role; the person's personal merits or qualifications are not determining factors.

b) *He speaks in God's name*: it is God who places words on his lips (Jer 1:9; 15:19), without this meaning that the prophet has to shed his own personality — which explains the sort of colourful language by prophets like Amos, Hosea, etc.

c) In the light of the Covenant he *acts as a judge*, taking the people to task for their immoral behaviour, their idolatrous or empty formal worship, their injustice, hypocrisy etc.

d) He *predicts divine retribution*; he is not afraid of being unpopular and he rejects any kind of adulation. Because of Israel's constant infidelity, the prophet is forever calling the people to conversion.

e) At the same time he opens a *vista of hope*, by foretelling a time when the "remnant" of Israel will achieve salvation. Over the centuries the prophets reveal more and more about the descendant of David, the *Immanuel* (= God-with-us), who will be born of a virgin, in Bethlehem of Judah; the servant of Yahweh who will go meekly like a lamb to the slaughter to be sacrificed for our sins; the Messiah, the Son of man, who through his sacrifice will achieve eternal redemption.

Although almost one third of the Old Testament is taken up by the books of the prophets, not all of them were writers nor did all have aides who wrote down their oral preaching. For example, in the case of Elijah or Elisha, all we have are a few isolated, fragmentary references. The books which have come down to us are, usually divided into major and minor prophets, depending on the length of the particular book. The major prophets are Isaiah, Jeremiah, Ezechiel and Daniel; the twelve others are the minor prophets.

A "remnant" will be saved   The theme of the "remnant" of Israel is one to be found often in the prophetic books of the Old Testament, but it is a concept which develops and leads on in the New Testament.[2]

Prior to the exile the prophets speak of two types of remnant: the *historical* one, that fraction of the people who survive a calamity which

2   Cf. F. Spadafora, op. cit., pp. 22-23; 30.

befalls Israel because of its breaking its pact with Yahweh; and the *eschatological* remnant, referring to that part of the people who will in the last times benefit from salvation. Only the latter type is called "holy" (cf. Mic 5:6ff; Is 4:4; Jer 23:3).

But after the exile we find a third idea: that of the *faithful remnant*, a portion of the people which is considered to be the heir and depository of the promises, a religiously fervent part pleasing to Yahweh. This is "my servant, Israel, in whom I will be glorified" (Is 49:3). From this Israel a unique, exceptional person will emerge — the *Servant of Yahweh*, who by his redemptive death will accomplish the mission entrusted to this "remnant".

Historically, however, the small community of Jews who returned from the exile referred to themselves as the "remnant" (Hag 1:12; Zech 8:6). But this should not be confused with the faithful remnant, because these returned exiles needed a further purification (Zech 13:8; 14:2), though not all of them. The Israel that constituted the "faithful remnant" was, then, that part which was pure in heart (Ps 72:1), the "poor of Yahweh" (Is 49:13).

All this clearly points to a later revelation, one which is clearer and more complete, that of the New Testament, where the expression "remnant" is applied to that part of the people of God which has believed in Jesus Christ (Rom 11:5). This faithful remnant, the only true Israel, is referred to in many texts and is latent in the whole Gospel message (cf. Mt 3:9; 22:14; Jn 1:11; 1:47; Rom 2:28;1 Cor 10:18; Gal 6:16); it ceases to exist separately because it becomes thenceforth the Church founded by Jesus Christ.

The theological signification of this identification ("faithful remnant" = the true Israel = the Church, the new Israel) is given in St Paul's Letter to the *Romans*, where he elaborates a theology of God's salvific plan for all mankind. Thanks to the remnant which has believed in Jesus Christ, Israel's unfaithfulness does not cancel out God's promises; he remains true to them (Rom 9:1-7). The existence of this "remnant", the only depository of God's promises, also shows the totally gratuitous nature of God's choice of each individual, within the context of the chosen people.

From this faithful remnant, which is the Church, the heir of the Israel of the promise, will flow salvation for all men. Jesus Christ, the Messiah, has given his life for the redemption of all men. Salvation therefore embraces not only Israel according to the flesh (Rom 11:26) but also the Gentiles (Rom 11:25), who are also called by grace to a new life in Jesus Christ.

Thus are two apparently contradictory factors reconciled — the

THE PROPHETS OF ISRAEL AND JUDAH

Assyria	Israel	a. C.	Judah	Prophets
	—JEROBOAM II	783	—UZZIAH	
		781		AMOS / HOSEA
—TIGLAT-PILESER III, invader, bears captives away	—ZACHARIAH / MENAHEM	743		
		740	—JOTHAM	ISAIAH
	—PEKAHIAH	738		
	—PEKAH	737		
		736	—AHAZ	MICAH
		732		
—Shalmaneser V besieges Samaria	—HOSEA	724		
—SARGON II conquers Samaria and takes prisoners	Fall of Samaria	721		
	Egypt			
	—SHABAKO	716	—HEZEKIAH	
—SENNACHERIB	—TAHZARQA	700	—Tunnel of Shiloah / —Taking of Lachish	
		687	—MANASSEH	
—ASSARHADDON		668		
—ASHURBANIPAL	—PSEMMITICHUS	663		
		642	—Amos	
		640	—JOSIAH	
Babylonia				
—NABOPOLLASAR		626		ZEPHANIAH / JEREMIAH
Fall of Nineveh		612		NAHUM / HABAKKUK
	—NECO	609	—JEHOAHAZ, JEHOIAKIM	

Rulers / Empires	Date	Events	Prophets
NEBUCHADNEZZAR	605		Jeremiah dictates to Baruch
	598	—JEHOIACHIN / Deportation of Jews to Babylon	Daniel
	598	—ZEDEKIAH	
HOPHRA (Apries)	587	—Jerusalem falls	EZEKIEL / Jeremiah imprisoned
		—Second deportation to Babylon	
	581	—Third deportation	
Persia			
-CYRUS	550		
	538	—Edict of Cyrus / —Return to Palestine	
CAMBYSES	529		
DARIUS I	522		
	515	—End of construction of the second Temple	HAGGAI AND ZECHARIAH
—XERXES I (Assuerus)	486		
-ARTAXERXES I	465		MALACHI AND OBADIAH
	458	—Mission of EZRA	
	445	—Mission of NEHEMIAH	
XERXES II	423		JOEL (?)
Artaxerxes II	404		JONAH (?)

necessary punishment of the people of Israel for breaking the Covenant, and God's fidelity to his promises, which man's sin, no matter how great it be, cannot undermine.

St Paul declares, however, that this whole matter is a great mystery, because although a part of Israel has fallen into unfaithfulness, this is not permanent; it will last "until the full number of the Gentiles come in, and so all Israel will be saved; as it is written, 'The Deliverer will come from Zion, he will banish ungodliness from Jacob' (Is 59:20; 27:9), and this will be my covenant with them when I take away their sins" (Rom 11:25-27).

This prophecy rounds off St Paul's teachings and gives us the right perspective on everything the prophets say in these books which originate long before the coming of the Messiah.

A. THE MAJOR PROPHETS

Isaiah

Isaiah (Yesá yāhū = Yahweh is salvation) is one of the most outstanding and most important of the prophets. He was born around the year 700 B.C. and lived in Jerusalem. There is a good basis for thinking that he belonged to a distinguished priestly and perhaps noble family, judging from his education and culture and from his contacts with the court and nobility of the kingdom of Judah. He was married, with two children. In the year 740, on the death of King Uzziah, he received his calling as a prophet in a vision[3] in the Temple of Jerusalem as he himself describes:

> I saw the Lord sitting upon a throne, high and lifted up; and his train filled the temple. Above him stood the seraphim; each had six wings: with two he covered his face, and with two he covered his feet, and with two he flew. And one called to another and said: "Holy, holy, holy is the Lord of hosts; the whole earth is full of his glory." And the foundations of the thresholds shook at the voice of him who called, and the house was filled with smoke. And I said: "Woe to me! For I am lost; for I am a man of

---

3   "Vision" refers to things seen or communicated. The *seraphim* referred to in the text are a choir of angels, which Pseudo-Dionysius places as the highest of the nine ranks of angels and the nearest to God. They are attendants of God who sing his praises. The name they are given here derives from the fiery coals with which they burn and purify Isaiah's lips.

unclean lips, and I dwell in the midst of a people of unclean lips; for my eyes have seen the King, the Lord of hosts!"

Then flew one of the seraphim to me, having in his hand a burning coal which he had taken with tongs from the altar. And he touched my mouth, and said: "Behold, this has touched your lips; your guilt is taken away, and your sin forgiven." And I heard the voice of the Lord saying, "Whom shall I send, and who will go for us?" Then I said, "Here am I! Send me." (Is 6:1-8).

From the moment Isaiah received his vocation he knew no rest. He was charged with proclaiming the downfall of Israel and of Judah in punishment for the unfaithfulness of the people and their failure to repent. In the second part of his book he goes on to announce the consecration of Israel which he describes in a prophetic vision of enormous importance.[4]

Historical background The prophecies contained in the first part of the book refer to the period in which Isaiah himself lived. In the year 738 the political horizon of the Near East was overshadowed by the growing threat of the military strength of Assyria, which was ruled at the time by Tiglath-pileser III (724-727). The northern kingdom (Israel) had fallen to the Assyrians in 721, and Judah, in the south, had become a vassal of Assyria and was about to succumb politically and spiritually in the reign of Ahaz. At this point the prophecy of the Immanuel is recorded (Is 7ff), the first announcement in this book of the coming of the Messiah, which will guarantee the continuity of the Davidic dynasty in line with the promise announced by Nathan (cf. 2 Sam 7ff).

On the death of Ahaz, King Hezekiah fostered a religious revival in Judah, albeit a rather external and superficial one which did not deeply affect the lifestyle of his subjects. Influenced by the aristocratic party, Hezekiah sought an alliance with Egypt against Syria and soon had to pay the price of his overlord's revenge; but just when everything seemed lost and exactly in the way that Isaiah had foretold, Yahweh's miraculous intervention in favour of his people destroyed the army of the arrogant Sennacherib.

In the second part of the book (chap. 40-55) the scene changes. In his prophetic vision Isaiah now sees Babylon, almost two centuries in the future, at a point when the exiled Jews are in need of consolation. The king, Cyrus the Great (555-528 B.C.), governor of Anzan, proclaimed himself king of Persia and Media around the year 549. His campaigns led him into Lydia, whose capital Sardis he took

4 Cf. A Vaccari, op. cit., I, pp. 15-197.

in 546, hence the panic referred to in Is 41:5; he continued northwards and eastwards, conquering as he went, and reaching Babylon in 539. The following year Cyrus issued a proclamation authorizing Jews in exile to return to Palestine; he restored to them the sacred vessels which Nebuchadnezzar had taken and permitted them to rebuild the Temple.

The third part (chap. 56-66) looks at the return of the Jews just at the point when they are taking steps to reform their lifestyle in keeping with the Covenant even though they are very exposed to foreign and idolatrous influences. By this stage the Jews apparently have an altar although they have not yet begun to rebuild the Temple or the city walls.

The book and its author   As Vaccari comments, a book like this is not the kind of thing written all at one go: different parts were written at different times over the fifty odd years of Isaiah's prophetic ministry.

When were those different parts brought together to make the book as we now know it? Is it possible to say that Isaiah was the human author of the entire book?

As far as the first question is concerned, three documents testify to the book having its present form between the third and second centuries B.C. These are the complete (Hebrew) text of *Isaiah* discovered in Qumran in 1947 (which scholars say goes back as early as the second century B.C.), which is endorsed by the Greek translations of the Septuagint and the praise of Isaiah made in the book of *Sirach* (48:24-25) referring to Is 40:1; 51:3, 12-19; 66:10-13).

As far as authorship is concerned, Jewish-Christian tradition has always recognized Isaiah as the human author of this entire book. However, some modern critics attribute chapters 40-66 to a prophet whose name is unknown and who lived in Babylon after the time of the exile, about a century and a half after Isaiah;[5] but this theory is based on historical and sociological arguments -- on the fact that the book refers to events occurring after Isaiah's lifetime, which in effect means questioning his prophetic abilities; and besides how could a prophet of this stature pass unnoticed in his own time?

---

5   From Döderlein (1775) and Eichhorn (1782) onwards two parts of the book of Isaiah began to be distinguished, with the second (40-66) attributed to a post-exilic prophet. Later, with Duhm (1892) came the hypothesis of a third Isaiah (56-66), also post-exilic. Kissane (1943) was of the opinion that an anonymous prophet at the end of the exile, a person fully involved with Isaiah's teaching, gave the book its present shape and even expanded its content.

The Pontifical Biblical Commission, in a reply of 28 June 1908 to a query on this subject, said that the arguments of the critics referred to were not strong enough to sustain the theory of there being a number of authors. However, some difficulties remain unresolved: for example, the fact that Cyrus is mentioned by name two centuries before he lived (this may be a matter of a later addition).

After the Psalms, *Isaiah* is the Old Testament book most quoted in the New Testament: 22 quotations and 13 references (six to the first part part of the book and seven to the second) and all referring to Isaiah by name.

There are 66 chapters in all, and these are usually divided up in three sections.

1. The Book of the Judgments of God (chap. 1-37). This consists of oracular statements about Judah and Jerusalem (1-12), not in any apparent chronological order; within this part falls the "Book of Immanuel" (chap. 7-12). Then come oracles against the nations (chap. 13-23), a series of apocalyptic prophecies; followed by the eschatological oracles (chap. 24-27), called the 'The Book of the Revelation of Israel', and the inauguration of the Kingdom of God, with the Six Woes (chap. 28-33), and a series of warnings to those who oppose God's plans.

Finally there is the destruction of God's enemies (chap. 34-35), and a description of Sennacherib's invasion, his defeat and the edict expelling the Jews.

2. The second part, called "The Book of the Consolation of Israel" (chap. 40-55), consists of oracles on liberation from Babylon (chap. 40-48) and others on messianic liberation (49-55). Of particular importance are the four poems of the Servant of Yahweh (42:1-7; 49:1-9; 50:4-11; 52:13 — 53:12).

3. The third part (56-66) contains a series of prophecies which extend the "Book of Consolation" although they also include a series of instructions to the returned exiles: this is the point at which they have to rebuild the Temple and restore its liturgy, all of this prefiguring the New Jerusalem, God's final calling of all the nations. The book closes with a hymn of thanksgiving for God's mercy, accepted readily by believers and rejected by unbelievers.

Prophecy and the unfaithfulness of Israel Chosen by God to be the spiritual guide of his people, Isaiah, like other prophets, receives as his main mission that of trying to get people to keep the Covenant made at Sinai, where they had committed themselves to adore Yahweh as the only true God and to keep his law. Given Israel's proneness to unfaithfulness, Isaiah's assignment was by no means an easy one. But God continues to watch over his people, as he tells Isaiah when he gives him his vocation as a prophet. The vision Isaiah receives in the Temple will exercise a profound influence on his ministry. Isaiah has an acute perception of the transcendence of God and a parallel sense of his own insignificance and unworthiness. Compared with the Holy One of Israel, as Isaiah likes to call God, man is stained by sin and unworthy to look upon God's infinite majesty.

The image of the Seraphim (described in chapter six when he gives the account of his vocation) who purifies his lips with a burning coal is meant to indicate on the one hand the infinite mercy of God who comes to man's aid out of pure love offering him the hand of friendship; but it also expresses fallen man's absolute need for hope of salvation: only through God's grace can man regain lost happiness. As the image of the burning coal shows, man's salvation is conditional on his recognizing his sins and shortcomings in all humility; only if he does this does the grace of forgiveness become effective.

It is interesting to note Isaiah's insistence that repentance is not merely an external, purely cultic or ritual exercise. He asks for more than that — purity of soul, sincerity of heart, strict fidelity to God's law; without this even the greatest sacrifices count for nothing.

Isaiah is a man of faith. All his forcefulness comes from his complete and unconditional faith in Yahweh. He asks the people to have the same kind of faith: they need it, because their relationship with God is tired and superficial. Isaiah tries to convert people by example, and he warns them to listen to what he says because he is speaking God's word, which never lies — and not to listen to human arguments, even if they come from powerful people, because salvation can come from God alone.

Isaiah knows that this time the testing which Israel will undergo because of its infidelity will be long and difficult. Soon they will be uprooted and sent to Babylon, with all the pain and anguish it involves, but they must not lose faith, they must keep hoping for deliverance. He prophesies that a "remnant" will survive and from it the Messiah will emerge to be universal King and Lord: cf. the announcement of Immanuel (Is 7:14).

This prophecy of Immanuel is one of the most important prophecies in *Isaiah* and in the entire Old Testament. The sign which the prophet announces is first the imminent birth of a son to Ahaz, the future King Hezekiah: this guarantees the continuity of the Davidic dynasty which has held the key to Israel's hope ever since the prophecy of Nathan. But because of the solemnity of the prophecy and the symbolism of the name (Immanuel = God-with-us) obviously here is something which goes beyond being a purely historical reference: it is a prediction of the birth of the future messianic king, Jesus Christ, the pinnacle of the Davidic dynasty and of Israel's hope.

The text expressly says that the Immanuel will be born of a virgin; in this unique kind of birth the Church sees a prophetic reference to Mary's perpetual virginity,[6] which was later to be the subject of a solemn definition.

The Anointed (= the Christ) who will be born of the virgin is the "Wonderful counsellor, Mighty God, Everlasting Father, Prince of Peace" (Is 9:6). These names applied to the child mean that the Anointed will possess to an eminent degree the outstanding virtues of those who went before him — the wisdom of Solomon ("Wonderful counsellor"); the fortitude and valour of David ("Mighty God"); the humility of Moses and all the virtues of the patriarchs, because he is "Everlasting Father, Prince of Peace".

But additionally the Messiah is the "Servant of Yahweh"* (Is 49) who gives his life to atone for the sins of men.

The final teaching in the second part of Isaiah is a dramatic account of how the very people whom the Servant of Yahweh comes to save are those who will rise up against him and heap opprobrium upon him:

> He was despised and rejected by men;
> a man of sorrows, and acquainted with grief;
> and as one from whom men hide their faces
> he was despised, and we esteemed him not.
>
> Surely he has borne our griefs and carried our sorrows;
> yet we esteemed him stricken, smitten by God, and afflicted.
> But he was wounded for our transgressions, he was bruised for our iniquities;
> upon him was the chastisement that made us whole,
> and with his stripes we are healed (Is 53:3-5).

6 The Hebrew text of Is 7:14 speaks of an *almah* (= young girl) to designate a young girl who is taken to be a virgin. This prophecy — veiled like all prophecies — will be made more explicit by Jewish tradition which in the Greek Septuagint translates it as "the virgin" (with the definite article); with the Gospel comes the authentic interpretation which sees this text as foretelling the virginal conception of Jesus Christ and, therefore, the perpetual virginity of his Blessed Mother (cf. Mt 1:23). On the basis of these texts the Lateran Council of 649 gave this definition: "If anyone does not confess according to the Holy Fathers that in the proper and true sense the holy, ever-Virgin, immaculate Mary is the Mother of God, since in this last age not with human seed but of the Holy Spirit she properly and truly conceived the divine Word, who was born of God the Father before all ages, and gave birth without any detriment to her virginity, which remained inviolate even after his birth: let such a one be condemned" (Dz 256).

It is impossible, Spadafora says, to argue against this prophecy referring to our Lord Jesus Christ. Even the most sceptical of exegetes is deeply moved by this passage which forms the climax of Isaiah's prophecies about the Servant of Yahweh and which is very reminiscent of Ps 22.

St Paul says that this is "a secret and hidden wisdom of God, which God decreed before the ages for our glorification. None of the rulers of this age understood this; for if they had, they would not have crucified the Lord of glory" (1 Cor 2:7-8).

Jeremiah

Jeremiah is the second of the four great prophets of Israel, a contemporary of Zephaniah, Nahum and Habakkuk. He was born in the last part of the reign of Manasseh (687-642), around the year 645 B.C., almost a century after Isaiah. He came from a priestly family in Anathoth, a town about five kilometres northeast of Jerusalem.

God called him in the thirteenth year of Josiah's reign (626) when he was still an adolescent (1:2). By express order of Yahweh he remained unmarried (16:2), embracing celibacy with generosity. A rather shy and extremely sensitive person, Jeremiah's own preference was for a quiet family life and small-town friendships (6:11; 9:20). God's call came to him at a time when the kingdom of Judah was about to collapse. He realized he could not contain the sentiments God had placed in his heart: "there is in my heart as it were a burning fire shut up in my bones, and I am weary with holding it in, and I cannot" (20:9).

For more than forty years, up to his death, he remained faithful to his vocation and prophesied until after the fall of Jerusalem in 587. Although his writings do not compare in quality and doctrinal depth with Isaiah, they overflow with spontaneity and simplicity and a most touching love for his people.[7]

Historical background Jeremiah lived in a very eventful period, the reigns of the last five kings of Judah. His book refers a few times to Josiah (638-609), Jehoahaz (609) and Jehoiachin (598), but it mainly

7 Cf. C. Lattey, 'Jeremias' in *CCHS*, sections 452ff.

has to do with the reigns of the proud and sceptical Jehoiakim (608-598) and of the weak-willed Zedekiah (598-587).

As we will remember from *1 and 2 Kings*, Josiah in his efforts to rebuild national unity opposed Pharaoh Neco III when he was trying to deal with the coalition of Medes and Babylonians. He went out to meet him at Megiddo and was slain. His son Jehoahaz was proclaimed king by the people but after ruling for three months he was taken prisoner and brought to Egypt. In his place Neco imposed Jehoiakim, Josiah's second son, as king; he was a proud, superstitious and cruel man. Jeremiah upbraided him for his servility towards the Egyptians, saying that it would cause his downfall and ruin the country. Jeremiah had not favoured pacts against the Medes: he had prophesied that the Chaldeans would prevail,[8] and that Jerusalem would be destroyed (20:1-3; 26:7-24).

Four years later as a result of the battle of Carchemish (605 B.C.) all Syria and Palestine came under the control of the new Babylonian empire and Egypt had been forced back to the narrow limits of its traditional frontiers.

Although he was Nebuchadnezzar's vassal Jehoiakim continued his own policy of alliance with the Egyptians. Hence his open opposition to Jeremiah who wanted the king to cooperate with the Chaldeans because he knew that the Babylonian empire was the instrument God planned to use to punish Israel for its unfaithfulness. When Jehoiakim very stupidly refused to pay tribute to Babylon, Nebuchadnezzar himself intervened, in 598, and declared war on Judah. On his death (possibly by assassination) Jehoiakim was succeeded by his son Jehoiachin, who three months later gave himself up to the Chaldeans when they began to besiege Jerusalem; he was deported to Babylon, and with him the queen mother, the entire court and many nobles and people of every class except the poorest. Jeremiah was among these exiles (597).

Nebuchadnezzar made Judas Mattaniah, Jehoiachin's uncle, king in his place; he changed his name to Zedekiah. Amazingly, he followed the same policy as his nephew despite all Jeremiah's efforts to bring him to his senses. After attempting to form a coalition in 593 (Jer 51:59-64), Zedekiah eventually did rebel against the Chaldeans in 588, with the support of the new Egyptian pharaoh Hophra. Nebuchadnezzar established his base at Riblah and launched a huge offensive against Jerusalem, the centre of the rebel coalition (Ezek 21:23-27). After a severe eighteen-month siege Hophra was defeated

8 Jeremiah refers to the Babylonians as "Chaldeans"; at this period the Chaldeans — a different race from the Babylonians — constituted the ruling class in Babylon.

and fled, leaving Judah to its fate (Jer 7:3-10). Finally, in July-August 587, Nebuchadnezzar took the city, sacked it and burned it.

The Chaldeans appointed Gedaliah, a man who enjoyed the emperor's trust, to govern the few who were left. He set about the task of building up the morale of his countrymen, a task in which Jeremiah supported him (chap. 40). Gedaliah's efforts were soon brought to an end because a group of fanatics led by Ishmael, open enemies of Babylon, treacherously killed him. Jeremiah and Baruch (43:6) were forcibly taken to Egypt when the remaining Israelites fled there.

In Egypt, in the city of Tahpanhes, Jeremiah contrived to prophesy against idolatrous Jews; he probably died there soon after, stoned by those same men, who could not stomach his criticism.

The book and its content   In the fifty-two chapters of this book oracles alternate with passages of history which confirm and illustrate the prophecies. The book as we have it does not follow a chronological or other order because it is, as St Jerome described, more a collection of writings than a book in the proper sense. These writings consist of a series of warnings and threats of divine retribution for the unfaithfulness of the chosen people and also for the behaviour of neighbouring peoples.

The book, which both Jews and Christians regard as protocanonical, begins with a prologue (chap. 1) which gives an account of Jeremiah's vocation, and it ends with an epilogue (chap. 52) which is a kind of historical summary of the whole collection. The rest of the book has three main parts:

a) The reprobation and condemnation of the Jewish people (2-19);
b) The execution of God's sentence against them;
c) Prophecies against foreign nations (46-51).

It is very probable that in its present form the book is the result of a recopilation of oracles dictated by Jeremiah to Baruch in 605, oracles which go back to the year 626 when he began his ministry. The content of the first scroll which was burned in a fit of anger by King Jehoiakim, was re-dictated by the prophet and expanded by him (36:32). Some of the additions which can be identified in the text date from after 605, and were probably begun by Jeremiah and later edited by Baruch, probably after the fall of Jerusalem in 587.

The interior drama of Jeremiah   Although this book is not essentially a didactic work, we can learn a lot from it. It shows us the drama of the interior life of a man whom God chose to be his spokesman — his prophet — to a people who persisted in their unfaithfulness to the Covenant of Sinai. Jeremiah, who is a man of peace and seeks the good of his people, has to preach the word of God tirelessly, often uttering threats and predicting wars. In spite of his natural shyness God chose him "over nations and over kingdoms, to pluck up and to break down, to destroy and to overthrow, to build and to plant" (1:10). He is changed, very much against his own inclinations, into "a man of strife and contention to the whole land" (15:10) through his fidelity to his prophetic calling.

Jeremiah finds it very difficult to understand why he has to suffer, why God is so slow in coming to his support. The greater his obedience to the task God has given him, the more he suffers. His life will remain forever as a symbol or sign of the route man must take to attain happiness. In Jesus Christ light is at last shed on this mystery: "If any man would come after me, let him deny himself and take up his cross and follow me. For whoever would save his life will lose it, and whoever loses his life for my sake will find it" (Mt 16:24-25).

The source of Jeremiah's faithfulness to God is his elevated concept of God, which is very similar to that found in *Isaiah*. The book vigorously asserts that there is only one God and it rejects idolatry and religious syncretism. Its oracles against the nations, for example, proclaim God's omnipotence: he is the creator and provider not only of Israel but of the whole world. However, Jeremiah takes pleasure in recalling the early faithfulness of the chosen people, describing it as the idyllic period of the betrothal (2:2; 3:4) of Yahweh and Israel. This is the same kind of language as the prophet Hosea uses and it echoes the *Song of Songs* where the love between Yahweh and Israel is compared with the love of husband and wife.

The New Alliance, of which Jeremiah speaks, is something which will come with the Messiah and it will be like a return to the fidelity and intimacy of the early times. Israel will again become the firstborn son of God, and Yahweh will be the tenderest of parents (31:9). However, the new Israel will grow only out of the "remnant" of the people which has stayed true (3:14).

Against this background of God's infinite love and tenderness, Jeremiah denounces sins of lust, injustice, dishonesty, false oaths, hypocrisy etc. He sees sin as a grave rebellion against God, which requires the sinner's "returning" humbly and sincerely to the fountain of living waters (3:7-14, 22; 4:1ff).

In this context it is easier to understand the energy with which he proclaims the need for a religion of the heart, in "spirit and truth" (Jn 4:23) as opposed to the empty formalism of worship not based on sincerity of heart (7:21ff). But it would be a mistake to think that this means that he does not appreciate ritual, external worship: his whole point is that it must be rooted in genuine interior worship (17:26; 33:18).

Jeremiah's insistence on the need to develop deep religious feelings is based on his appreciation of the value and power of prayer. He has recourse to prayer when he sees the danger that threatens his nation (7:16; 11:14; etc); he begs men to join him in extolling divine justice (12:1-5) which punishes the evil doer.[9] He asks God to come to his own aid (18:19) because he realizes he can do nothing without God's favour. He gratefully acknowledges — and teaches others — that humble, trusting prayer is always effective (27:18; 37:3).

In view of all this it is correct to say that Jeremiah's life was not a failure, as some people superficially make out. On the contrary, his whole life is a wonderful lesson on the close terms on which a person like him can be with God, despite contradictions, sufferings and misunderstanding. That was simply the route God wanted him to take in order to carry out his important mission. Indeed, his experiences make him a figure of Jesus Christ and a precursor of the New and definitive Covenant.

Lamentations

This canonical book of the Old Testament is made up of five elegies on the destruction of Jerusalem (587 B.C.). In the Greek translation of the Septuagint, as in the Vulgate, this book is located after *Jeremiah*, to whom they attribute it, whereas in the Hebrew Bible it is included among the writings (*Ketûbîm*) and is part of the "Five Scrolls" (*meghillôth*) which were read out in the liturgical ceremonies of the principal Jewish feasts — the *Song of Songs*, at the Passover; *Ruth*, at Pentecost; *Lamentations*, on the day of fasting to commemorate

---

9 These people had committed the sin which, according to St John, deserves death; it serves no purpose to pray God to help such people (cf. 1 Jn 5:16). Commenting on this passage, St Jerome says: "If we persisted in our vice and thought we could be pardoned through promises and sacrifices, we would be wide of the mark, because we would be expecting God to act unjustly. . . . That is why the prophet is told there is no point in his praying for something that cannot be obtained with prayers" (cf. Jer 14:10-12).

the fall of Jerusalem; *Ecclesiastes* on the feast of Tabernacles; and *Esther* at Purim.

Up to the eighteenth century, both Jewish and Christian tradition regarded it as an undisputed fact that Jeremiah was the author of *Lamentations*, the basis for this being 2 Chron 35:25 and the internal evidence of the poems themselves. But then doubts were cast on this attribution on the grounds that it was difficult to see how Jeremiah could praise Zedekiah[10] in *Lamentations* yet reproach him in his own book, or how he could hope for aid to come from the Egyptians (4:17) in view of the fact that he bitterly opposed the policy of the kings of Judah to ally with Egypt. However, the relationship between this and the period and teachings of Jeremiah cannot be doubted, except for the passages mentioned. Therefore, there is a good basis for thinking that it was written in Palestine, shortly after the fall of Jerusalem in 587, if not by Jeremiah himself, then by a secretary of his, in which case the question of authorship is a secondary one.[11]

Lamentations is much admired for its content and poetic beauty. The structure of the first four poems is alphabetical, that is to say, each of its stanzas begins with one of the twenty-two letters of the Hebrew alphabet, a device frequently used in the Bible to help memorization of the text. The fifth lamentation is not alphabetical, although it also has twenty-two stanzas.

In the course of each of these lamentations the drama of destruction of Jerusalem and its Temple is described in tones of deep pathos; but what they mainly stress is divine punishment of its inhabitants for betraying and abandoning Yahweh. In spite of this terrible punishment the poems recognize that it has served to awaken the people to their sin (5:16) and cause them to desire to turn back to God: "Restore us to thyself, O Lord, that we may be restored" (5:21).

The main teaching in this little book is summed up in the following point which well warrants meditation: faults and sins, no matter how enormous they be, can, if they are humbly recognized and confessed with true repentance, help to lead one back to God and be pardoned by him. Hence the hope of forgiveness in this poem:

Rejoice and be glad, O daughter of Edom,
dweller in the land of Uz;

---

10 Although the text — Lam 3:20 — deals with Zedekiah, it can also be applied to Jesus Christ, God's anointed Messiah, whose death and resurrection will open the way to eternal life.

11 Cf. Robert Feuillet, op. cit.; F. Spadafora, op. cit., p.360.

> but to you also the cup shall pass;
> you shall become drunk and strip yourself bare.
>
> The punishment of your iniquity, O daughter of Zion, is accomplished,
> he will keep you in exile no longer;
> but your iniquity, O daughter of Edom, he will punish,
> he will uncover your sins (Lam 4:21-22).

This is a canticle appropriately used in the Church's Holy Week liturgy. Through the passion and death of our Lord, provided man recognizes and confesses his sins, he is enabled to rejoice and to share in the glory of the resurrection of his Lord.

Baruch

The book of *Baruch*, a deuterocanonical book of the Old Testament comes after *Lamentations* in the Vulgate, but the Septuagint puts it after *Jeremiah* because of its obviously close connexion. Although it is not part of the Hebrew canon it was read in the synagogue, like *Lamentations*. The Fathers of the Church (Athenagoras, St Irenaeus and Clement of Alexandria, among others) considered *Baruch* to be an inspired book. This is the official position of the Church, which ever since the Council of Trent lists it in the canon of Scripture.

Baruch (= blessed) was the secretary and disciple of Jeremiah (Jer 32:12ff). After the assassination of Gedaliah he was forcibly taken, with Jeremiah, to Egypt (Jer 43). Later, as he himself tells us, he left Egypt (1:1-2) and joined the Jewish exiles in Babylon, where he wrote his book and gave a public reading of it on the fifth anniversary of the destruction of Jerusalem (581). He returned to Jerusalem that same year with monies collected for those remaining in the city, for burnt offerings and sin offerings; he brought with him some of the sacred vessels which Nebuchadnezzar had plundered from the Temple, and must surely have read out the book on the occasion of the feast of Tabernacles (1:6-14).

The book consists of six chapters, the last of which gives the text of the Letter of Jeremiah. After a short historical introduction (1:1-14), there are three fairly distinct parts to the book: the first (1:15 - 3:8) consists of a long prayer in which the people confess their sin and beg God's mercy and forgiveness; the second (3:9 - 4:4) is a hymn of praise to divine wisdom, an attribute of God which is inaccessible to man unless — as is the case with Israel — God makes his mind known in the form of his eternal law,[12] the source of life; the third part (4:5—5:9) is an exhortation in which Jerusalem, cast in the role of a good mother, invites her children to have hope and confidence in God, and in which the enemies of Israel are threatened with dire punishment. The book ends with a passage announcing the end of the exile and the return to Jerusalem.

The Letter of Jeremiah (chap. 6), whose original text according to scholars was in Hebrew is, St Jerome thinks, psuedoepigraphic, since he assigns it a date much later than that for the editing of the writings of that prophet. It probably comes from the third century B.C. when the worship of the gods was being reestablished in all its ancient splendour at Babylon. This, however, does not mean that it is not an inspired text: the Fathers recognized it as such and it is in the Church's canon.

This sixth chapter, which is very beautifully written, is an argument in popular language in favour of the one true God. It ridicules idolatrous worship as vain and empty; the exiles have no need to fear it, no matter how decked out in gold or silver these idols are; they are only pieces of wood[13] which cannot move and can do nothing to help themselves. The prophet cleverly proves that the gods the Babylonians adore are idols, on which no one can rely:

> They cannot save a man from death or rescue the weak from the strong. They cannot restore sight to a blind man; they cannot rescue a man who is in distress. They cannot take pity on a widow or do good to an orphan. These things that are made of wood and overlaid with gold and silver are like stones from the mountain, and those who serve them will be put to shame. Why then must any one think that they are gods, or call them gods? (Bar 6:36-40).

The teaching contained in this letter is in line with the prophetic writings we have already seen, even if it is of a later date: the only one in whom they should place their trust is the God of Israel, transcendent, eternal, unique — not the idols of Babylon which people were trying to enthrone once again.

---

12   The Law is said to be eternal as far as its moral precepts go but not as far as liturgical rites are concerned. Jesus will carry it to fulfilment.

13   Obviously one cannot adore a piece of wood as such, no matter how much gold and silver adorn it. If we venerate icons and other sacred images it is because they represent the true God, the Mother of God, the angels or the saints.

Ezekiel

Ezekiel is the third of the major prophets. His name, which in Hebrew is Yehezq'el (= God strengthens), was very much in keeping with the mission God planned for him. A member of a priestly family, he was taken to Babylon in the first deportation (597), along with his wife, King Jehoiachin and all his court (cf. 2 Kings 24:16).

Like most of these deportees, Ezekiel settled down near the Naru-Kabaru or Great Canal between Babylon and Nippur, in southern Babilonia. There the exiles established the farming community of Tel-Abib, but later on many of them were employed in the grandiose building schemes then underway in the country.

Five years after his arrival (592), when he was around thirty years of age, Ezekiel received his great vision, a theophany or vision of God (1:1ff), and was called by God himself to be a prophet to his people (2:1ff). So generous was his response that from that point onwards, for about twenty-two years, Ezekiel was the spiritual guide of his fellow-exiles. His life was full of suffering and misunderstanding, even though he was a man of peace and sought only his people's welfare, but he remained ever optimistic and full of hope in the power of Yahweh. His wife had died shortly after their arrival in Babylon and he himself died in exile, probably at the hands of one of the Jewish leaders whom he criticized for idolatry — that at least is the opinion of St Athanasius and St Epiphanus.

The content of the book[14] Ezekiel's prophetic and spiritual mission all turns on one central event — the destruction of Jerusalem (587). Prior to that date the prophecies all have to do with warning the people and exhorting them to repent and to trust in God rather than in pacts with Egypt or any other neighbour. Ezekiel keeps insisting on a point which may seem rather unusual: namely, that, by a special disposition of providence, Babylon is to be the instrument God will use to punish Judah; there is no escape from this punishment but its purpose is medicinal, because it will purify people's souls and set them again on the road of faithfulness to Yahweh. Are they sure to turn in that direction? The will of God, when it is absolute, is always fulfilled; however, when people are warned of it, as in this case, God conditions his will when instructing man's will to do something, leaving man free to do it or not. Judah will indeed be

---

14 On the whole question of the formation of this book and modern scholars' doubts about its authenticity, cf. discussion in A. Robert and A. Feuillet, op. cit.

purified, but only part of it — the "remnant" who will experience the suffering of separation from Yahweh and from his Temple during the long years of exile.

The first part of the book, up to chapter 32 inclusive, announces God's judgments against both the people of Israel and the idolatrous nations. After a short prologue in which Ezekiel describes how God called him, he uses a series of symbols to predict the — now inevitable — destruction of Jerusalem and identify its causes.

In the second part, with those prophecies already come true, he puts on the mantle of a prophet of hope.[15] He consoles and encourages the exiles and tells them of God's determination to set them free and bring them home. These prophecies, full of majestic symbols, look forward to the era when the New Covenant will be made, in the kingdom of the Messiah to come:

> They shall dwell in the land where your fathers dwelt that I gave to my servant Jacob; they and their children and their children's children shall dwell there for ever; and David my servant shall be their prince for ever. I will make a covenant of peace with them; it shall be an everlasting covenant with them; and I will bless them and multiply them, and will set my sanctuary in the midst of them for evermore. My dwelling place shall be with them; and I will be their God, and they shall be my people. Then the nations will know that I the Lord sanctify Israel, when my sanctuary is in the midst of them for evermore (Ezek 37:25-28).

The book is written almost entirely in prose, with a didactic and descriptive purpose, using symbolism to catch the attention of his listeners. He is obviously addressing a people strongly inclined to be sceptical. His language is extremely rich, colourful and descriptive, sometimes rising to poetic heights.

Although the Hebrew text which the Vulgate follows is defective in some parts, it is superior to that of the Greek translation of the Septuagint and to the Masoretic text, though both the latter do help to clarify obscure passages.

Ezekiel, prophet of hope Ezekiel is the prophet of the exiles. He shared the hardest years the Jews spent in Babylon. All his energies were directed towards keeping the exiles' hopes alive, just at the point at which, on hearing the news of the fall of Jerusalem, they were liable to feel that God had abandoned them forever.

15 From chapter 36 onwards hopes for a possible return from exile are in the ascendant. The mountains will become fertile and clean water will flow. It is to another later era that Ezekiel is referring, a time when all these messianic hopes will be realized, the era of the New Alliance in which the "heart of stone" — hard, rebellious and not very docile to God's grace — will be renewed and guided by the Holy Spirit (Ezek 36:25-27).

The first point the prophet emphasizes is that Yahweh is not confined to Jerusalem or even Palestine: his power extends as far as Babylon and to the ends of the earth. His majesty is infinite, his presence universal. Thanks to his omnipotence and infinite love, he will once more show mercy to his people and by a totally gratuitous act he will work their conversion. What seems so difficult will soon become a reality, as shown in the symbolic vision of the bare bones which are clothed again with flesh and changed back into men.[16] Nothing is impossible to God.

> Then he said to me, "Son of man, these bones are the whole house of Israel. Behold, they say, 'Our bones are dried up, and our hope is lost; we are clean cut off.' Therefore prophesy, and say to them, Thus says the Lord God: Behold, I will open your graves, and raise you from your graves, O my people; and I will bring you home into the land of Israel. And you shall know that I am the Lord, when I open your graves, and raise you from your graves, O my people. And I will put my Spirit within you, and you shall live, and I will place you in your own land; then you shall know that I, the Lord, have spoken, and I have done it, says the Lord" (Ezek 37:11-14).

Ezekiel then goes on to preach about personal responsibility and everything it implies in the case of the exiles. What he teaches marks an advance on the revelation contained in previous books. People took it as normal for a city or a whole nation to be punished collectively — just men as well as sinners — and for the sins of parents to be visited also on their children. Ezekiel speaks of individual responsibility: a man's salvation or condemnation depends on him alone, on his personal attitude to God, that is, his response to the grace he has been given, as it was in the beginning.

Ezekiel therefore explains the meaning and purpose of divine punishment and teaches that it is possible for each individual to be reconciled with God, going on to explain further about individual retribution. Since man is responsible for his actions, he must suffer the consequences of his unfaithfulness, although — even in exile — he can recover lost grace by being converted, which is the true purpose of any punishment God metes out:

> But if a wicked man turns away from all his sins which he has committed and keeps all my statutes and does what is lawful and right, he shall surely live; he shall not die. None of the transgressions which he has committed shall be remembered against him; for the righteousness which he has done

---

16 The resurrection of the bones (Ezek 37:7-9) symbolizes the people of Israel becoming a nation once again; but it is also a symbol of the resurrection of the body which will take place before the Last Judgment (cf. Dan 12:2; 2 Mac 7:9-14; Mt 22:29-32; 1 Cor 15).

he shall live. Have I any pleasure in the death of the wicked, says the Lord God, and not rather that he should turn from his way and live? (Ezek 18:21-23).

Ezekiel's work did much to regroup the exiles around the priests and the Law; it revived their religion, making it more interior and personal; it gave new hope to those who stayed faithful to Yahweh; it gave them a vision of their future and, in particular, it showed them a new spiritual horizon, a type of renewal deeper than anything they had so far experienced.

In this future which Ezekiel predicts, it will be God himself who purifies and renews their hearts:

I will sprinkle clean water upon you, and you shall be clean from all your uncleannesses, and from all your idols I will cleanse you. A new heart I will give you, and a new spirit I will put within you; and I will take out of your flesh the heart of stone and give you a heart of flesh. And I will put my spirit within you, and cause you to walk in my statutes and be careful to observe my ordinances (Ezek 36:25-27).

In the messianic times God will seek out the individual person, as a shepherd seeks his sheep.[17] Our Lord, in his parable of the Good Shepherd, interprets this passage of Ezekiel:

As a shepherd seeks out his flock when some of his sheep have been scattered abroad, so will I seek out my sheep; and I will rescue them from all places. . . . I myself will make them lie down, says the Lord God. I will seek the lost, and I will bring back the strayed, and I will bind up the crippled, and I will strengthen the weak, and the fat and the strong I will watch over; I will feed them in justice (Ezek 34:12-16).

Ezekiel concludes his prophecies, as we have seen, by announcing that there will be a New Covenant:

I will make a covenant of peace with them; it shall be an everlasting covenant with them; and I will bless them and multiply them, and set my sanctuary in the midst of them for ever more (Ezek 27:26).

The book closes with a description of the future city: "The circumference of the city shall be eighteen thousands cubits. And the name of the city henceforth shall be, Yahweh is there" (48:35). This prophecy looks first to the reconstruction of Israel, symbolic of the future messianic kingdom, the Church.

---

17 For both Jews and Christians this shepherd is the Messiah, also called David by Jeremiah (30:9) and Hosea (3:5) because David is a figure and ancestor of the Messiah.

Daniel

In both the Greek version of the Septuagint and the Vulgate, the book of *Daniel* is mentioned as the fourth of the major prophets, after *Ezekiel*. The Hebrew includes it among the *Ketûbîm* (Writings), between *Ezra* and *Esther*, but only its protocanonical part (chap. 1-12). Probably prior to the first century B.C. it was located among the *Nebîîm* (Prophets), which is the source the Septuagint would have used.

Everthing we know about Daniel (= God is my judge) comes from the book that bears his name.[18] He belonged to the royal family of Zedekiah and was taken, by order of Nebuchadnezzar, in captivity along with other Jewish children, to Babylon in 605 B.C. Like certain other young men he was later chosen by the king to be brought up and educated at court, where he was given the name of Belteshazzar. God endowed him with special wisdom which soon led him to enjoy the king's favour; he was so successful in interpreting the king's dreams that he was appointed ruler of the province of Babylon. King Darius wanted to make him prime minister (6:4), but the envy of his other ministers frustrated this plan; they plotted his death but God saved him in a miraculous way (6:23).

As regards the language of the book, chapters 1-2:4a and 8-12 were written in Hebrew and 2:4b — 7:28 in Aramaic. Some scholars think that the original text was written in Hebrew and that the Aramaic parts were the result of later changes made to fill in for damaged or lost portions. Others think that the original text must have been written in Aramaic but that it was later translated into Hebrew in order to get it into the canon. In any event, there is no doubt about the canonicity of the "interpreted" passages, or about that of the deuterocanonical parts. All this is guaranteed by Jewish Alexandrine tradition and by Christian tradition and was solemnly sanctioned by the Council of Trent.

The structure of the book   The aim of the book is to show that the God of Israel, the one true God, is greater than the pagan gods. This is proved by Daniel's personal experiences and by the prophecy, which runs through the book, of the establishment of the kingdom of God, a universal, eternal kingdom, a kingdom of peace and justice for all who prove faithful to him.

18   Cf. P. P. Saydon, *CCHS*, sections 494ff; F. Spadafora, op. cit., pp. 141-145.

Daniel recognizes that human wisdom can never penetrate the mystery communicated to the king in his dreams. It can be explained only by the God of Israel, the lord of heaven and earth. The mystery has to do with the future messianic kingdom, the kingdom of heaven which the Messiah, Jesus Christ, will inaugurate through his incarnation.

There are two quite distinguishable parts in the book: in the first (1-6) Daniel tells of his personal experiences at the royal court, to show that the God of Israel is almighty and is the only God that lives. To do this he interprets the king's dreams, with the help of a special revelation from God. In his vision of the image or statue (chap. 2) he predicts the four successive kingdoms which will precede the coming of the Messiah.

These four are: the Babylonian kingdom (gold), that of the Medes and the Persians (silver), the Greek (bronze) and that of iron (the Ptolemy kingdom). The main meaning of all this is that the kingdom of God inaugurated by Jesus Christ (cf. Mt 4:17) will oppose the various pagan kingdoms, which are the personification of the kingdom of Satan. This kingdom of God, which is the Church is, St Augustine thinks, symbolized by the stone "which was cut out by no human hand ... and smote the image" (2:34-35). Beginning in a small, unsignificant way, the Church will spread all over the world, thanks to the power of God who sustains it. This, in summary, is the content of Daniel's interpretation.

The king is so amazed by Daniel's great wisdom — which far exceeds that of all his wise men — that he recognizes the power and justice of Daniel's God. The cryptic words (*Mene, Tekel, Parsin*: Dan 5:25) which a mysterious hand writes on the wall are also interpreted by the prophet,[19] and immediately his prediction comes true: Babylon falls to the Persians.

This first part of the book ends with an amazing episode which can only be explained as a special intervention by God: Daniel is saved from a lions' den, without a scratch, just as his three companions were saved from the fiery furnace where they had been put for refusing to worship the golden image.

The second part (chap. 7-12) relates four prophetic apocalyptic visions which Daniel received.

In the first vision (chap. 7) in the first year of King Belshazzar's

---

19 *Mene* means number(ed); *Tekel*, weight, weighed; *Parsin*, division or divided. Scholars offer various interpretations of this passage. It probably is a reference to the descending fortunes of the three next empires — Babylonian, Medean and Persian — or else to the empires' three kings — Nebuchadnezzar, Evil-Merodach and Belshazzar.

reign, Daniel sees four great beasts coming out of the sea. They represent the four successive kingdoms, from the last of which a king will emerge who will try to exterminate the people of God, but he will be destroyed and "the people of the saints of the Most High" will be given "an everlasting kingdom" (7:27).

The second vision (chap. 8), in the third year of Belshazzar's reign, symbolizes the downfall of the empire of the Medes and the Persians, the arrival of the empire of Alexander the Great, and the sacrilegious arrogance of its successor, Antiochus IV Epiphanes, who will attack the people of God and profane and destroy the Temple.

In the third vision (chap. 9), in the first year of Darius the Mede, while Daniel is meditating on the prophecy of Jeremiah about the seventy years which Israel will spend in exile in Babylonia, the angel Gabriel reveals to him that the full restoration will come about after seventy weeks of years (490 years), with the coming of the kingdom of God. The opening date of this prophecy is the prophecy of Jeremiah (cf. Jer 25:12; 29:12) about the return of Israel from exile in Babylon. The end date is the persecution by and death of Antiochus IV Epiphanes. At the end of the seventy weeks, sacrifice and offering will cease until the decreed destruction of the destroyer. Then there will be an end to sin and the kingdom of the Messiah will come.

The fourth vision (chap. 10-12), in the third year of Cyrus, is a revelation of the course of events involving the rulers of the people of God up to Antiochus IV, whose conquests and last persecution are described very vividly. In spite of this, the people must keep hoping, because the hour of their deliverance is at hand, the predicted messianic era. Is Daniel in chapter 12 referring to the resurrection of all men prior to the Last Judgment? Some commentators think that this text does refer to the resurrection, which Isaiah had already spoken of (cf. Is 26:19). However, it is more likely that the passage refers to the time the departed will spend in Hades (*sheol*),* after which the blessed will go to heaven and the unjust will be condemned, which will take place much later, when Jesus Christ after his resurrection visits those in "hell", in the bosom of Abraham.

The book closes with an appendix (chap. 13-14) containing the stories of Susanna and of Bel and the Dragon,. both of which have a happy outcome thanks to Daniel's prudence and sagacity.

The providence of God and the future messianic kingdom The entire book derives from one main teaching — the God of Israel, the one true, all-knowing and almighty God, the sovereign Master of human affairs, is the King of kings and the Lord of heaven and earth, who in his infinite wisdom and power governs the course of human history, saving those who are faithful to him and overthrowing kings who try to frustrate his plans. Any resistance offered him ends in war and destruction; whereas obedience and faithfulness to his laws will always, despite any obstacles that may arise, lead to victory and eventual peace.

Without it in any way taking from his transcendence, Daniel teaches, God governs the world and lovingly cares for his creatures. To do this he makes use of angels, whose mission is to protect men. Should God on occasions allow the just man to be persecuted, it is only to test his faithfulness and reward him for his good works. Daniel is distressed to see Israelites suffering in exile, but his sadness is mitigated not so much by the memory of past glory but by the hope of a much more secure future.

"This *messianic* teaching differs noticeably from that of the other prophets in that it is almost totally wrapped up in the eschatological side of the kingdom of God. Before the coming of the Messiah all hostile powers and particularly the great persecutor of the people of God (Antiochus IV) will be destroyed. The messianic kingdom, imperceptible at first, will in time spread all over the world. It will be a spiritual kingdom based on peace and justice and acknowledgment of the one true God. The messianic king will not conquer the world by the sword; he will be the 'Son of man'* and will receive royal authority from the hands of God himself, who is the only who has the right to give it to whomever he chooses."[20]

The prophecy of Daniel marks the culmination of God's intervention in history prior to that time. Now new horizons are opened up, a future history is predicted in which the kingdom of God (the Church) will spread, during its earthly phase, to all peoples and become in effect the stage prior to the final, definitive heavenly stage, which will last forever. That is the scenario for the book's teaching on the resurrection of the dead, when the just receive their reward and the reprobate their punishment — a doctrinal advance compared with what had been revealed in the earlier prophets.

B. THE TWELVE MINOR PROPHETS

The twelve shorter prophetic books in the Old Testament are

20 P. P. Saydon, art. cit., sections 503f.

attributed to "minor prophets" — a title which refers to the shortness of the books, which of course were written under the same divine inspiration and contain teaching which is on a par with that in the preceding books.

The New Vulgate — like the Vulgate before it — gives these books in the same order as the Hebrew Bible, a chronological order based on the traditional opinion as to when they were written; they come from a period extending over some five hundred years.

Here we will discuss them in an historical order and comment on what we consider to be the more important features of each book, with a view to elucidating the biblical message as a whole.[21]

a) *Before the fall of the kingdom of Israel (eighth century B.C.).*

Amos

Amos was the earliest of the writer prophets. He was born in Tekoa, near Bethlehem, probably around the beginning of the eighth century. While he was shepherding his flock he was called by God to prophesy in the northern kingdom. Amos makes it quite clear in his book that God's choice of him was quite unmerited, because he was neither "a prophet nor the son of a prophet". He ministered in the reign of Jeroboam II (783-743), using as his base the schismatic shrine at Bethel. Therefore, he was a contemporary of Hosea.

At that time the northern kingdom, thanks to its conquests, was enjoying a period of great prosperity, but there were sharp contrasts between rich and poor and many instances of inequity and injustice; the spirit of true religion was difficult to find. Amos, a deeply religious man, zealous for God's glory, condemns dissolute city life, social injustice and insincerity of religious worship (5:21-22). He exposes those who exploit the poor (8:6) and upbraids judges for their venality (5:10-15).

The book is a hymn to God's omnipotence and to the permanence of the Covenant. It is full of rich imagery and vivid parables based on the pastoral and rural life with which Amos was so familiar. Through this he passes on God's message; if the people do not change their ways they will soon be punished by Yahweh: the kingdom will

---

21 For a more extensive commentary on the minor prophets, cf. G. Rinaldi, *I Profeti Minori* (Turin 1953); J. Coppens, *Les Douze Petits Prophètes: brevaire du prophetisme* (Bruges-Louvain 1950); A. Van Hoonacker, *Les Douze Petits Prophètes* (Paris 1908).

collapse and its inhabitants will be sent into exile. This is the last chance God will give them to avoid this outcome. In spite of all the criticism the prophet levels at his people, there is still, as always, a shaft of hope; in the context of the repentance to which he calls them, he speaks of future salvation for the "remnant of Joseph" (5:15) who with the "remnant" of Judah will experience the grace of messianic restoration.

Hosea

Hosea (= salvation) was a citizen of the northern kingdom whose prophetic mission began in the reign of Jeroboam II, king of Israel (783-743) and probably continued until just before the fall of Samaria in 721.

In this book the prophet describes his own life, surrounded as he was by moral corruption, in the form of a personal drama which symbolically represents the dramatic story of Yahweh and Israel his spouse. To God's generous and even passionate love, Israel's response is ingratitude and indifference.

This religious infidelity, which takes the form of worshipping false Gods, thereby breaking the Covenant, is described by him in terms of adultery, prostitution and fornication.

The entire eighth chapter of the book is a denunciation of Israel whom Hosea charges with breaking the Covenant; with having kings who are illegitimate because they contravene God's will; with adoring the golden calf; and with making foreign alliances rather than relying on God's aid — all of which will lead to enslavement in a foreign land (cf. Deut 26:68).

Yahweh, who had contracted marriage with Israel, has discovered her to be unfaithful and feels the natural jealousy of a wounded spouse. Despite her unfaithfulness he still loves his wife. Even though he does at times punish her, his only purpose in doing so is to attract her back to himself: he is merciful and desires that she mend her ways and experience once more the delight of their first love.

The teaching is clear: Yahweh is a jealous God and he wants his love to be reciprocated. Love is the very foundation of man's relationship with God, the only thing which guarantees the sincerity of his spiritual life: "For I desire steadfast love and not sacrifice, the knowledge of God, rather than burnt offerings" (Hos 6:6).

This teaching will be echoed by later prophets who, like Hosea, exhort people to a more personal and more interior relationship with God, based on love of him: genuine faith in God leads to moral uprightness. The use of marriage as a comparison to describe God's relations with Israel will acquire its fullest meaning in the pages of the New Testament: Jesus' intimacy with his Church is very appropriately described in these terms (cf. Eph 23-32).

Micah

The prophet Micah (= Who is like Yahweh?) was a native of Moresheth, a village near Israel's border with the territory of the Philistines, about forty five kilometres from Jerusalem. He ministered as a prophet in the reigns of Jotham, Ahaz and Hezekiah. He was a contemporary of Hosea in his youth, and also of Amos and Isaiah. His rural background reminds us of Amos — witness the vivid, expressive language, rich in imagery, which he uses to illustrate his teaching.

We do not know anything about Micah's life. The inspired text does show him to be a true prophet, chosen by God to perform this mission. Micah does nothing to ingratiate himself with the people, yet they listen to him nevertheless; his main message has to do with the sentence God is going to pass on the Israelites and the punishment they will experience if they do not repent. In a dialogue alternating with threats and promises, this book, like *Amos* and *Hosea*, warns them that "the day of Yahweh" is near at hand. Contrary to what many people think, it will be a day of darkness, not of light. However, he tells them, after a period of purification, a new light of hope will shine out.

As regards this purification, what God wants of man, is not so much material offerings as acts of the virtues of humility, justice and charity: for that proves a person's faithfulness. Any worship and any purification which stem from this deep humility will have the effect of rendering material offerings pleasing to God (cf. Hos 6:6; Amos 5:24-25).

God's promises to Abraham (7:20) will come true in that "remnant" of the people which will be purified (4-5). From this remnant will be born — in Bethlehem Ephrathah — him whose origin is from ancient days, from eternity (5:1). The birth of the Messiah of a woman (5:2) implies that Micah is aware of the prophecy of Isaiah: "The virgin shall conceive and bear a son, and shall call his name Immanuel" (Is 7:14). The New Testament sees in this passage a reference to the virginal birth of Jesus, the Son of God, from a particular woman, Mary, in Bethlehem (Mt 2:6; Jn 7:42).

b) *From the fall of the kingdom of Israel (721 B.C.) to that of the kingdom of Judah (587 B.C.).*

Zephaniah

From the opening verse of this book we learn that Zephaniah (= Yahweh protects) prophesied in the time of Josiah, king of Judah (640-609 B.C.). Since Josiah's religious reform took place in 622 and Zephaniah in his preaching continues to make reference to sins of idolatry (1:4-6) and exhorts the people to conversion, his ministry should probably be dated prior to 622, which would make him a contemporary of Jeremiah, Nahum and Habukkuk.

The book of *Zephaniah* and its message can be summed up in terms of its announcement of the "day of Yahweh". This "day", which the preceding prophets referred to so much, implies a clear invitation to penance, extended to pagan nations and more particularly to Judah itself. Yet, when it does come God will give his people — that is, the faithful remnant — a new hope and confidence. This remnant will, as Amos and Isaiah had earlier foretold, consist of the poor, the humble and all those who put their trust in God. Clearly this teaching has a reference to the New Testament. No matter how seriously they have sinned, these humble people are being promised salvation, for the Redeemer is coming to heal them (Mt 11:5). They are the poor in spirit referred to in our Lord's first beatitude (Mt 5:3).

Nahum

The prophet Nahum (in Hebrew "consoler") was a veritable consoler of Judah: in his short oracle he communicated God's message of the downfall of its greatest enemy, Assyria. That kingdom's capital would be destroyed, as happened previously in the case of Thebes (663 B.C.), in just punishment of its sins.

Like Jonah, Nahum does not address Israel directly: he speaks to the people of Nineveh in an attempt to move them to repent. This sacred book stresses the justice and mercy of God, who always comes to the defence of these who love him and keep his commandments.

The fall of Nineveh in 612 built up Judah's hopes for a short while, but soon Judah itself was punished for its unfaithfulness and its own capital, Jerusalem, destroyed.

Habakkuk

Somewhat earlier than Nahum and like him a contemporary of Jeremiah and Zephaniah, Habakkuk (the origin of the name is unclear) lived at an important point in history when the Chaldeans, after the victory of Nebuchadnezzar at Carchemis (605 B.C.), extended their control over vast areas of the Near East and now threatened Judah.

In this short book Habakkuk poses the problem of evil and how it fits in with divine justice. In his prayer he accepts that God has chosen the Babylonians to be the instrument of justice against Judah. But, he asks, how can God allow them to be so brutal, how can he permit them to commit such terrible crimes? (1:13ff). One can detect in his lament, which is also a prayer of entreaty, an echo of the book of *Job*, which, as we shall soon see, posed a similar problem.

His reply confirms that God has acted justly, even though man finds it difficult to see it that way. The chastisement Judah will receive is medicinal; therefore it is temporary and is proportional to its faults, because "he whose soul is not upright in him shall fail, but the righteous man shall live by his faith" (2:4). The book ends with a prayer and a canticle of hope and faith or abandonment in God. He who trusts in the word of Yahweh may suffer and bemoan his state for a while, but in the end, if he perseveres in his fidelity, he will rejoice in the God of his salvation.

c) *After the return from Babylonian captivity (537 B.C.)*

Haggai

Haggai (= festive) was the first of the post-exilic prophets. With him began the last prophetic period, that of the restoration which followed the end of the Jewish exile. Haggai began his preaching in the second year of the reign of Darius (522-486 B.C.). His book has a different kind of content from that of the previous prophets: instead of threats of punishment for unfaithfulness and words of hope and consolation for the exiles, now it is a positive desire for restoration that the prophet is encouraging them to have.

They had started rebuilding the Temple with this frame of mind, but they soon ran into opposition from the Samaritans, their greatest enemies. The Samaritans prevailed on the Persian authorities to put a halt to the rebuilding. On top of this there were bad harvests. The net effect was that the Jews' initial enthusiasm was beginning to wane, if it had not indeed disappeared.

Haggai's exhortations, in the months of August and September 520, were aimed at reversing this trend — as Zechariah's would be, some time later. Haggai inspired new energies in the people and encouraged Zerubbabel to start work again on the Temple. What he says is: God has permitted the harvest to fail because his Temple is still in ruins and no one is doing anything about it; on its rebuilding depends the future prosperity and plenty of Judah. Although the new Temple will not be as magnificent as Solomon's, it will surpass it because of its close connexion with the Messiah, the descendant of David. St Paul later used Haggai's prophecy to show the permanence of the New Covenant, which has come to replace the Old (Heb 12:26ff).

Zechariah

The book of Zechariah (= Yahweh remembers) comes chronologically after that of Haggai. The prophet Zechariah, the son of Berechiah and grandson of Ido, belonged to a priestly family which had returned from exile to Babylon. Like Haggai, he was called by God in 520, the second year of the reign of Darius. He probably lived until very near the time the new Temple was finished.

Working in a literary style quite different from Haggai's but with the same doctrinal content, Zechariah describes in the first part of his book (chap. 1-8), by means of eight sublime visions, God's plan for the restoration of the Temple and of the city of Jerusalem, and promises God's blessing on Israel. As a prerequisite God asks his people for moral rectitude, to be shown in acts of justice and mercy and obedience to his commandments. It should be pointed out that in Zechariah's time the Jews gave much importance to fasting but their motivation was at fault because they were more concerned about appearing to others to be good that about seeking God's favour. The prophet tells them that fasting is pleasing to God if it stems from genuine piety.

The second part of the book (chap. 9-14), referring to a later period, is also important for its messianic teaching. It describes in detail the reestablishment of the house of David (chap. 12); the advent of the Messiah, humble and riding on an ass (9:9-10); his passion and death, with the remarkable prophecy of his being pierced (12:10); his priesthood (13:9) and, finally, the calling of the Gentiles to the Church (14:16). In his Gospel St Matthew sees these prophecies being fulfilled in Jesus Christ, who enters Jerusalem meekly mounted on an ass (Mt 21:2-9) at the start of the week in which God's plan for salvation reaches its climax.

Malachi

Malachi in Hebrew means "my messenger", and is the prophet's real name and not that of some anonymous person. We know nothing about Malachi other than what can be gleaned from the text. He must have begun his prophetic ministry after the exile, during the period of Persian domination, given the laxity of morals noted in the text and the continued lack of devotion on the part of priests. Along with this there was the proliferation of mixed marriages consequent on the return from exile, and many divorces among the Jews, which fuelled the prophet's indignation.

The spiritual renewal worked by Haggai and Zechariah has come to a halt. The people are very easygoing and weak in the practice of their faith. In a style reminiscent of Ezechiel, Malachi energetically exhorts them — particularly the priests — to practise religion in a more wholehearted manner, based on the love of God. He foretells the coming of the Messiah — the angel or messenger of the Covenant, he calls him — who himself will be preceded by another messenger, a precursor (3:1), which is clearly a prophecy about John the Baptist (cf. Mt 11:10).

With Jesus, the Messiah, to whom all the books of the Old Testament, and particularly this one, refer, the era of salvation will begin. In that era the moral order will be reestablished (3:5) and proper worship (3:4), and above all the sacrifice of the New Covenant will take place, a perfect offering made to God on behalf of all men (1:11) by Christ, who is both Victim and Priest.

This comes true and is renewed each day in the holy sacrifice of the altar, the only sacrifice of the messianic era, offered to God by all people all over the earth.

Obadiah

Obadiah (= servant of Yahweh) was perhaps a contemporary of Ezekiel, but profane history can tell us nothing about him. His "book" of 21 verses is the shortest of the minor prophets. However, St Jerome says of him: "a little prophet as far as words go, but not little in terms of ideas".

Obadiah's prophecy operates on two levels — that of the chastisement of Edom and that of the ultimate triumph of Israel on "the day of Yahweh". The Edomites incurred the prophet's anger because they had foolishly applauded the destruction of Jerusalem and had gone to play a part in the sacking of the city and the persecution of its refugees (cf. Jer 49:7-22; Ezek 25:12ff). Parallel with the punishment of Edom, Judah will receive the reward of being restored and of recovering its treasures. All this should be understood in terms of its ultimate messianic restoration.

Joel

The name Joel means "Yahweh is God" in Hebrew. Joel prophesied in Judah, in Jerusalem, and most scholars think that he operated around the year 500, after the return from exile.

There are two parts to the book. The first describes a plague of locusts, a sign of the sentence God will deliver on the "day of Yahweh". Is this day close at hand? The prophet describes a series of calamities which will precede it; these include the locust plague. Is this a symbol or something which will actually happen? Even if it is a real event, it is also a symbol of invasion by enemy peoples, invasion of the Holy Land by pagan foreigners, in chastisement of Israel's unfaithfulness. The people will do penance and God will call a halt to the plague and restore prosperity.

The second part, written in apocalyptic style, describes God's judgment of the nations and his final victory, and therefore the victory of Israel. The "day of Yahweh" refers to the messianic era, at the end of time, prior to the Last Judgment, which will, Joel says, be accompanied by a cosmic disaster. However, since the book is apocalyptic in style, what it says does not have to be taken literally. Its teaching can only be understood in the light of the New Testament.

The book's main doctrinal contribution is its prophecy of the outpouring of the Spirit, who will descend on all the people of God in the messianic era (3:1-5). St Peter actually quotes this text on the day of Pentecost (Acts 2:16-21), asserting that this prophecy has come true in the Church.

Joel concludes by speaking of the judgment which will take place in the valley of Jehoshaphat,[22] an eschatological vision shot through with messianic hope.

Jonah

The author of this book used to be identified as the prophet of the same name, the son of Amittai (1:1), who in the times of Jeroboam II (783-743 B.C.) prophesied the reestablishment of the ancient frontiers of Israel (2 Kings 14:25). Scholars are in disagreement as to the book's date of composition, but it seems to be around the end of the fifth century.

The book starts with Yahweh's command to Jonah to go to Nineveh[23] to preach penance. Jonah makes excuses and in fact disobeys. He flees on board ship but is thrown into the sea during a storm. A huge fish swallows him (chap. 1) and he spends three days and three nights in the fish's belly.[24] Then the fish vomits him out and he finds himself safe and sound on the coast of Palestine (chap. 2). Yahweh repeats his command and this time Jonah obeys. When he reaches Nineveh he tells the people that the city is now to be destroyed in forty days time (3:4). But the Ninevites do penance, and God in his mercy forgives them (chap. 3).

Basically what the book says is that God's plan for salvation embraces everyone, Gentiles as well as Jews. All have need of God. That is why the prophet is sent to a "foreign" city — to show that

---

22 Popular belief that the universal judgment will take place in the valley of Jehosaphat derives from the book of *Joel* (Joel 3:2, 12), which contains the only passages in the Bible that refer to it. An ancient tradition, which goes back to the fourth century A.D., locates the place of the Last Judgment on the eastern side of the valley of the Kidron river, facing Jerusalem. Commentators, however, are of the view that given the etymology of the word Jehosaphat (= Yahweh judges) it is a symbolic name. Cf. P.J. Morris in *CCHS*, section 522.

23 Nineveh was the capital of Assyria, on the left bank of the Tigris. According to tradition it was surrounded by high walls. However, in order to understand the text properly, we should not lose sight of the literary genre used here (common after the exile), which consists in starting from a known datum (2 Kings 14:25, for example) and then developing a moral message (cf. A. Robert and A. Feuillet, op. cit).

24 This may have been a sperm whale. These are to be found in the Mediterranean and are quite capable of swallowing a man. "Three days and three nights": in Hebrew usage, one full day and part of the other two (cf. Esther 4:16; 5:1; Mt 12:40). Jesus uses this story when referring to the three days his body will spend in the tomb prior to his resurrection (Mt 12:39-40).

God is no respecter of persons but loves everyone, without exception. He takes pity on Jonah (2:7) and on the people of Nineveh — but only when they do penance. His love even extends to infants — people "who do not know their right hand from their left" (4:11). This book prepares the way for a more exalted and definitive revelation — whereby Jesus explains the essence of God's inner life by telling us that God is love (1 Jn 4:8).

The wisdom books and poetical books of the Old Testament

When they returned from captivity in Babylon, the people of Israel were in need of guides who, speaking in God's name, would reawaken their dormant religious consciousness and teach them how to live up to the Covenant of Sinai. This guidance came first from the prophets, but after the death of Malachi, an already established literary form began to play an important part — wisdom writing; that is, the oral and written work of "wise men" of Israel after the exile.

Although this kind of writing is not exclusive to Israel or even Israelite in origin — for centuries it was already to be found all over Egypt, Babylon, Phoenicia and the East generally — it is still true to say that biblical wisdom writing has features of its own: it is based on revelation and on personal experience illuminated by faith, since knowledge of God is the ultimate basis of all wisdom. This knowledge of God underlies all the moral teaching contained in the wisdom books of the Bible.[1]

Wisdom in Israel As a literary form, wisdom writing goes back to the very earliest times. Jotham's fable (Jud 9:8-15) and proverbs to be found right through the Bible confirm this. But its real beginning stems from Solomon's time; obviously external influences played a part but there is no doubt about Solomon's own extraordinary wisdom, the fame of which extended to the countries neighbouring Israel. As the book of *Kings* puts it: "God gave Solomon wisdom and understanding beyond measure, and eagerness of mind like the sand on the seashore, so that Solomon's wisdom surpassed the wisdom of all the people of the east, and all the wisdom of Egypt" (1 Kings 4:29-30).

After the exile, wise men of Israel and wisdom writing came into its own. This material is to be found in the books of *Job*, *Proverbs*, *Sirach*, *Wisdom* and many of the *Psalms* and, among others, the *Song*

---

1 On this subject cf. R. A. Dyson in *CCHS*, section 313ff; Profesores de Salamanca, op. cit., II, pp. 2-12; P. de Surgy, op. cit.

of Songs, although the book will be treated separately. All these writings have one main theme — that of perfect knowledge which teaches men how to gear all their activity to the goal God wishes them to reach.

The "wise man" in Israel   From reading these writings, we can say that the wise man is above all a man of faith, a prudent man, interested in the cultural and religious development of his people; a genuine teacher, whose mission is one of counselling and is different from that of a priest or a prophet. The book of *Jeremiah* contains this reference: "the law shall not perish from the priest, nor counsel from the wise, nor the word from the prophet" (Jer 18:18).

These, among others, are features which distinguish the wise man of Israel:

a) He is a *man of faith*, deeply religious, who nourishes his spirit by reading and meditating on the Law of Yahweh. From that Law he draws moral principles which he then applies by giving his advice in the form of maxims and proverbs.

b) He is also a *realist*: he really understands the problems of the time he lives in. He studies what is happening and shows how events and behaviour fit in with the moral precepts of the Covenant.

c) He does not lay down the law: rather, *he proposes counsels and teachings* in a gentle way, suggesting the right line of action. He respects the freedom of his listeners and tries, by simple but effective reasoning, to build up their convictions.

d) He clearly shows the need for *consistency* between faith and living, because he is conscious that true wisdom should lead a person to obey God in everything — in high spiritual matters and also in the prosaic activities of everyday life.

The following text from *Sirach* sums all this up very well:

> Consider the ancient generations and see:
>   who ever trusted in the Lord and was put to shame?
> Or who ever persevered in the fear of the Lord and was forsaken?
>   Or who ever called upon him and was overlooked?
> For the Lord is compassionate and merciful;
>   he forgives sins and saves in time of affliction.
>
> Woe to timid hearts and to slack hands,
>   and to the sinner who walks along two ways!
> Woe to the faint heart, for it has no trust!
>   Therefore it will not be sheltered.

> Woe to you who have lost your endurance!
> What will you do when the Lord punishes you?
> Those who fear the Lord will not disobey his words,
> and those who love him will keep his ways (Sir 2:10-15).

Wisdom writing The wisdom books, with the exception of the later ones — *Sirach* and *Wisdom* — do not generally go into the main themes of the Old Testament — the Law, the Covenant, God's choice of Israel, and Israel's salvation. They are concerned not so much with the history and future of the chosen people as with the destiny of the individual. Until the second century B.C. there is no clear revelation about the immortality of the soul and the reward of eternal life, although from very early days the hope existed of the just in Sheol achieving union with God. There is an even deeper theme running through these writings — the meaning of the pain and suffering the just man experiences in his lifetime. The wisdom books progressively explore this subject.

Job

The book of *Job* is included among the wisdom writings precisely because it teaches man that pain and suffering are a mystery of divine wisdom. According to the sacred writer, the truly wise man should realize that "the fear of the Lord, that is wisdom; and to depart from evil, that is understanding" (28:28).

Job, a foreigner, not descended from Abraham, is the central character of the book that bears his name. A wise and wealthy man a native of the Idumean city of Uz, located between Edom and northern Arabia, a region famed for its wise men (cf. Jer 49:7), he believes in the true God, whom he adores and to whom he offers sacrifice, even in the midst of severe suffering.

We do not know for certain who wrote the book of Job; the text suggests that it is by an educated Jew, familiar with the prophets and the teachings of the wise men of Israel. He probably lived in Palestine, although he did visit and even lived for a while abroad, mainly in Egypt.

We can only conjecture as to when the book was written. Due perhaps to the patriarchal tone of the prose narrative it was thought for a long time to have been written by Moses. But the book is later than *Jeremiah* and *Ezekiel* as evidenced by similarity of expression and thought; its elegant style and language laden with Aramaic terms lead us to suppose that it was written shortly after the exile (587-538). This was a period when preoccupation with Israel's future as a nation gave way to concern about the individual destiny of the Israelite. We might place the book tentatively around the end of the fifth century B.C.[2]

It should be noted that of all the different versions of this book, the Vulgate of St Jerome (recently slightly changed in the New Vulgate edition, which is the official text of the Church) is particularly clear and elegant and seems to have the best grasp of the original.

The structure of the book　The book of *Job* is one of the most beautiful and accomplished poems in world literature. It has been compared with Dante's *Divine Comedy* and Goethe's *Faust*. As Vaccari says, it deals with an absorbing subject, a deeply human and divinely sublime drama, with such colour and warmth of feeling and such variety of form that language and art have here reached their zenith.[3]

The poem is divided into three parts: a prologue (chap. 1-2); a dialogue, taking up the main body of the book (chap. 3-42:6); and an epilogue.

The *prologue* introduces us to the characters and summarizes the theme of the book. Job, a pious and blameless man, is perfectly happy and contented. The adversary (Satan) insinuates himself among the angels of God's court and argues that Job's virtue is not genuine. So God permits Job to be tested. Blow after blow falls on Job, depriving him of his possessions and of his children. But Job remains faithful, and then is attacked personally; he becomes gravely ill and disfigured. However, he accepts with resignation the physical evil which God sends him, just as he had previously accepted the contentment he enjoyed. Such is Job's faith that Satan is defeated. But Job's suffering is so deep that he utters a cry of lamentation — not of despair — when his three friends seek to console him after his being plunged into silent for seven days.

Job starts the *dialogue*, provoked by his friends' failure to understand why he is suffering like this. They consider suffering to be punishment for sin (this was the general view at that time), yet Job keeps insisting that he is blameless. They in turn invite him humbly to recognize his fault and beg God's forgiveness.

At no stage does Job say that he is completely free from sin; what he does maintain is that his suffering is far greater than his faults

2　Cf. A. Robert and A. Feuillet, op. cit.
3　Cf. A Vaccari, op. cit., IV, pp. 13-110.

deserve. One might think that this means he is accusing God of being unjust; but that is not so: he simply cannot make out why God is sending him these sufferings. In fact, in this life God does not reward everyone according to his merits: that happens in the life to come. Therefore, if he sometimes causes suffering to someone who is known to be blameless, his purpose in doing so is to train him in virtue, to make his merits shine even more through the patience he shows.

Job's three friends, Eliphaz, Bildad and Zophar, keep interrupting him to try to convince him that he *is* at fault, but Job knows otherwise and refuses to plead guilty to a sin he did not commit.

After addressing himself to divine wisdom, confident that God will hear him (chap. 28), Job appeals to the Supreme Judge, who is the only one who can give him justice and declare his innocence. God hears him and he uses Elihu, a young man who up to this has not taken part in the dialogue, to come in on Job's side. To everyone's surprise he says something entirely new: Job should not be saying that God has condemned him, because the reason God sends evils and sufferings is not only to punish people: their primary purpose is to purify man of his faults and prevent him from committing worse sins. By saying this Elihu consoles Job: he argues that Job is blameless and he also shows him why he has had to suffer in this way. Finally, Yahweh himself enters into the discussion, on Job's side. Job cannot find words; he feels so insignificant. As he says himself:

> I know that thou canst do all things,
> and that no purpose of thine can be thwarted.
> "Who is this that hides counsel without knowledge?"
> Therefore I have uttered what I did not understand,
> things too wonderful for me, which I did not know.
> "Hear, and I will speak;
> I will question you, and you declare to me."
> I had heard of thee by the hearing of the ear,
> But now my eyes sees thee;
> therefore I despise myself,
> and repent in dust and ashes (Job 42:2-6).

In the *epilogue*, in which God takes Job's three friends to task, Job is declared innocent. To reward his virtue God restores all his property to him, twice over:

> And the Lord restored the fortunes of Job, when he had prayed for his friends; and the Lord gave Job twice as much as he had before. Then came to him all his brothers and sisters and all who had known him before, and ate bread with him in his house (Job 42:10-11).

There is a happy ending and the moral is quite clear, even if Job does not grasp it. But he does realize now that there is no reason why God should have to account to anyone for what he does: man cannot grasp the mysterious ways of divine providence. In permitting the innocent to suffer and even die and in not punishing the evildoer during his lifetime, God has his reasons, even if man cannot grasp them.

The questions raised in the book of Job The book does not answer the initial question posed; indeed no answer is forthcoming until almost the era of the New Testament. According to Vaccari it does advance to the position of realizing that God has wisely but mysteriously disposed that sometimes even the just are made to suffer despite their innocence. However, God will eventually reward their virtue. The problem posed by Job is, basically, what is the origin and purpose of suffering?

Job's question remains unanswered: he does not discover the reason why innocent people suffer. The furthest he gets is to realize that suffering is part of God's plan; that it has to be accepted as long as it lasts; and that God does not abandon the sufferer. In this connexion it raises other basic points which later revelation — especially that of the New Testament — will be more specific about:

a) suffering tests the genuineness of a person's virtue;

b) it protects him from pride and makes him more humble;

c) when suffering comes a person's way he should abandon himself completely into God's hands.

The entire book opens up a new perspective — that of the reward which awaits, in heaven, those who do God's will on earth. Job's suffering, the suffering of a just man who bears it patiently and continues to seek mercy and forgiveness, acquires its fullest meaning in the New Testament. Thus, this text of St Paul provides an answer to Job's complaints:

> I consider that the sufferings of this present time are not worth comparing with the glory that is to be revealed to us (Rom 8:18).

In other words, no matter how much we may suffer on earth, it is nothing compared with the vision of God which awaits us in heaven. Job did not realize that the just man does not attain fulfilment through possession of material things, and never attains it completely in this life. He also knew nothing about what happens to souls after they leave the body. Happiness and immortality are totally connected to one another; but it took human reason centuries to discover this.

Without Christ's passion, without his death on the cross, man would

have never managed to understand the apparent paradox which our
Lord expressed in these words:

> If any man would come after me, let him deny himself and take up his
> cross and follow me. For whoever would save his life will lose it, and
> whoever loses his life for my sake will find it. For what will it profit a
> man, if he gains the whole world and forfeits his life? (Mt 16:24-26).

The lives of the early Christians were, from the very beginning,
based on identification with Christ in his passion. St Paul, who
understood all this very well, put it in this way:

> in my flesh I complete what is lacking in Christ's afflictions for the sake
> of his body, that is, the Church (Col 1:24).

In this life, every Christian, as a member of the Church, is called
to spread the kingdom of God in the world. To do this he must
supernaturalize all his sufferings and difficulties and see them as
something very precious which God puts in his hands. By uniting
himself to the sacrifice of Christ, he will turn all these adverse things
into a source of supernatural light and will find in them the peace
and the joy which no created thing can provide.

Proverbs

This protocanonical book of the Old Testament, attributed to
Solomon, is the oldest collection of inspired texts in the corpus of
wisdom literature. The book takes its name from the Hebrew word
masal, which means a provocative saying, a popular saying or a maxim
which arrests the listener's attention. In the early stages, these sayings
were short in form; later on they tended to take the form of a parable
or allegory or a reasoned discourse. Being short and pithy it was easier
for people to remember them and this meant that they were very
useful in oral teaching: in fact parents used them for teaching their
children (1:8; 4:1; 31:1).

As to the date of composition, it should be borne in mind that the
maxims in the second collection (see below) were already part of a
long tradition when the men of Hezekiah collected them around 700
B.C. This part therefore can be dated well before the exile, as can
the central part of the book (chap. 10-29). What is unclear is when
chapters 30-31 were collected: certainly chapters 1-9, which form
a kind of introduction to the whole book, must be much later —

perhaps around the fifth century B.C. It was in this last period, after the exile — that the book was given its final form.

The division of the book The main nucleus of this book consists of two collections of proverbs attributed, in the main, to Solomon (chap. 10-22 and 25-29), of whom the Bible says "he uttered three thousand proverbs; and his songs were a thousand and five" (1 Kings 4:32) and who was considered to be the wisest man in Israel. The book seems to be a collection of maxims or proverbs put together in a particular order. However, scholars usually distinguish different parts, along these lines:

The first part (chap. 1-9) gives the purpose of the book and summarizes it by pointing out that the fear of God is the beginning of wisdom. It exhorts people to follow wisdom, which means avoiding bad company, foolishness, hasty marriage, indolence and other vices. The "wisdom" referred to really has to do with the practical and moral sense necessary for directing one's life towards the will of God, and thereby being happy in this life. Often important aspects of this wisdom are described by key words such as discipline, insight, instruction, prudence, vigilance, righteousness, etc.

In the second part (10-22:16) we find the first collection of the proverbs of Solomon,[4] including aphorisms about life and morality. In chapters 10-15 the verses are in antithetical form and from chapter 16 forward in the form of parallelisms. An example of this is where it speaks of the righteous man (10:16) who works hard and makes good use of his earnings: he knows that his work is the route to true life; whereas the aim of the man who rejects God is to indulge himself; he will never be happy because the more materialistic he becomes the further he goes away from God who is the origin of all happiness.

The third part (chap. 22:17 — 24:22) is a collection of "sayings of the wise men", consisting of various counsels on duties to one's neighbour and on temperance with the emphasis throughout on prudence:

> Incline your ear, and hear the words of the wise,
>   and apply your mind to my knowledge;
> for it will be pleasant if you keep them within you,
>   if all of them are ready on your lips.
> That your trust may be in the Lord,

4 A certain parallelism has been found between this collection and "The Teaching of Amenemope" (a tenth century B.C. Egyptian papyrus) and "The Wisdom of Ajikar" (from the same period). It should come as no surprise to find that man, through other ways than that of supernatural revelation, should have learned deep truths about human nature similar to those given through revealed wisdom.

I have made them known to you today, even to you

(Prov 22:18-19)

The fourth part (24:23-34) is an appendix with more "sayings of the wise men." This develops the same argument and stresses the malice of idleness.

The fifth part (25-29) contains the second collection of proverbs of Solomon, taken down by the men of Hezekiah, king of Judah. It runs on the same lines, content-wise, as the first collection (10-22) and in almost the same form, literally, although the sayings contain more comparisons and antitheses.

The sixth part (30:1-33) is the sayings of Agur, which describe the wisdom of God and man's mediocrity. Although this is wisdom writing, it is not couched in proverbs: it begins with a monologue, which is at first a confession and then a prayer; it continues with a proverb in the proper sense of the term and concludes with a kind of lamentation (11-14) followed by five numerical proverbs and a proverbial saying.

The seventh part (31:1-9) is an exhortation to princes. These words of Lemuel, "which his mother taught him"(v. 1) contain three recommendations of a mother to her son.

The eighth part (31:10-31) praises the virtues of a good wife, painting a picture of the ideal woman, who is lacking nothing in terms of perfection and integrity. This part is different in style from the rest of the book but it provides it with a fine epilogue. It is a poem which describes a wife's beauty as consisting primarily in the virtues which should adorn her — humility, strength, family feeling, moral probity and trust in God. With these qualities and God's grace she can face the future with optimism, knowing that God will watch over her and hers because she is so good. Obviously if mothers are faithful to their obligations society is going to have a good base.

Teachings It is important to remember that wisdom literature did not originate in Israel — as indeed can be deduced from the fact that this book contains virtually no reference to salvation history.

The book is a sort of manual aimed at teaching people to live in accordance with the moral law — divine and human — and become good, honest people, as a first step towards holiness of life. The righteous man is the truly wise man, who knows exactly what life is about because he is gifted with practical common sense which enables him to form sound judgments about all aspects of life. It studies wisdom and foolishness, riches and poverty, love and hate, work and idleness; it explores in depth the relationships between God and man, children and parents, king and subjects, husband and wife, master and servant, friend and enemy.

These proverbs also get across a series of moral values, recommending fear of God, love of one's neighbour, charity, truthfulness, temperance, prudent speech, suffering in silence while being aware of God's friendly providence.

A person who has these virtues has wisdom. Thus, the wisdom revealed in this book has to do with practical education for living. At the base of this lies fear of the Lord, the beginning of wisdom, the essence of wisdom (1:7). The book does go somewhat further than earlier wisdom writings: for example, it stresses the use of freedom, for a person can resist and even reject wisdom (1:24-25). It also asserts that wise men possess all the virtues, whereas foolish men pile one vice on another; the former follow the way leading to life, the latter to death and ruin; but it makes it plain that it is not just personal effort that brings the wise man to the goal of happiness: "the blessing of the Lord makes rich" (10-22).

The wisdom of *Proverbs* is not simply a speculative idea: it is highly practical. But the book goes further than this: it presents wisdom as a person: a person who possesses the word of God and awaits people at the city gates and in the streets (1:20-21), inviting all to attend his banquet in a well-appointed room (9:1-11), implying that what he has to offer is the only thing worth having.

It also shows this wisdom revealed by God to have been present with God for all eternity; it had a part in the creation of the world; it is wisdom who joyfully takes the initiative in seeking men's company (8:22-31). Training oneself to receive wisdom is a matter of life and death for men (8:32-36). It must have been difficult to grasp the full meaning of the book but with hindsight we can recognize in it the presence of the Logos, the Word, of St John. The Fathers of the Church see the mystery of wisdom as outlined in this book as a clear reference to the mystery of the Second Person of the Blessed Trinity.

Ecclesiastes (Qoheleth)

This is the fourth of the wisdom (or sapiential) books of the Old Testament. In the Hebrew title it forms part of the *ketûbîm* (= writings), and is one of the five *meghillôth* (= scrolls or volumes) which were read on the feast of Tabernacles, along with the *Song of Songs, Ruth, Lamentations* and *Esther.*

It takes its name from the Greek translation of the Hebrew word *qoheleth* at the start of the book: "The words of the Preacher [*Qoheleth*], the son of David, king in Jerusalem" (1:1). *Qoheleth* is not a proper name; it describes the position of one who speaks in an assembly (*qahal*). Hence Ecclesiastes is usually understood to be a qualified teacher, the leader of an assembly of wise men.[5] The reference to his being the son of David is typical of pseudoepigraphical literature's tendency to attribute the work of an unknown author to some illustrious person in order to give it greater credence In this instance, the sacred writer chose to put the fruit of his reflexions under the patronage of the most outstanding of Israel's wise men.

The teaching given in the book and its use of numerous Aramaicisms and late-Hebrew expressions mean that it cannot be dated prior to the exile in Babylon. All the indications are that it was given its final form between 250 and 200 B.C.

The book's twelve chapters all deal with the same theme — the uselessness of human things, which it describes as "vanity of vanities" (1:2; 12:8). The word translated here as vanity means in Hebrew, wind, puff or vapour; metaphorically, as used here, it refers to the barrenness, impermanence and illusory nature of things and, therefore, the way they deceive anyone who puts his trust in them. It is not saying that things are essentially bad, but that they cannot provide man with the contentment he tries to find in them (cf. Rom 8:20).

The book follows no particular plan; like the books that go before it — *Job* and *Proverbs* — and like *Sirach*, which follows it, it consists of a series of observations on life and everything connected with it — knowledge, pleasure, wisdom, human striving, ambition: none of these can bring man true happiness, which is why they all appear as vanity. Thus:

1. The vanity of knowledge (1:12-18). Here a wise king seeks out all that is done under heaven and, after acquiring great wisdom, he is disenchanted: all his wisdom is in vain.

2. The vanity of pleasure (2:12-26). He now seeks new experiences — the pleasures of life. He gives himself everything his eyes fall on, and indulges his heart (v. 10), but the result is the same — vanity.

3. The vanity of wisdom (2:12-26). What benefit does he derive from acquiring so much wisdom, and striving so hard to get it? None,

5 A. Robert and A. Feuillet, op. cit.

all is vanity. However, being a man of faith, he asserts that true wisdom and knowledge and joy come only from God (v.26).

4. The vanity of human striving (3:1-22). All human things have their season. Providence in its infinite wisdom governs all creation. Although we cannot see it, everything has a cause, a reason for being, which only God knows. God himself invites us to penetrate these mysteries, to have us realize our intellectual limitations and his sovereign power. If man refuses to recognize God's lordship, even social order begins to break down (4:1 — 5:8) envy and jealousy alienate man from his brother and cause him to exploit the poor (5:7-8).

5. The vanity of riches (5:9 — 6:12). Further experience shows him that wealth cannot bring happiness; on the contrary, it can take away his peace of mind (vv. 9-11). To his dismay he discovers that wealth is impermanent: it is someone else who benefits from all his effort (6:1-6).

Further on he realizes the value of wisdom (7:1-2) but asserts that this virtue cannot assure him of happiness (7:13 — 9:10). Prosperity and adversity seem to be distributed without reference to a person's merits (9:11-12); life itself is a risky business which calls for prudence (11:1-6).

Finally he speaks of the happiness of youth, comparing it with the failings of old age (11:7 — 12:8). But he warns young people that God will judge their actions when the body turns into the dust from which it came and the spirit returns to God its maker (12:7).

The book ends with an epilogue recommending fear of God and the keeping of his commandments. They will be the standard against which God will judge our actions, good or bad, even our hidden actions.

After all these somewhat pessimistic observations, *Ecclesiastes* reminds us that happiness can only be found in material things if we use them in accordance with God's will (5:17). That is to say, they must be used in moderation; we should not be greedy for the things which God gives us in this life; this virtue of temperance can be attained only with the help of God's grace. No matter how many possessions a man acquires, they will never fully satisfy him; for his spiritual and immortal soul aspires to higher things which are to be found in God alone.

The inadequacy of human answers *Ecclesiastes* is a kind of treatise on moral conduct, with specific observations about the vanity of things and their incapacity to satisfy the deepest yearnings of the human heart. It only hints at the way to true happiness. The basic problem posed by Ecclesiastes is the same as that posed by Job: Do the just receive their reward, and evildoers their punishment, in this life? The answer is no: experience shows that it just does not happen like that, as people used to think.

Unlike *Job*, *Ecclesiastes* does not discuss the problem of the just man's sufferings. He certainly emphasizes that material things in themselves do not provide happiness; indeed, all is vanity. But his attitude is not really a pessimistic one; his faith leads him to see prosperity and misfortune as both coming from God (7:14). He recommends the just mean[6] — not defeatism or mediocrity, but a mode of conduct inpired by devotion to and confidence in God. However, he does not yet give the answer which revelation will later give to the question under discussion; in fact he seems to give no answer, for he says: "there is a righteous man who perishes in his righteousness, and there is a wicked man who prolongs his life in his evil-doing" (7:15).

God uses this perplexity to stress that man has to concentrate more on his eternal destiny. The book, in recognizing man's ignorance and his inability to reach true knowledge and wisdom by his own efforts, invites God to communicate a final and fuller revelation.[7]

However, the Preacher does make a number of points which are worth bearing in mind. For example, when he says that riches can never satisfy our unlimited desires for happiness he stresses that detachment from earthly, perishable things, is essential. But eternal goods he does not clearly describe because he as yet knows little about the immortality of the soul and, therefore, about man's eternal destiny in the kingdom of God.

He also points out the transitoriness of human life — in a famous passage which begins in this way:

> For everything there is a season, and a time for every matter under heaven:
> a time to be born and a time to die;
> a time to plant, and a time to pluck up what is planted;
> a time to kill, and a time to heal;
> a time to break down, and a time to build up;

6 According to the philosophy of the just mean (cf. Eccles 7:16), man should not rashly devote himself to the scrupulous practice of religion, nor irresponsibly neglect his religious duties: neither of these excesses leads to happiness. St Augustine comments: "He does not censure the justice of the wise man but rather the pride of the presumptuous man; he who is too righteous becomes unrighteous by excess", especially, when his behaviour is not inspired by charity.

7 Cf. A. Robert and A. Feuillet, op. cit.

a time to weep, and a time to laugh;
a time to mourn, and a time to dance;
a time to cast away stones, and a time to gather stones together;
a time to embrace, and a time to refrain from embracing;
a time to seek, and a time to lose;
a time to keep, and a time to cast away;
a time to rend, and a time to sew;
a time to keep silence, and a time to speak;
a time to love, and a time to hate;
a time for war, and a time for peace.
What gain has the worker from his toil?

(Eccles 3:1-4).

Although Qoheleth does contribute to the religious education of the people of the Old Covenant by making them reflect on their own destiny, he is still far from the teaching Jesus Christ would bring three centuries later in his Sermon on the Mount:

Blessed are the poor in spirit, for theirs is the kingdom of heaven.
Blessed are those who mourn, for they shall be comforted.
Blessed are the meek, for they shall inherit the earth.
Blessed are those who hunger and thirst for righteousness, for they shall be satisfied.
Blessed are the merciful, for they shall obtain mercy.
Blessed are the pure in heart, for they shall see God.
Blessed are the peacemakers, for they shall be called sons of God.
Blessed are those who are persecuted for righteousness' sake, for theirs is the kingdom of heaven.
Blessed are you when men revile you and persecute you and utter all kinds of evil against you falsely on my account. Rejoice and be glad, for your reward is great in heaven, for so men persecuted the prophets who were before you (Mt 5:3-12).

Sirach

In the Greek version of the Bible, the first title of this book was "The Wisdom of Ben Sirach", but from the time of St Cyprian — early third century — the Latin title, *Ecclesiasticus*, was used. It received this name from the fact that, after the Psalms, it was the book most used in the liturgy; in fact, in the early Church it was a kind of official catechism used in the catechumenate.

Sirach was originally written in Hebrew, as the Greek translator says in the prologue. St Jerome was acquainted with the Hebrew text, which was used up to the Middle Ages. In the eleventh century the Hebrew disappeared and could not be used again until about two thirds of it was discovered in an old synagogue in Cairo in 1896. The archaeological evidence given by that manuscript, together with the portions of the same which survive in rabbinical literature, proves that the Hebrew text dates from before 132 B.C. The New Vulgate conserves the Old Latin text which was made from a Greek codex containing some interpolations, to which certain glosses and retouches were added.[8]

According to the prologue and other passages in the book, the inspired author was a learned scribe, a humble and zealous man, who lived in Jerusalem. Through application and response to grace, from an early age he had meditated deeply on Sacred Scripture. As an adult he was an indefatigable traveller and always kept his eyes and his soul open to test "the good and the evil among men" (34:12; 39:5). He eventually settled in Jerusalem, where he opened a school to give moral and civic education to all comers; there, under the inspiration of God, he wrote this book. His grandson — the Greek translator — arrived in Egypt in the thirty-eighth year of the reign of Ptolemy Euergetes (170-116 B.C.). He began on his translation in the year 132, working on the Hebrew text, which probably was written prior to 170 B.C., since it contains no reference to the persecution of the Jews by Antiochus IV Epiphanes.

A mosaic of situations Like *Proverbs* and *Ecclesiastes*, this book has no particular structure. Subjects arise in delightful and even planned disorder — praise of wisdom, fortitude in temptation, filial piety, praise of parents, friendships; he parades before the reader a whole series of themes taken from the world around him, in a period on the threshold of the heroic age of the Maccabees — things to do with family life, with work, situations affecting old people, the rich, people in power, parents and children etc. Alongside this Sirach also deals with typical wisdom themes — the origin of evil, human freedom, creation, sin, penance etc. In treating each of these he uses the classical sapiential form of the *mashal*[9] — numerical (25:7-11), parallel 21:16-19 and anaphoristic (2; 4; 7:20-16).

The book closes with hymns giving thanks to God the Creator, who has arranged things in the best possible way to benefit the just and punish the evildoer; these are followed by a hymn praising the patriarchs for having lived in accordance with the laws God gave

8 On the formation of the text, see Profesores de Salamanca, op.cit., pp 1081-1083.

9 The ensemble of sayings or sapiential statements formed into the collections which have come down to us, particularly that of *Proverbs*.

them, from Adam up to Simon, the son of Onias, the high priest in Ben Sirach's time.

The practical purpose of the book   As happened with all the wisdom books of the Bible, the Greek translator puts special emphasis on the practical purpose of *Sirach*. Firstly, he advises everyone to live in accordance with divine Law, which should be the highest rule and main aspiration of man's behaviour. But as he says in the prologue, Ben Sirach wanted to write this book for those living abroad "who wished to gain learning, being prepared in character to live according to the law".

This book played an important part in shaping the faith of the Jewish people to equip them to cope with the imminent menace of hellenism, which ran completely counter to the monotheism of the people of the Old Covenant. At the basis of his teaching, Ben Sirach puts fear of God. In concrete terms this means fleeing from sin, as a first step on the road to virtue, and then walking that way in humility, which is the basis of all the other virtues; through humility a person accepts himself and recognizes his defects, while also respecting his neighbour and never engaging in defamation and calumny (7:12-17). This follows logically from obedience to God's commandments and implies total trust in God's power and majesty. This sense of trust grows the more a person is tested and tempted — an experience he needs if he is to develop a strong character and temper his spirit.

However, the main enemy which people encounter — an enemy which is an ally of hellenism — does not come from outside. This enemy is to be found in easygoingness and a lack of moral vigilance, in indolence and neglect of the duties the Law imposes. Ben Sirach, therefore, argues energetically in favour of pursuit of righteousness and consideration for others. He asks people to aim at consistency between their faith and their everyday actions, and to give special attention to things to do with the worship of God.

Chapter 24 marks a high point in the book's teaching. It presents wisdom in the form of an actual person who is ever alongside God, man's creator and supreme lawgiver. Now, in his infinite goodness and mercy, wisdom speaks directly[10] to the people of Israel; he speaks like a person, as befits the personification of a divine attribute:

> I came forth from the mouth of the Most High,
> and covered the earth like a mist. . . .

10 Cf. Prov 8; Wis 7.

Then the Creator of all things gave me a commandment,
and the one who created me assigned a place for my tent.
And he said, 'Make your dwelling in Jacob,
and in Israel receive your inheritance.'
From eternity, in the beginning, he created me,
and for eternity I shall not cease to exist

(Sir 24:3, 8-9)

This text clearly represents a development of the revelation given
in earlier books: Wisdom is shown as intimately united to God, though
distinct from him, and has characteristics which will later be attributed
to the person of the Word. Once the eternal Word of God becomes
man it will be much easier to understand what this book as yet only
hints at. It was this text which led the Liturgy to describe our Lady
— in an allegorical spiritual sense — as "the seat of wisdom" a wisdom
which God communicates to all men but to Mary in a very special
way.

Finally, Sirach prepared the way, a short while before the schism
between the Saduccees and the Pharisees, for a devout and faithful
people to accept the revelation which Jesus Christ would bring.
Although the book is doctrinally a considerable distance from the
Sermon on the Mount, it does contain features which are later to
be found fully formed in the New Testament — as, for example, when
Ben Sirach, for the first time in Old Testament tradition, addresses
his prayer to God, calling him Father:

O Lord, Father and Ruler of my life,
do not abandon me to their counsel,
and let me not fall because of them! ...
O Lord, Father and God of my life,
do not give me haughty eyes,
and remove from me evil desire

(Sir 23:1-4).

He even says that this Father will not pardon our sins unless we first
pardon those who offend us:

Forgive your neighbour the wrong he has done,
and then your sins will be pardoned when you pray.
Does a man harbour anger against another,
and yet seek for healing from the Lord?
Does he have no mercy toward a man like himself,
and yet pray for his own sins?

(Sir 28:2-4)

11 Cf. Jn 1:1-14; 1 Col 15ff.

Wisdom

This book, which the Vulgate calls "Wisdom" and the Septuagint Greek 'The Wisdom of Solomon", is one of the most typical books of wisdom literature. Its literary beauty and particularly its depth of doctrine brings us to the threshold of New Testament revelation. Although the book itself claims that it was written by Solomon it must be pointed out that here as in the case of *Ecclesiastes* we have an example of recourse to pseudonimity, a device often used in the ancient world to highlight the importance of a literary work; here the author used the prestige of Solomon, the greatest of the wise men of Israel.

The inspired writer wrote the entire book in Greek, including the first five chapters which were once taken to have been originally in Hebrew. This is demonstrated by the language used, which is elegant and cultured, by its thematic unity and even by its consistency of style. We can therefore say that he was a hellenist Jew, who wrote out of his great faith in God (9:1). He abominates any kind of polytheism and is proud to belong to a "holy and blameless race" (10:15). In view of his many references to Egypt, he probably wrote it in Alexandria, the capital of hellenism in the Ptolemy period, which was then the cultural focus of the Jews in the Diaspora.

We do not know exactly when the book was written but we can say that it was written later than the Septuagint translation of the Bible and before Philo of Alexandria (20 B.C.-54 B.C.), with whom the author is not acquainted. The references to the persecution undergone by the Jews (2:1-20; 15:14) lead us to suggest that the most likely date of composition was around the last years of the reign of Ptolemy Dionysius (80-52 B.C.), very close to the Christian period but before the Roman conquest, to which no reference is made.[12]

Division of the book   The book can be divided into three parts.

The first part (chap. 1-5) is prophetic in style and somewhat Hebraic in the concepts it uses. It exhorts people to practise righteousness and sincerely seek God. As a first step towards this it stresses the need for a pure and upright heart, and for avoidance of all sin. Against this background it contrasts the reward that ultimately awaits those who are faithful to God with the punishment that evildoers will receive and their unhappy fate after death.[13]

---

12 Cf. A. Robert and A. Feuillet, op. cit.

13 Some commentators make the mistake of interpreting in a dualist sense what *Wisdom*

The second part (chap. 6-9) concentrates on the source of wisdom and the need to obtain wisdom. Speaking as Solomon, the sacred writer explains what he means by wisdom:

> For in her there is a spirit that is intelligent, holy,
> unique, manifold, subtle,
> mobile, clear, unpolluted,
> distinct, invulnerable, loving the good, keen,
> irresistible, beneficent, humane,
> steadfast, sure, free from anxiety,
> all-powerful, everseeing all,
> and penetrating through all spirits
> that are intelligent and pure and most subtle.
> For wisdom is more mobile than any motion;
> because of her pureness she pervades and penetrates all things.
> For she is a breath of the power of God,
> and a pure emanation of the glory of the Almighty
>
> (Wis 7:22-25).

It is this wisdom that lies at the basis of all other good things. The author stresses that it is something to be sought through prayer, because we cannot attain it by our own efforts:

> O God of my fathers and Lord of mercy,
> who has made all things by thy word,
> and by thy wisdom hast formed man,
> to have dominion over the creatures thou hast made,
> and rule the world in holiness and righteousness,
> and pronounce judgment in uprightness of soul,
> give me the wisdom that sits by thy throne,
> and do not reject me from among thy servants. . . .
> for even if one is perfect among the sons of men,
> yet without the wisdom that comes from thee he will be regarded as nothing
>
> (Wis 9:1-8)

The third part (chap. 10-19), written in a very original style, speaks of the magnificence of wisdom as demonstrated by the history of the chosen people. In contrast to this it describes the origin of polytheism and the moral consequences of idolatry:

> For all men who were ignorant of God were foolish by nature;
> and they were unable from the good things that are seen to know him
>   who exists,
> nor did they recognize the craftsman while paying heed to his works;
> but they supposed that either fire or wind or swift air,
> or the circle of the stars, or turbulent water,

says about the origin of evil. However, although the body is not evil in itself, it can become, through the weakness consequent on original sin, an instrument of evil and exercise a tyranny over the soul (cf. Rom 7:14; Jn 8:34).

or the luminaries of heaven were the gods that rule the world. . . .
Afterward it was not enough for them to err about the knowledge of God,
but they live in great strife due to ignorance,
and they call such great evils peace. . . .
They no longer keep either their lives or their marriages pure,
but they either treacherously kill one another, or grieve one another by
    adultery. . . .
For the worship of idols that should not even be named
is the beginning and cause and end of every evil

                        (Wis 13:1-3; 14:22-27)

By natural reason they could have discovered that the universe is
not the result of chance; it could not cause its own existence or keep
itself in being, because it needs — as pagan philosophers like Plato
and Aristotle realized — a first principle or cause which would give
every existing thing its being and which does not depend on any other
cause for its own being or activity. But they, who considered
themselves to be so wise, failed to grasp the truth because of their
moral corruption, which led them finally to idolatry. This is true
not only of pagans but also of members of the chosen people and
of many Christians when they idolize created things. Immediate
consequences follow:

> Therefore God gave them up in the lusts of their hearts to impurity,
> to the dishonouring of their bodies amongst themselves, because they
> exchanged the truth about God for a lie and worshipped and served
> the creature rather than the Creator (Rom 1:24-25).

It is easy to conclude, as the writer does, that revealed wisdom
is far superior to pagan wisdom — which is what he is trying to do
in the three parts of the book which we have outlined. In each he
deals with wisdom from a different angle: in the first he shows wisdom
as a moral virtue, identifying it with the pursuit of righteousness;
in the second, as the mother of all virtues, personifying it as a divine
attribute; in the third he emphasizes the objective character of wisdom,
which is the source of riches for those who attain it.

The message of Wisdom   The whole background of this book
is profoundly religious. God wished to put the Jews of the first century
B.C. on their guard against the temptation they might experience
in Egyptian culture — an attractive culture but one which inevitably
deflected man from his ultimate goal. Instead of giving them genuine
knowledge it would woo them away from the faith and from true
wisdom. Therefore, the sacred text is continually exhorting the reader
to search for higher knowledge which comes from God, not from

man; God is the source of all good things. Wisdom, as we have seen, is a "reflection of eternal light, a spotless mirror of the working of God, and an image of his goodness" (7:25-26). It is God himself who, in an act of his mercy, gives wisdom to men, made in his image and likeness.

With *Daniel* and *2 Maccabees, Wisdom* provides an adequate answer to the problem of the *reward of the righteous*. All the pains and sufferings a man experiences in this life find their explanation in the *revelation of the immortality of the soul*:[14]

> But the souls of the righteous are in the hand of God,
> and no torment will ever touch them.
> In the eyes of the foolish they seemed to have died,
> and their departure was thought to be an affliction,
> and their going from us to be their destruction;
> but they are at peace.
> For though in the sight of men they were punished,
> their hope is full of immortality.
> Having been disciplined a little, they will receive great good,
> because God tested them and found them worthy of himself;
> like gold in the furnace he tried them,
> and like a sacrificial burnt offering he accepted them.
> In the time of their visitation they will shine forth,
> and will run like sparks through the stubble.
> They will govern nations and rule over peoples,
> and the Lord will reign over them for ever
>
> (Wis 3:1-8).

This is the answer to the great questions posed in *Job* and *Ecclesiastes*. On the one hand it explains why the just man suffers; on the other, it points up the inadequacy of earthly things to satisfy man's yearnings for happiness. In other words, everything that happens to man in this life needs to be seen through the prism of eternal life, where the just man will be forever happy, whereas the ungodly will suffer the punishment their sins deserve (3:9-10).

Wisdom, then, brings us to the threshold of the Gospel message. Therefore, it comes as no surprise to find the Apostles quoting it often in their preaching. To describe the work of the Word of God Incarnate, St Paul refers to wisdom as a divine attribute (Wis 9:11-19; 1 Cor 2:7-16), as does St John in the prologue to his Gospel (Jn 1:1ff). The same thing happens in other places in the New Testament dealing with the eternal life of the just (Rom 8:18; 1 Cor 6:2); and where

---

14 At no point does the sacred text mention the Platonic doctrine of the pre-existence of the soul. On the contrary, it make it quite clear how man is created. In Wis 15:1 it states that it is God who infuses the spiritual soul into the human body (cf. Dz 203 and 236).

it asserts that man, by the use of natural reason alone, can from evidence of created things come to discover the existence of God (Rom 1:20; Wis 13:4-9), and that of divine mercy and providence (Rom 9:19-23; Wis 12:12-15).

In view of all this and because of the ground it lays for the revelation of the mystery of the Blessed Trinity, the book of *Wisdom* offers the Christian spiritual and doctrinal material of the first order, which the Church in its liturgy uses as an unequivocal announcement of the messianic era, which from this point onward was seen as imminent.

Psalms

Like its neighbours (Egypt and Babylonia especially) Israel had a very ancient tradition of lyric poetry in all its forms. This treasure is conserved in the Psalter, a collection of 150 psalms which has come down to us in the book of *Psalms*. The word "psalter" derives from the Greek *salterion*, the stringed instrument used to accompany these songs (psalms). In Hebrew the book is called *Tehil-lim* (Hymns), although this name only suits a certain number of the psalms — for example Psalm 145, the most typical.

Although, as we have said, there are 150 psalms in all, the Hebrew version, which is the one the New Vulgate follows, is one ahead from Psalm 10 to Psalm 148 of the Greek version, the latter's number being usually given in parentheses in the more recent editions of the Bible. Here are the variations:

HEBREW		SEPTUAGINT
9-10	=	9:1-21 9:22-39
114-115	=	113:1-8 113:9-26
116:1-9 116:10-19	=	114-115
147:1-11 147:12-20	=	146-147

Efforts have been made to deduce the authors of the psalms from the titles which head them up. On this basis, 73 are attributed to

King David, 12 to Asaph, 11 to the sons of Korah, 2 to Solomon, one to Moses, and others to Heman and Ethan. It was soon realized that the original titles contained a mere reference to particular people and that in fact something over a half should be attributed to David (which is what tradition does), even if they were given their final form in a later period. This is not surprising if one bears in mind King David's policy of systematizing the use of music and poetry in divine worship (cf. 2 Sam 1:19-27; 3:33-34).

Different kinds of psalms   The Psalter is the most complete and most treasured collection of religious songs used by the people of Israel over a period of centuries. An uninterrupted tradition confirms that psalms, hymns and canticles were sung in the synagogues. In the Gospel there is reference to the psalms and hymns which were sung after the paschal meal (cf. Mt 26:30).

However, some psalms were initially used outside the liturgy — for example the *Miserere* (Ps 51), composed by David to ask God's forgiveness for his sins.[15] In time, and due to their symbolic beauty, these psalms were brought into the liturgy and used as prayers by the entire community of Israel. Others, didactic in content, were originally a kind of popular catechism, made up of edifying narratives with prayer formulae added, designed to preserve knowledge and worship of the true God. It is also known that these psalms gradually passed from private use to public use, since only a few were composed especially for use in liturgical ceremonies in the Temple.

Originally, many of these psalms were *royal* songs, composed in honour of the king, in the form of prayer and thanksgiving. These go back to the period of the monarchy and reflect court language and ceremonial. The "anointed" referred to in many of these psalms is the king, who at that time was anointed and was described in Hebrew as *masîah*.

The fact that there are various levels of meaning in the Psalms should not confuse us. God's promises to the Davidic dynasty clearly gave rise to expectation of an absolutely unique descendant of David — a messiah, a son of David, who would reign forever (cf. 2 Sam 7). This prophecy of Nathan was the first link in a string of prophecies about the Messiah and was interpreted in the psalms as a promise

---

15   Not only does David confess his sins: he recognizes something deeper — a tendency to sin, which he was born with. All the Fathers see these words of Psalm 51 (50) as confirming the existence of original sin, which each person contracts through generation (cf. Rom 5:12; Eph 4:22). Although man's nature is weakened by this, he is still free and therefore capable of actions which are naturally good (cf. Dz 817).

of stability for the house of David (Ps 89 and 132). If we associate with it certain clearly messianic psalms, such as 16 and 22, we discover a perfect profile of this unique person, the Anointed, Jesus Christ our Lord. However, it must be said that these psalms, like many others, attain their full meaning in the light of the New Testament. St Peter and St Paul speak of Psalm 16 (15) when referring to Jesus Christ's death and resurrection and the salvation his sacrifice would bring to those who believe in him (Acts 2:25-32; 13:35-37). And our Lord himself, when he was dying on the cross, used the words of Psalm 22 (21), giving it back its authentic meaning (Mt 27:46).

Some of the old royal psalms, which were much used after the fall of the monarchy, were modified slightly and put into the Psalter, and became what are known as messianic psalms in the strict sense. For example, this happened in the case of Psalms 2, 72 and 110 (in fact Psalm 110 is the one most quoted in the New Testament).[16] This is also true of Psalm 45 which describes the union of the Messiah with the new Israel, following the line of the marriage allegories of the prophets: *Hebrews* (1:8) applies this psalm directly to Jesus Christ. In other words, the messianic hopes which are scattered throughout the Psalter would at last be realized in the great mystery of the Incarnation of the Word and specially in his redemption of man.

The Psalms, the prayer of a believing people *Psalms* contains a unique religious and spiritual treasury, without equal in world literature. It provides a synthesis of all the teaching of the Old Testament and reflects the consciousness of an essentially believing people, a people who, in spite of all sorts of vicissitudes, stayed faithful to God. In each of the psalms we can find the sensitive and extraordinarily sincere soul of a man who prays by singing because he feels that is the best way to praise God. The Jewish people were always at risk of being tempted or forced into idolatry by the neighbouring peoples. But the whole climate of the psalms is one of strict monotheism — faith in one God, who is personal, who rewards man, who is creator and lord of the whole universe, its king and sovereign judge. It is he who regulates the course of history; nothing can resist him; he is infinite and almighty; he is in need of nothing. His only purpose is his own glory. He has no rivals.

16 Both Jewish and Christian tradition regards these psalms as messianic. They are closely connected with one another, especially Psalms 2 and 110. The Church's liturgy uses Psalm 2 on feasts to do with the Incarnation, especially those of Christmastide. The fact that the Word is the Son of God and therefore Jesus Christ is the Son of God, emerges in these psalms, particularly when they are read in the light of the New Testament.

Although God is of course transcendent and invisible — the Psalms will say — he continually reveals himself to man through his works. From these man can plainly see his main attributes — holiness, goodness, justice, mercy, power and truth. Of these they especially stress his mercy. They mention God's mercy more than one hundred times, almost always connecting it with God's faithfulness to his promises — the mercy and fidelity of a good Father, who is shown in the history of Israel as a husband, king and shepherd of his people, a people whom he has loved with preferential love. Not only has he chosen Israel in preference to others: he protects Israel with a jealous love.

In this context it is easy to see how the Psalms nourished, for centuries, the prayer of so many men and women of the Old Testament thirsty for God. He wanted to teach them to trust him and to abandon themselves to him in prayer, for he is the God of mercy, ever ready to forgive, console and encourage his children.

And not only in the Old Testament. The Psalms were also recited by Jesus and by Mary, by the Apostles and the first Christian martyrs. The Church has taken them as its official prayer, to be recited every day by priests and religious in the liturgy of the hours.

The words have not changed, but their meaning has developed. In the light of the New Alliance they reveal new treasures. Christians praise and thank God for revealing his inner life through his Son, who by his death on the cross has redeemed us, made us children of God and sent us the Holy Spirit to set our souls aflame. This is why we conclude each psalm with the trinitarian doxology glorifying the Father, the Son and the Holy Spirit. The old entreaties, Gelineau comments, become more ardent now that the Supper, the Cross and the Resurrection have shown man the infinite power of God, the gravity of sin and the heavenly life that awaits the just. The messianic hopes about which the Psalmist sang have been realized; the Messiah has come; he reigns; and all nations are called to praise him.[17]

The Song of Songs

In the Hebrew Bible this book was the first of the five volumes or scrolls (*meghillôth*) used by the Jews on important feast days. It was the book read on the eighth day of the Passover.

17 Cf. J. Gelineau, *Biblia de Jerusalén* (Bilbao 1967).

The title comes from the literal translation of the Hebrew term *Sir hassirim*, a very common grammatical form used in Hebrew to describe a superlative degree of some quality: as, for example, "holy of holies" instead of "holiest" (cf. Ex 26:33). This is why Origen called this book the Song *par excellence* or the Greatest Song, or just the Song.

The very title of the book (1:1) attributes it to Solomon. But as we have seen in the case of *Proverbs, Ecclesiastes* and *Wisdom*, this is used in substitution of the writer's real name. The true author of this beautiful lyrical-dramatic poem remains unknown.

The many Aramaicisms and the serene and optimistic tone of the narrative allow us to give the first part of the fourth century as the likely time of composition. This was the period immediately following the religious reform introduced by Ezra and Nehemiah, when all Palestine was at peace, a situation which would continue up to the overthrow of the Persian empire by Alexander the Great (331 B.C.).

The theme of the Song   A reading of this book shows that it is a poem of married love, presented in alternating songs. Most commentators say that it was written as an allegory, because its background is that of the relationship between Israel and the God of the Covenant: it is a song in praise of the reestablishment of theocracy, the renewal of the alliance between Yahweh and the "remnant" of Israel returned safe and sound from captivity in Babylon.

Vaccari[18] explains it as a parable and a contrast, a parable in an idyllic setting and a contrast between two lives, two loves. A simple shepherdess tenderly loves her young husband, also a shepherd; and he loves her no less tenderly.... The setting is pastoral, rural, unspoilt countryside, where they have grown up together. Up to this point, the book is an idyll.

Contrasting with this simple life, this pure affection, lies the city with its hubbub, the court with its blandishments, a powerful king (personified in Solomon, the richest and most ostentatious of all the kings in the history of Israel) who seeks to win the love of the shepherdess, to be his consort and enhance his court. But the generous shepherdess disdainfully rejects the approaches of the king and is content with the simple rural life. She wishes to remain forever faithful to her shepherd, the only object of her pure love.

Throughout this vivid narrative, very rich in images, the faithfulness

18   Cf. F. Spadafora, op. cit., pp. 104-106.

of the couple symbolizes the relationship between God and his people. They had been put to the test in their exile by all the sparkle of life in Babylon, but they still felt the claims of faithfulness to the God in the Covenant. Many did succumb, but a "remnant" chose to stay true to Yahweh and are ready to persevere in that fidelity. These are those who have returned, and in gratitude to God they sing a song in his praise.

Man's relationship with God Probably no other Old Testament book is open to so many interpretations. However, from the beginning Jews, and later Christians, have taken this book mainly as an allegory, as we have said. The love between the couple represents Yahweh's love for his people — the same metaphor as used by the prophets from Hosea onwards (cf. Hos 2; Is 54:6ff; 62:4ff; Jer 2:2; Ezek 16:1-58), and the same as used in the New Testament to symbolize the relationship of Jesus Christ with his Church,[19] whom he deeply loves and on whose behalf he readily goes to his death, death on a cross (cf. Mt 9:15; 22:1-14; Jn 3:29).

The sacred author also uses the image of the vineyard (Song 2:15) to describe the love God expects of his people; but there are little foxes in the vineyard, who continually try to undermine their fidelity. St Gregory says that this is a warning to those who aspire to holiness, to be on the watch against faults and defects which may seem to be very minor but which must be uprooted at the outset and not allowed to grow stronger and eventually utterly destroy their souls.

If he reads it attentively and meditates on it with faith, the Christian will discover in this book teachings of benefit to his spiritual life, giving him consolation and optimism. Along with the drama of sin and human wretchedness, he will discover the great value of repentance, which always leads to God's forgiveness. For although sin breaks the limits of love, sincere repentance restores the soul's friendship with its Lord.

This is how mystics like St John of the Cross understand the poem. He uses it in his *Spiritual Canticle* to show all who aspire to holiness the way to attain it, even those who, not wanting to withdraw from their daily affairs, want to turn all their activities into a prayer pleasing to God.

19 St Paul applies this image to the Church, Christ's spouse, whom our Lord presents to himself "in splendour, without spot or wrinkle or any such thing, that she might be holy and without blemish" (Eph 5:27).

PART TWO

THE NEW TESTAMENT

Introduction to the New Testament

"The Word of God, which is the power of God for salvation to everyone who has faith (cf. Rom 1:16), is set forth and displays its power in a most wonderful way in the writings of the New Testament. For when the time had fully come (cf. Gal 4:4), the Word became flesh and dwelt among us full of grace and truth (cf. Jn 1:14). Christ established on earth the kingdom of God, revealed his Father and himself by deeds and words; and by his death, resurrection and glorious ascension, as well as by sending the Holy Spirit, completed his work. Lifted up from the earth he draws all men to himself (cf. Jn 10:32), for he alone has the words of eternal life (cf. Jn 6:58)."[1]

In the times of the Old Testament God used Israel, the Jewish people, to prepare the way for the Messiah. In the New Testament the centre of attraction is that Messiah, Jesus Christ, and the Church, the new people of God. The process of revelation begun under the Old Alliance, the Old Testament, reaches its climax in the New Testament. Commenting on this St Ambrose, a fourth-century Latin Father of the Church, wrote in his commentary on the psalms: "In the Old Testament you will find a feeling of compunction; in the New, true joy. These are the two cups which you must drink [. . .], for in both you drink Christ [. . .]. Do drink Christ, and make his words your own; for his word is the Old Testament, and his word is also the New."

Jesus Christ, the promised Messiah   At the centre of the whole mystery of our salvation foretold by the prophets stands Jesus Christ — the Word made man, the Son of God born of the Virgin Mary, the Immanuel announced by Isaiah (7:14), "the son of David, the son of Abraham" (Mt 1:1). He is the long-awaited Messiah, and his coming means that God has kept the promise he made centuries earlier to Abraham: as Mary proclaims in the *Magnificat*, God "has helped his servant Israel, in remembrance of his mercy, as he spoke to our fathers, to Abraham and to his posterity for ever" (Lk 1:54-55).

1   Vatican Council II, Dogm. Const. *Dei Verbum* 17.

Jesus (whose name means "the Lord is salvation") is not simply the latest in the long line of Old Testament prophets. He has come to save everyone from their sins, irrespective of nation or race. Many Jews of his time envisaged an earthly Messiah, who would bring salvation to the Jewish people only. But Jesus came to save all men from the slavery of sin — which went far beyond just bringing a message of peace or a few good answers to the sort of philosophical questions people are always raising about the meaning of life and the way to attain happiness. The New Testament is very clear on this; one would really have to mutilate it to make out (as some people try to do) that Jesus was in fact an earthly Messiah, a "revolutionary" more interested in radical reform of social and political structures than in the true happiness of people, which they obtain through being sons and daughters of God. As St Paul exclaims:

> Blessed be the God and Father of our Lord Jesus Christ, who has blessed us in Christ with every spiritual blessing in the heavenly places, even as he chose us in him before the foundation of the world, that we should be holy and blameless before him [. . .]. In him we have redemption through his blood, the forgiveness of our trespasses, according to the riches of his grace which he lavished upon us. For he has made known to us in all wisdom and insight the mystery of his will, according to his purposes which he set forth in Christ as a plan for the fullness of time, to unite all things in him, things in heaven and things on earth (Eph 1:3-10).

Jesus, as we said, is the centre of God's plan of salvation; he is "the Saviour of the world" (Jn 4:42). Outside of him there is no grace, no redemption. We cannot find true peace or happiness without him; but if we are joined to him all our needs are met: "I am the vine, you are the branches. He who abides in me, and I in him, he it is that bears much fruit, for apart from me you can do nothing" (Jn 15:5).

Jesus is able to say this because he is completely obedient to the will of the Father who has sent him. He is the obedient new Adam (Rom 5:14) who sacrifices his life to atone for our sins and merit justification and superabundant grace, in contrast with Adam's disobedience, which sowed sin and death: Christ "became obedient unto death, even death on a cross" (Phil 2:8), thereby sealing in his blood the new, definitive alliance between God and men. That is why he says, "this is my blood of the new covenant, which is poured out for many for the forgiveness of sins" (Mt 26:28).

Jesus died on the cross as head of the human race, offering himself for each and every one of us. His resurrection from the dead is palpable proof that his Father accepts his sacrifice. Because he did rise, St

Paul says, our faith is not futile (cf. 1 Cor 15:17-20). Through faith and through obtaining a share in his death by receiving Baptism, we are born again to a new life befitting the sons and daughters of God, who are "born not of blood nor of the will of the flesh nor of the will of man, but of God" (Jn 1:13).

The Church, the new Israel   The new people of God, then, does not derive from flesh or blood and is not limited to any particular territory. God's grace is its origin, and it is spread throughout the whole world, in obedience to the charge Christ gave his Apostles:

> Go therefore and make disciples of all nations, baptizing them in the name of the Father and of the Son and of the Holy Spirit, teaching them to observe all that I have commanded you; and lo, I am with you always, to the close of the age.

The New Testament contains the word of God preached by Jesus Christ and passed on by his Apostles. The same word is in the keeping of the Church, which untiringly proclaims it so that all men may be saved and come to the knowledge of the truth (cf. 1 Tim 2:4).

The Church, which Christ established, is therefore the other central axis of the New Testament; in perfect continuity with the plan of salvation begun in the Old Testament, the Church is the new Israel, the successor of the people of the Old Covenant; in St Paul's words, "If you are Christ's, then you are Abraham's offspring, heirs according to promise" (Gal 3:29). For, if we have Abraham as our father, we form "the Israel of God" (Gal 6:16), the Christian people who make up the Church. For centuries the people of Israel lived in hope of salvation; that salvation is now attained in the Chuch, the new people of God.

Faith in Jesus Christ is what binds together this new people. They belong to the Church who believe and are baptized and obey the successor of St Peter, the visible head of the Church. However, being born again into the new life of grace also means that a Christian should steadily grow in grace: it is not enough to simply "be" in the Church: God wants us to be living members of the Church; he wants each of us, in his or her own circumstances, to put to good use the treasure we have been given. Jesus does want his Church to spread throughout the world, but everyone has to achieve personal spiritual growth and has to develop his talents to the maximum.

To help us to do this, the Church comes to our aid by nourishing us with the Eucharist, that is, the very Body of Christ, which binds

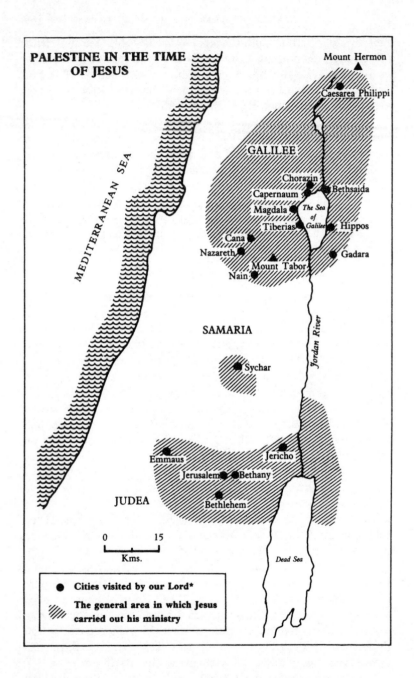

Map 9

us together in the bond of charity. The Eucharist acts as the deepest root of our spiritual growth; it is what makes us effective and on it depends the spreading of the Church. In this connexion St Paul recommends to the first Christians at Ephesus not to be any longer

> children, tossed to and fro and carried about with every wind of doctrine, by the cunning of men, by their craftiness in deceitful wiles. Rather, speaking the truth in love, we are to grow up in every way into him who is the head, into Christ, from whom the whole body, joined and knit together by every joint with which it is supplied, when each part is working properly, makes bodily growth and upbuilds itself in love (Eph 4:14-16).

God's revelation closed with the death of the last of the Apostles, St John; but we continue to develop a deeper understanding of the New Testament with the help of the grace of the Holy Spirit who continuously enlightens the Church and keeps it from error.

Palestine in the time of Jesus   In Jesus' time all Palestine was under the control of the Romans. It was divided into regions under three governors who reported directly to Rome. Archelaus was ethnarch of Judea and Samaria; Herod Antipas was tetrarch of Galilee and Peraea, and Philip tetrarch of Gaulanitis, Trachonitis and Ituraea. All three were sons of King Herod the Great, who had ruled Judea from 37 B.C. to 4 A.D. Through political astuteness, Herod had made himself absolute monarch of Judea and, at its high-point, his rule extended over most of the territory of the ancient kingdom of David.

Herod Antipas and Philip held power for a long time, but Archelaus was deposed by Emperor Augustine in 6 A.D., and Judea became a Roman province which was usually controlled by a procurator appointed by Rome.

Herod's Temple and the fall of Jerusalem   The Temple of Jerusalem, where Jesus prayed and taught, had been rebuilt by Herod the Great in an attempt to win favour with the Jews. Work on the Temple began in 20 B.C. and was not completed until many years after Herod's death.

Although the basic plan of the Temple was on the lines of that of the Temple of Solomon, Herod's building — which was on the site of the earlier Temple — was more magnificent and on a grander scale. Built of white stone, the facade encrusted with gold, it rose in a series of stepped courtyards each surrounded by columns and walls, with a huge defensive wall round the perimeter of the buildings. Inside this wall was the Court of the Gentiles; it was around the edge of this that money-changers and dealers set up shop. On the north-eastern corner of the Temple complex Herod built the Antonia fortress.

Roman rule in Judea was corrupt, inefficient and abusive of Jewish civil rights. This situation worsened in the reign of Emperor Nero, who was extremely hostile towards Jews, and eventually open and initially successful rebellion broke out in Judea. This was finally put down by Titus, son of the Emperor Vespasian. The Temple itself was the last outpost of Jewish rebellion and, although Titus wanted to preserve the building, a Roman legionary started a fire which proved uncontrollable. Titus then razed the temple and the city and enslaved such prisoners as he took.

Thus was fulfilled the prophecy Jesus made to his Apostles one day when leaving the Temple buildings: "You see all these, do you not? Truly I say to you, there will not be left here one stone upon another, that will not be thrown down" (Mt 24:2).

The historical books of the New Testament

THE FOUR GOSPELS

The word "gospel" means "good news," good tidings of some important event — in this case the message of that salvation proclaimed and accomplished by Jesus Christ. The book containing this message, and reporting the main events of our Lord's life and the things he said is therefore called the Gospel. However, it is important to remember at the outset that the Gospel does not contain the full life-story of Jesus or an exhaustive account of his teaching. In fact Jesus did not commission his disciples to write down what they had seen and heard: he asked them to spread the teaching he had given them (cf. Mt 28:19-20).

In the first instance, the "Good News", the Gospel, was preached orally by the Apostles, in keeping with our Lord's commandment: his words, the miracles he worked and the main events of his life were spontaneously memorized by the early disciples (with the aid of the Holy Spirit, who protected them from error) and were spread to others through oral preaching. This was the pattern for quite some time, until the beginning of the second half of the first century, when early catechesis began to become more systematic and structured — forming that Tradition which, some years later and only partially, the evangelists put down in writing. This one and only Gospel has come down to us in four editions, which are in a sense complementary to one another.

"The Church", the Second Vatican Council says, "has always and everywhere maintained, and continued to maintain, the apostolic origin of the Four Gospels. The Apostles preached, as Christ charged them to do, and then, under the inspiration of the Holy Spirit, they and others of the apostolic age handed on to us in writing the same message they had preached, the foundation of our faith — the fourfold Gospel according to Matthew, Mark, Luke and John."[1]

1 *Dei Verbum* 18.

Although it is true that God is the principal author of the Gospels, as he is of all Sacred Scripture, he chose to use certain men, whom he first endowed with the charism of inspiration, to put down in writing everything that he wanted them to write, and no more. They did not approach their task in a mechanical sort of way (they had minds of their own and free will); God respected their personal qualities — their individual character, culture, talent, literary style, etc. Each dedicated himself to the service of the truth, seeking to pass on the truth which is unique and unchangeable; but each went about this in his own way, in his own style, choosing to highlight certain aspects of Christ's life and teaching, and to pass over others, depending on what he thought best suited to his readers: sometimes these were of Jewish, sometimes of Gentile, background.

In writing the Gospels, the evangelists did not attempt to describe what Christian life was like, or what it meant, in the early days of the Church. Nor did they seek to give a theological analysis of the faith, using concepts which people could easily understand. They immediately zone in on what Jesus said and did, and particularly they recount his miracles: they did not have to think anything up, but simply tell what happened. Therefore, the "Church has firmly and with absolute constancy maintained and continues to maintain, that the four Gospels just named, whose historicity she unhesitatingly affirms, faithfully hand on what Jesus, the Son of God, while he lived among men, really did and taught for their eternal salvation, until the day when he was taken up (cf. Acts 1:1-2). For, after the Lord's ascension, the Apostles handed on to their hearers what he had said and done, but with that fuller understanding given them by the glorious resurrection of Christ and the teaching of the Spirit of truth."[2]

St Matthew

We know that Matthew was a tax-collector, a "publican."* He was, it would seem, quite well-to-do and popular among the people of Capernaum, where, St Luke tells us, he had many friends (Lk 5:29). This was all the more significant in view of the fact that the Jews had a very low opinion of tax-collectors in general; they regarded them as extortionists, in addition to being collaborators with the Roman regime.

2 *Dei Verbum* 19.

Matthew was a warm-hearted person; he responded quickly and generously when Jesus called him the day he passed by his office (Mk 9:9). He immediately left everything and followed him. He was later chosen to become one of the Twelve (Mk 10:1-4) and to the very end of his life he was a faithful witness to the passion, death and resurrection of our Lord.

According to the Fathers of the Church, the *Gospel according to St Matthew* was written in Palestine, almost certainly in Aramaic, and was addressed mainly to Jews living in that region. It is thought that it was first written around the year 50, but that this version disappeared soon after the destruction of Jerusalem in the year 70. Immediately after this a Greek translation of *Matthew* — the one we now possess — began to be used; this is regarded by the Church as canonical, authentic and substantially the same as the original Aramaic.

The "Gospel of the Kingdom" St Matthew, under God's inspiration, set out to show that Jesus of Nazareth was the Messiah foretold by the prophets, the Son of God. This is why his Gospel has been called "the Gospel of the fulfillment." It stresses all the prophecies of the Old Testament which announce the coming of the Messiah: he is of the house of David (1:6); he is born of Mary, a virgin, to fulfil what Isaiah foretold (1:22-12); and now, in the fullness of time, he makes his appearance, preaching "the Gospel of the Kingdom".

In the Sermon on the Mount Jesus tells us about this kingdom, promulgating the beatitudes (5:3-11), which give us a whole programme for Christian living. No one can enter the kingdom without first selling what he has and buying this precious treasure, a hidden treasure (13:44) which, because it is as small as a mustard seed (13:31), a person really has to seek out: despite its inherent strength and power — it will grow to fill the whole world — one can possess it only through detachment from material things.

Jesus wants those who follow him to be poor and to trust in providence; in other words, no Christian should become so taken up with material things that he cuts himself off from God. Possessions go against God if a person turns them into an absolute value and makes them (whether consciously or not) his god, his only goal in life. The Lord wants us to use material resources as means to an end; we should therefore be able to do without them when they in any way prevent us from doing his will.[3]

3 Vatican II, Dogm. Const. *Lumen gentium* 42.

Because this kingdom should be constantly on the increase, we should pray for it with faith and hope, using the best prayer of all, the *Our Father* (6:9-13). In fact, if it is to fully influence our lives we need to be permanently united to the successor of Peter, whom Jesus appointed as administrator of the treasures of the kingdom of heaven, conferring on him the fullness of the primacy, with responsibility for teaching and governing the whole Church (16:18-19).[4]

Moreover, this kingdom founded by Jesus Christ on earth, his Church, will last until the end of time. Jesus himself, after his resurrection, promised that this would happen: "Go therefore and make disciples of all nations, baptizing them in the name of the Father and of the Son and of the Holy Spirit, teaching them to observe all that I have commanded you; and lo, I am with you always, to the close of the age" (28:19-20). In this passage, which we find also in Mk 16:16, it is expressly stated that the Apostles (the Church) receive from Jesus the same mission as he received from his Father — to save all men through preaching and the ministry of the sacraments. First among these is Baptism, which is absolutely necessary for salvation. However, if someone is physically unable to receive Baptism, then its place may be taken by baptism of desire, in the case of adults; and also by martyrdom, which is called baptism of blood, should this extreme situation arise.

Preaching and Baptism　　Thus Jesus confers on his disciples and on those who succeed them in the apostolic ministry the power to baptize in the name of the Blessed Trinity and to admit into the bosom of the Church those who have faith. But to do this they must first proclaim the Gospel to all the nations, teaching them to practise, by word and example, the faith they have received. The Second Vatican Council confirmed this in these words: "And so the apostolic teaching, which is expressed in a special way in the inspired books, was to be preserved by a continuous succession of preachers until the end of time. Therefore, the apostles, handing on what they themselves received, warn the faithful to hold fast to the traditions which they have learned either by word of mouth or by letter (cf. 2 Thess 2:15) and to fight in defence of the faith handed on once and for all (cf. Jude 3). Now what was handed on by the apostles includes everything which contributes to the holiness of life and the

4　Since he is the visible head of the Church, Peter is supported by the charism of infallibility (which his successors also have) in everything to do with faith and morals. This is why solemn definitions made by the Pope are irreversible and do not depend on any kind of majority consent (cf. Vatican I, Dogm. Const. *Pastor Aeternus*, c. 1, 2 and 4).

increase of faith of the people of God; and so the Church, in her teaching, life, and worship, perpetuates and hands on to all generations all that she herself is, all that she believes."[5]

Jesus also promises that he will stay with his Church forever. We rely on this assurance. Although the Church is a fragile vessel which can feel threatened by the waves of atheism and materialism which seek to wreck it, it will always survive and develop: our Lord will say to us what he said that day on the lake to his disciples: "Take heart, it is I; have no fear" (14:27), referring to that sort of fear the disciples experienced even when they saw Jesus being glorified at the transfiguration (17:6); the same fear they felt in Gethsemani, which caused them all to flee and abandon him (25:56). This fear is the darker side of their behaviour prior to Pentecost: yet they later became witnesses to the life and resurrection of Jesus, no longer afraid to preach in his name.

There is one important detail which Matthew does not fail to observe: "the curtain of the temple was torn in two, from top to bottom" (17:51). This was the curtain separating the sanctuary from the Holy of Holies (cf. Ex 26:31); on Jesus' death it was torn, indicating (this has been the traditional interpretation of the Church) that the old Mosaic cult had come to an end and a new era had begun, that of the New Alliance, sealed with the blood of the Son of God. Through this New Alliance man can be born again to a new life, leaving behind fear and any kind of pessimism, for death has been overcome by Life.

St Mark

The tradition of the early Church is unanimous in attributing the second Gospel to Mark, the disciple and interpreter of St Peter the Apostle. The historian Eusebius quotes Papias, a disciple of St John, as stating this in writing around the year 125: "Mark, having been the interpreter of Peter, wrote accurately, though not in order, all that he remembered of the things said or done by the Lord. For he had neither heard the Lord nor been his follower, but afterwards, as I said, he was the follower of Peter, who gave his instructions as

5   Vatican II, Dogm. Const. *Dei Verbum* 6.

circumstances demanded, but not as one giving an orderly account of the words of the Lord. So that Mark was not at fault in writing certain things as he remembered them. For he was concerned with only one thing, not to omit anything of the things he had heard, and not to record any untruth in regard to them".[6]

We know that St Mark was born in Jerusalem and that his mother's name was Mary. The first Christians used her house as a meeting-place. It was there that St Peter sought refuge after being miraculously freed from prison (Acts 12:12). Quite probably the Apostle himself baptised Mark in his own home; he refers to Mark as his son (1 Pet 5:1); and some authorities identify Mark's house with the cenacle.

Mark accompanied St Paul on his first apostolic journey, around the year 45, but after reaching Perga in Pamphylia he headed back to Jerusalem (Acts 13:13). At the time of St Paul's second journey St Barnabas took Mark, his cousin, on a separate journey. A few years later Mark joined St Peter who gave him a first-hand account of "all that Jesus said and did." The Holy Spirit used this to inspire him to write the Gospel which bears his name; it was probably written about the year 60.

The "Gospel of Miracles"   St Mark addressed his Gospel to Christians of Gentile origin living in Rome: but, of course, being a Gospel it had a universal purpose — the spread of the good news of salvation to all the nations. Within the framework of the gift of inspiration, Mark's aim was not so much to show that Jesus was the promised Messiah (which was St Matthew's approach in writing for Jews, because he wanted to show how the Old Testament promises had been fulfilled in Jesus); his aim, rather, was to give an account of Christ's life based on what he had heard directly from St Peter. Therefore he lays the emphasis on those events or miracles which will help the Roman Christians to see more clearly the divinity of Jesus, in whom they already believed.

Mark insists so much on our Lord's miracles that he omits, for example, the Sermon on the Mount and many parables which Jesus used to explain important aspects of the hierarchical organization and life of the Church. This, perhaps, is why his Gospel has been called "the gospel of miracles". Despite its brevity (16 chapters) he deals with almost all the miracles referred to by the other evangelists, but he adds two which they do not report — the curing of the deaf

6   Eusebius, *Ecclesiastical History*, III, 39, 15.

and dumb man (7:32-37) and of the blind man whom Jesus cured with his saliva (8:22-26).

St Mark tries to show (this is part of divine revelation) that Jesus was able to work all these miracles (healing of the sick, control of the elements, authority over unclean spirits, etc.) because he was the Son of God, the supreme master and lord of all creation. Anyone who reads this Gospel in a spirit of faith and sees the wonderful range of supernatural phenomena it contains will be inclined to exclaim like the centurion at the foot of the cross: "Truly this man was the Son of God" (15:39).

However, the scribes and Pharisees argued that if Jesus really were the Messiah he would always obey the Mosaic Law even when working miracles. But when one of them asked, for example, "Which commandment is the first of all?" (12:28), Jesus replied by making the law subject to himself and by interpreting it with full authority: "The first is, 'Hear, O Israel: The Lord our God, the Lord is one; and you shall love the Lord your God with all your heart, and with all your soul, and with all your mind, and with all your strength.' The second is this, 'You shall love your neighbour as yourself.' There is no other commandment greater than these" (12:29-31).[7] Jesus, as befits the Son of God, enunciates this first commandment in all its force and purity, while joining it inseparably to the second commandment, which he quotes according to Lev 19:18. But now he no longer limits it to a provincial, nationalist Jewish context. As he tells them in the parable of the good Samaritan (Lk 10:29-37), 'neighbour' for him means anyone in need of help: there are no exceptions. This is why he has come: he wants to heal everyone, to save everyone.

Our Lord's Prayer   St Mark, however, lays his main stress on the importance of prayer, especially at three key moments in Jesus' life — at the beginning of his public ministry (1:35), after the multiplication of the loaves (6:46) and at the beginning of his passion in Gethsemani (14:32). On these three occasions Jesus goes away to a private place to speak alone to his Father God. This is the prayer of the beloved Son of God in whom the Father is well pleased (1:11).

---

7   The commandment to love God with one's whole heart and soul and might (Deut 6:4) was very familiar to the Jews, for it formed part of the prayer knows as the *Shema*, a profession of faith in one God which every pious Jew recited twice a day. But the essence of the commandment might have become somewhat obscured due to the fact that the Shema went on to include additional verses of Deuteronomy (6:10-11) which make clear reference to the material prosperity God promises his people.

By giving us this example, our Lord wants to teach us how a son of God should pray: it should be filial, trusting conversation which we can have at any time, in any situation. In addition to praising God and asking him for graces, prayer must above all aim at identifying our will with that of our Father God.

We can see this very clearly in his prayer at Gethsemani (Mk 14:32). Jesus goes off again to be alone. He addresses his Father calling him *Abba*, a name which shows Jesus' spiritual childhood and his absolute conviction that he is being listened to. His human nature reacts against what he sees is going to happen — the chalice of pain; yet, in his prayer and as a result of his prayer, he identifies his human will with his divine will in the unity of his own Person (as St Thomas Aquinas puts it), for that is the aim of all prayer — to identify our will with God's, and to do so in a free and ready manner, full of love, as befits a son of God.

By revealing this high point of divine sonship, St Mark, aided by the gift of inspiration, wants to stress the central thing in Jesus' life — the fact that he is the redeemer. Readers may be surprised to see how, despite Jesus' very explicit miracles, the Son of God, in the full light of day and in the presence of crowds of people, was rejected by the very people he had come to save. Indeed, they went as far as to cause his death.

Jesus is scourged and put to death Superficially, the crucifixion might seem to be the great failure of Christ; but St Mark immediately explains that it was necessary for Christ to suffer this ignominy, with the scourging, insults and pain, in order to ransom men from the slavery of sin (10:45).[8] The Jewish people were wrong, therefore, in expecting a victorious warrior-Messiah who would liberate them from the Roman yoke as if he were an earthly king. They failed to see in Jesus the meek and humble Servant whom Isaiah had foretold, who would come to serve and not to be served; who chose to save us by way of pain and self-denial, even to the extremity of giving his life, as a spotless lamb, out of love for men. Jesus' apparent failure was turned into victory over the prince of this world. Finally, through his resurrection, the greatest miracle of all, Jesus proved both his divinity and the Father's acceptance of his sacrifice.

The Christian life, the life which truly leads to heaven, necessarily

8 Jesus himself explains the purpose of his death: "a ransom for many" (Mk 10:45). Any attempt to explain Christ's death as other than a true, redemptive self-sacrifice would contradict the Gospel and the unanimous thinking of the Church (cf. Paul VI, *Creed of the People of God*, 12).

involves the acceptance of the cross. Through their failure to understand these words — "a stumbling block to Jews and folly to Gentiles" (1 Cor 1:23) many people reject happiness. "They have no wish to know anything about the cross of Christ. They think it is sheer madness. But in fact it is they who are insane, for they are slaves of envy, gluttony and sensuality. They end up suffering far more, and only too late do they realize they have squandered both their earthly and their eternal happiness in exchange for meaningless trifles."[9]

St Luke

St Luke, a Syrian from Antioch, was the inspired author of the third Gospel. A physician by profession, a man of culture with perfect Greek, he was a disciple of St Paul (an early Gentile convert — from about the year 40). He accompanied St Paul on his second journey (49-53) from Troas to Philippi (Acts 16:10-37), remaining there for some years, until he again joined Paul towards the end of his third journey (53-58). He stayed with the Apostle when he was imprisoned in Caesarea; he was with him on his adventurous trip from Caesarea to Rome and during his first Roman captivity (Col 4:14; Phil 1:24).

We can be sure that Luke wrote his Gospel after the Aramaic original of Matthew and definitely after Mark; but it is not so easy to establish the precise date. According to the Pontifical Biblical Commission (26 June 1912) it must have been written before the destruction of Jerusalem in the year 70. And, since it was written before *Acts* and since *Acts* finishes with a description of St Paul's ministry towards the end of his first captivity in Rome (the year 63), this Gospel can be dated at the latest at the end of 62 or the beginning of 63. The same Commission confirmed the inspiration and canonicity of the third Gospel, and its authenticity. As regards some particular points: it also said that it was not "lawful to doubt the inspiration and authenticity of Luke's narrative of Christ's infancy (Lk 1 and 2) or of the appearance of the angel to comfort him, or the fact that he sweated blood (Lk 22:43-44): nor are there solid reasons to indicate — as some early heresies, supported by certain modern critics, try to make out — that these narratives do not belong to the authentic Gospel of Luke."

9   J. Escrivá de Balaguer, *Friends of God* (Dublin 1974; 1983), 130.

St Luke was not an eyewitness of our Lord's life. Therefore, when he refers in his introduction to the sources he has used, he includes those "who from the beginning were eyewitnesses and ministers of the word" (1:2), among the most outstanding of whom was the Blessed Virgin Mary. It must have been she who provided most of the information Luke gives in the first chapters of his Gospel. Luke liked to get order and chronology right — not just to satisfy his own or anyone else's curiosity but to pass on to others precisely what the Lord wanted him to write, that is, "the truth concerning the things of which you have been informed"(1:4), the true history of our salvation. That is what his Gospel contains — and the same is true of *Acts* : although these two books are independent they do form a perfect doctrinal and literary unity.

With reference to his literary style we can notice (St Jerome, for example, points it out) that Luke has a much better grammatical grasp of the Greek language than any of the other evangelists. Conscious that he is addressing people with a Gentile background, he usually avoids expressions which they might find jarring — and whenever possible he uses Greek equivalents for Aramaic terms. This is one reason why he is silent on some subjects which might have sounded indelicate to his readers.

The New Testament's continuity with the Old   St Luke stresses certain specific aspects of doctrine. He begins by emphasizing the continuity of the work of salvation begun by God in the Old Testament and brought to fulfilment in the New. He does this by recording a series of very revealing facts:

1. The announcement by the archangel Gabriel about the birth of John the Baptist (1:5ff), to Zechariah, a priest officiating in the Temple at the time of sacrifice prescribed by the old Law. The names of the protagonists in this scene are particularly significant: Zechariah (= Yahweh has remembered); Elizabeth (= God has sworn); John (= Yahweh is merciful).

2. John's future role as precursor of the Lord; a mission foretold by the prophet Malachi (4:5-6) and now presented by the angel as an accomplished fact (1:16-17).

3. The announcement by the same angel Gabriel of the virginal conception by Mary, who is full of grace. She will conceive the Saviour himself,[10] by the power of the Holy Spirit. This is directly linked

---

10 Mary's *fiat*, her total acceptance of God's will, was sufficient for the Word, at that

to the conception of the Baptist, his precursor (1:36).

All these events speak of continuity: they link past with present, promise with fulfilment. The promised Messiah, who for centuries had filled the hopes of the patriarchs and prophets and of all the Jewish people, is he who is now entering human history to bring salvation. It is not surprising, therefore, that the Virgin Mary should rejoice in God her Saviour (1:47) after being greeted by her cousin Elizabeth;[11] or that the angels should tell the shepherds "of a great joy which is to come to all the people; for to you is born this day a Saviour, who is Christ the Lord" (2:11); or that Simeon in his old age should bless God when, seeing Jesus coming into the Temple, he recognized him as the Messiah. There was no need for him to live any longer "for mine eyes have seen thy salvation which thou has prepared in the presence of all the people" (2:30). Jesus came to save all men, Gentiles and Jews, rich and poor, healthy and sick.

It had been prophesied (cf. Is 61:1-2) that the Messiah would redeem his people from every kind of affliction. Jesus actually said that this prophecy found its fulfilment in him (Lk 4:21). He came to redeem man from sin, to free him from slavery to the devil and from eternal death. But although he did rid many people of their physical illnesses and on occasions relieved the hunger of huge crowds, he did not seek to suppress pain or illness; God's plan is that these should have a clearly redemptive purpose; this is why the poor and the sick are his favourites, and we should see them as a reflexion of Jesus himself.[12]

Salvation is offered to all St Luke stresses the universal character of salvation; however, salvation starts in Jerusalem, the centre of all Jesus' activity. Luke starts his Gospel there, and there he concludes it. The infancy narrative finishes with the scene in the Temple in which our Lord, still an adolescent, talks to the teachers of the Law and leaves them amazed at the wisdom of his answers (cf. Lk 2:46-47). For Luke Jesus' public life is a continuous progress towards Jerusalem.

---

instant, to become man: in other words, God at that moment formed a body from the Virgin Mary by the work of the Holy Spirit and created a soul out of nothing; to this body and soul were joined the Son of God, who thus took on our human nature. This was defined by the Council of Ephesus in the year 431 as a dogma of faith (cf. Dz. 111).

11 Mary's soul overflowed with joy and gratitude in the *Magnificat*, in which she humbly recognizes that everything that has happened in her is the work of God. The canticle of Hannah (1 Sam 2:1-11) and Ps 103:17 — which Mary must have known very well — are reflected in the *Magnificat*.

12 Vatican II, Dogm. Const. *Lumen gentium* 8.

It is significant that the Last Supper takes place in the Holy City. This is a particularly important point in Jesus' life when he performs the miracle of transubstantiation, turning bread and wine into his Body and Blood so that he is really, truly and substantially present in the Eucharist: he does this as a form of sacrifice to God and then of nourishment for men. The institution of the Eucharist anticipates, through the consecration of the bread and wine, what Jesus was going to carry out a little later in his sacrifice on Calvary — just as the Mass is a sacramental renewal of the sacrifice of the cross. In both cases the victim sacrificed and the priest offering the sacrifice are one and the same — Jesus Christ.

It is in Jerusalem also that Jesus completes the mission which brought him among us, by obediently surrendering himself to the Cross, through which we have been freed from our sins. And, after the Ascension, the disciples themselves "returned to Jerusalem with great joy" (24:52).

St Luke leaves over to his second book — the *Acts of the Apostles* — the account of the spread of the Church. There also he stresses how the Church expanded outwards from Jerusalem, spreading throughout the known world and reaching Rome where the blood of Peter and Paul and many other Christian martyrs constitutes the seed of the Church. In this way is fulfilled what Isaiah prophesied in the seventh century before Christ: "out of Zion shall go forth the law, and the word of the Lord from Jerusalem" (Is 2:3).

The need to imitate Christ   St Luke sees this prophecy of salvation as fulfilled in Christ. The long period of waiting for the Messiah has come to an end. Now that Christ has brought salvation, the Christian must imitate him and follow in his footsteps. Jesus insists that no one can be his disciple unless he denies himself and takes up his cross daily (9:23). This is not easy, for good will is not enough; a person needs the help of grace and must cooperate with grace. Because we can easily grow tired, St Luke speaks of the endurance and perseverance involved (21:19); or what amounts to the same thing, the need for fortitude so as to be detached from anything which could separate us from God (18:29).

In making this effort to imitate the Master, Christians need virtues — such as justice, temperance, chastity, charity. These, St Luke tells us, are obtained firstly by prayer and then by sacrifice and mercy (6:27-38), by doing the work of each day in the presence of God.

Every Christian, therefore, must strive (unless his vocation takes

him away from the world) to combine action and contemplation and
not to make the mistake of counterposing these two aspects of life
(cf. the dialogue between Jesus and Martha: Lk 10:41-42). Every kind
of honest work helps us maintain continuous conversation with God:
we can serve him "in and from the ordinary, material and secular
activities of human life. He waits for us everyday, in the laboratory,
in the operating theatre, in the army barracks, in the university chair,
in the factory, in the workshop, in the fields, in the home and in
the immense panorama of work."[13]

Mary, the Mother of God   St Luke introduces us to our best ally
in this effort to imitate Christ — Mary, the Mother of God. She is
the holiest of all creatures — "full of grace" (1:28), sensitive, tender,
resolute, strong. Her love for us is so strong that we find it easy to
go to her with the love and abandonment of a child. Her faith and
self-surrender are so complete that everything our Lady asks for in
prayer — as on that day at Cana — Jesus grants her. This is how
Pope John Paul II put it: "Mary is always at the very centre of our
prayer. She is the first to pray. And she is *Omnipotentia supplex*: all
powerful in her prayer. This was the case in Nazareth, when she
conversed with Gabriel. We find her there, deep in prayer. In the
depth of her prayer she speaks to God the Father. In the depth of
her prayer the eternal Word becomes her Son. In the depth of her
prayer the Holy Spirit comes down upon her, and she brings this
same deep spirit of prayer from Nazareth to the Cenacle at Pentecost,
where all the apostles join her in united, devout and constant
prayer."[14]
    Although the New Testament does not give us information about
the birth and childhood of the Blessed Virgin Mary, Christian
tradition has passed on some details which tells us more about her.
For example, that she was the daughter of St Joachim and St Anne,
and from childhood had been dedicated to the service of the Lord
in his Temple until the time of her betrothal to St Joseph. Starting
at the Annunciation, St Matthew and St Luke give us the revealed
teaching about Jesus' virginal conception and miraculous birth which
were an object of the faith of the early Christian community. It is
in Mary that the Immanuel prophecy was fulfilled: "The Lord himself
will give you a sign. Behold, a virgin shall conceive and bear a son
and shall call his name Immanuel" (Is 7:14).

13 J. Escrivá de Balaguer, *Conversations* . . . 114.
14 21 October 1979.

The Second Vatican Council begins its exposition of doctrine on Mary by saying that "the Virgin Mary, who at the message of the angel received the Word of God in her heart and in her body and gave Life to the world, is acknowledged and honoured as being truly the Mother of God and of the Redeemer.... She is endowed with the high office and dignity of the Mother of the Son of God, and therefore she is also the beloved daughter of the Father and the temple of the Holy Spirit."[15]

The privileged place which Mary holds in Christian devotion and its liturgical expression led to her having a very special place in sacred art. Representations of her are to be found in the Roman catacombs, but it is not until the period between 400 and 900 that she comes into full view in Byzantine art. Devotion to her was further expressed in this way in the Gothic period — first as the Virgin of Sorrows, then as our Lady of Mercy. At the beginning of the seventeenth century the image of the Immaculate Conception, drawn from the book of *Revelation*, comes into its own. These are but a few of the many advocations of our Lady which arise at different times and in different places as expressions of the love and veneration Christians have for her.

St John

St John the Apostle, the son of Zebedee and Salome and the brother of James the Greater, was probably a native of Bethsaida, a city in Galilee on the shore of Lake Gennesaret. His family was fairly well off and he worked in the family business, fishing. As a very young man he became a disciple first of John the Baptist and then of Jesus: he followed Jesus when he heard the Baptist say, "Behold, the Lamb of God!" (1:36). That very afternoon, as he tells us himself, after following Jesus on the lakeshore and asking him where he lived, he spent many hours in his company (1:38-39). After that conversation, which he never forgot, he left his father in the boat with the hired men and threw himself into the new life to which our Lord had called him (Mk 1:20). He might have been twenty years old at the time.

He remained faithful to the Lord his whole life long. As a young

15 *Lumen gentium* 53.

man, in his total commitment of love and his passion for the things of God, he and his brother earned the nickname of 'sons of thunder' (cf. Lk 9:54). He did not allow difficulties get in his way. He alone of the Apostles, together with the Blessed Virgin and the holy women who accompanied her (Mk 15:40-41), remained at the foot of the cross. And Jesus showed his confidence in John by entrusting him with the care of his Blessed Mother, the person he loved most in the world.

The tradition of the Church, as witnessed by St Polycarp, tells us that John moved from Palestine to Ephesus and that he was exiled, during Diocletian's persecution, to the island of Patmos, where he wrote the *Apocalypse*. After the death of that emperor he returned to Ephesus, where he wrote his three Letters and Gospel.

St John is the inspired author of the fourth Gospel: this is explicitly recognized by tradition and witnessed to by, among others, Papias, St Irenaeus, the Muratori fragment, Clement of Alexandria, Tertullian and Origen. It is also borne out by internal evidence of the text: the author's familiarity with Jewish customs and his policy of pointing out how the Old Testament prophecies were fulfilled (the cleansing of the Temple, the entry of Jesus into Jerusalem, the unbelief of the Jews, the distribution of Jesus' clothes and the casting of lots for his tunic, the piercing of his side with a lance); the vivid eyewitness quality of many of his accounts; his detailed knowledge of the topography of Jerusalem (he knows that the portico of Solomon is part of the Temple; that there was a pavement in the praetorium called Gabbatha; that the pool of Bethzatha has five porticoes and is located near the Sheep Gate); and, finally, by the wealth of detail which gives the narrative a special freshness and originality which could only come from an eyewitness.

To this should be added the fact that whereas the Synoptics expressly mention St John (St Matthew three times, St Luke seven and St Mark nine), the fourth Gospel never gives his name, and never refers to his family, except on one occasion when it mentions the sons of Zebedee (21:2). However, because the author seems to hide his true identity by using the literary form of 'he whom Jesus loved' (13:23) and this could only refer to our Lord's three most intimate Apostles (Peter, James and John: Mt 17:1-2 Mk 14:33), we can conclude by process of elimination that this disciple was John, because we know St James was already dead (he died in the year 44, in the reign of Agrippa) and Peter asked this disciple a question (13:24) but Peter had also died a martyr's death in Rome during Nero's persecution of the Church, which began in 64.

Jesus Christ, the Son of God   In writing his Gospel — under the charism of inspiration — St John had a clear purpose in mind: "These [signs] have been written," he says, "that you may believe that Jesus is the Christ, the Son of God, and that believing you may have life in his name" (20:31). He seeks to strengthen the faith of those early Christians of the young churches of Asia Minor, who are threatened by the latent danger of going astray and even falling into doctrinal error about who Jesus Christ is and what is the true story of his life. St John goes straight to the point: Jesus is the Messiah, the Son of God made man. His account has a structure similar to that used by the other Apostles in their oral teaching (cf. Acts 10:36-43), but he fills out the account given in the Synoptic Gospels, with which Christians were already familiar. Like them, St John's aim is not to write a complete biography of Jesus: he selects (21:25) only the material necessary for explaining the main truth he wishes to get across to his readers — that Jesus Christ is the Son of God made man.

His Gospel consists essentially of a prologue and two main parts:

The prologue (1:1-18)   This contains a revelation extremely important from the doctrinal point of view. St John presents the Word — the Logos — as eternal, distinct from the Father, and yet identical with him because he shares the same divine nature. The Logos is "the eternal Word of the Father before time began, one in substance with the Father, *homoousios to Patri*, through whom all things were made. He was incarnate of the Virgin Mary and was made man; equal, therefore, to the Father according to his divinity, less than the Father according to his humanity, his unity deriving not from some impossible confusion of substance but from his Person."[16]

The Word, the Second Person of the Blessed Trinity, in addition to being eternal and consubstantial with the Father, is the Creator of the world, together with the Father, by whom all things are made.[17] He is the Saviour, the true light which enlightens every man — light against the darkness of the world of those who refuse to receive him. He came to his own people (Israel, the chosen people), but they too chose not to receive him. However, to those who do receive him through believing in him he gives eternal life, the power

16 Paul VI, *The Creed of the People of God*, 11.

17 Everything created is created by the Word, but it is not as if he were an instrument in the hands of the Father, for in that case he would be a creature himself (which was Arius' error). The Word, therefore, is the active principle of creation, but every *ad extra* action of God is an action common to the three divine Persons (cf. Dz. 421).

(grace) to be children of God. In the fullness of time, the Word became man, in the pure womb of the Blessed Virgin Mary, ever virgin: he came, as Jesus of Nazareth, to save all men, living among us full of grace and truth. All are called to share in his fullness. The Old Alliance gives way to the New, which will be sealed by the sacrifice of the Son of God on the Cross. The teaching contained in this prologue is a summary of St John's entire Gospel.

The first part (chapters 1-13) St John devotes mainly to presenting Jesus as the promised Messiah, whom the people of Israel have so long awaited. To prove that he is the Messiah, he describes a number of miracles in detail. The first of these is the changing of water into wine at Cana in Galilee (2:9): in response to the faith and humility of his Mother he acts before his "time has come."[18] There follows the cure, also in Cana, of the son of the royal official who is lying ill in Capernaum (4:46-54). Here again we can see the faith our Lord awakens in those who approach him with good will. There follows the curing of the paralytic at the pool of Bethzatha (5:1-18), the multiplication of the loaves (6:5-13), Jesus walking on the water (6:19), the curing of the man born blind (9:1-8), the raising of Lazarus (11:1-45) and his own resurrection (20:1-18). To these should be added the miraculous draught of fish after his resurrection (21:11).

By means of these miracles, Jesus shows that he is the true Messiah, the Saviour of the world. He wants people to realize that only God can work such miracles. That is why he works cures on the sabbath: he is the Lord even of the sabbath. He restores sight to the blind, to show that he is the light of the world. He does these miracles so that people can see that his preaching goes further than mere words. And, after his death, he rises by his own power, to dispel any doubt the Apostles might have about his divinity.

The second part The second part of the Gospel (chapters 13:21) covers, in three acts, the most intimate and significant events of our Lord's life — the Last Supper, his passion and death, and his

---

18 The Mother of Jesus was one of the guests at the wedding (cf. Jn 2:2-3). St John mentions her only twice — here, at Cana, and at the foot of the cross (Jn 19:25), that is to say, at the beginning and at the end of Jesus' public ministry. In both instances he wants to underline her role as co-redeemer. By her humble prayer, full of faith, she gets Jesus to work his first miracle before time; and it is her faith which makes her, as she stands beside her son on his cross, Mother of all believers (cf. Dogm. Const. *Lumen gentium* 58).

resurrection. In each of these acts we can see the realization of the plan of salvation which the Father has given to the Son. Through them the Son's love shines forth: so great is it that he gives up his life on the cross. It is followed by the profound joy of the resurrection. Thus, love, sacrifice and joy are the keynotes of this second part of the Gospel.

Last Supper, Death and Resurrection   1. St John opens his account of the Last Supper with a passage which summarizes Christ's whole purpose during the episodes which follow: "Now before the feast of the Passover, when Jesus knew the hour had come to depart out of this world to the Father, having loved his own who were in the world, he loved them to the end" (13:1). The limitless love of Jesus is the key to understanding his later sacrifice on the cross; it fulfils, as it were, what John says at the beginning of his Gospel: "God so loved the world that he gave his only Son" (3:16). Genuine love implies surrender, self-denial, to the point of giving oneself: it needs to be expressed in actions. Thus, Jesus will say that no one loves better than he who lays down his life for his friends (15:13), even if that love is not reciprocated. Jesus' love is not a matter of empty words or superficial gestures: he sacrificed himself. In the face of this completely disinterested, pure and generous love which God has for him, man — every one of us — can only feel ashamed; he is unable to reply.

But Jesus Christ, in his priestly prayer at the Last Supper, has prayed for his disciples (17:6-19), for each one of us (17:20), to enable us to respond to his love. The ground of God's love for men is to be found in the intimate life of the three divine Persons. Therefore, Jesus prays "that they all may be one; even as thou, Father, art in me, and I in thee, that they also may be in us, so that the world may believe that thou has sent me" (17:21). This is the content and scope of the new commandment Jesus gives his disciples: "that you love one another, even as I have loved you, that you also love one another. By this all men will know that you are my disciples, if you have love for one another" (13:34-35).[19] With the help of God's grace it is easy to keep this commandment; but when a person isolates himself and distances himself from God, he also ruptures his

19   Although the commandment of brotherly love was promulgated before (cf. Lev 19:18), Jesus Christ not only ratifies the commandment but gives it a deeper, a completely new dimension — "as I have loved you." It is not simply a matter of loving our enemies also (Ex 23:4-5) but of loving in a disinterested way: everyone must love in this way, because our Lord has given himself up for all men.

attachment to his brothers and can even come to despise them and hate them if they get in the way of his self-centred plans; whereas love unites and smoothens one's neighbour's way to holiness. This is why Christian life can be summed up as love of God and love of one's neighbour. Living by love is living the life of God, because "God is love" (1 Jn 4:8).

Jesus Christ reveals himself as the expression of the Father's love. He is the vine and we are the branches. "He who abides in me, and I in him, he it is that bears much fruit, because apart from me you can do nothing" (15:5).[20] To strengthen our union with him he institutes the sacrament of the Eucharist, remaining with us in order to make our way easier. In the synagogue of Capernaum he promised he would do this when he said, "My flesh is food indeed, and my blood is drink indeed. He who eats my flesh and drinks my blood abides in me, and I in him" (6:55-56). The Eucharist maintains our union with our Lord, enabling us to live as sons of God (1:12-13) and, despite our weaknesses, to hope confidently in attaining possession of God in heaven.

2. In his account of the passion and death of our Lord, beginning in chapter 18, St John writes in a very personal style and seeks to fill out or nuance the Synoptic version of these events. His approach is different from that of the Synoptics. They give special importance to certain circumstances surrounding our Lord's death — the darkness that envelopes the earth from midday onwards, the sundering of the veil of the temple; the Jews who witness his death and are overcome by terror; the dead rising out of their graves; etc. They obviously want to stress the transition that is taking place from one era to another, from the Old to the New Alliance. St John lays the emphasis on one feature of the events which he regards as fundamental: Christ's death brings about the foundation of the Church. This is the key, as it were, to understanding the whole Redemption. Hence the importance he gives to the wound in Christ's open side, caused by the lance, with blood and water coming out (cf. 19:35). From the Church flow the sacraments, in the same kind of way as from the open side of Jesus, our Saviour, water (Baptism) and blood (Eucharist) flow — blood being a symbol of expiation, and water a symbol of purification. The sacraments, and the Church itself, flow from Christ's death. As Vatican II puts it, "the Church — that is, the kingdom of Christ — already present in mystery, grows visibly in the world

20 If we do not stay united to Jesus Christ through grace, there is no way we can have supernatural life. Our desires would be ineffective and our deeds would have no value as far as our salvation is concerned (cf. Council of Trent, *Decree on justification*, chap. 16).

through the power of God. The origin and growth of the Church are symbolized by the blood and water which flowed from the open side of the crucified Jesus."[21]

A Church-meaning is also to be seen in the details given about casting of lots for the seamless tunic, which is a symbol of the unity of the Church (19:23-24); as are Jesus' farewell words, when he entrusts his last and most precious possession, his Blessed Mother, to the disciple whom he loved (19:25-27). St John stands for all of us, the entire Church. And Mary, who had entered into the plan of salvation by the express will of God, becomes through this last act of her Son, mediatrix of all graces, the Mother of the Church. As Vatican II puts it, "she endured with her only begotten Son the intensity of his suffering, associating herself with his sacrifice in her mother's heart, and lovingly consenting to the immolation of this victim who was born of her."[22]

3. Jesus' resurrection and everything connected with it can be said to be the best-recounted of all Gospel events, and the best testified to, as we can see from St John's Gospel. We should not forget that he was a personal witness of the death and subsequent burial of our Lord: he was the only Apostle who stayed on Calvary and was present at the burial, until the entrance stone was sealed. He reports all the details which he considers basic to our belief. That, he says, is why he wrote his account — "that you may believe that Jesus is the Christ, the Son of God, and that believing you may have life in his name" (20:31).

Because the resurrection of Christ is the basis of the Christian faith (20:28), John takes the trouble to recount everything relevant to guaranteeing the historic truth of the resurrection and to strengthening our faith — the discovery of the empty tomb (20:1-10), and the physical reality of the body of the risen Jesus, who three times lets himself be seen and touched by those who were to act as witnesses for all whom faith would later lead into the Church.

Despite the little faith shown by the Apostles (Thomas did not believe until he saw and touched Jesus), the facts are so overpowering as to make it impossible to deny that the resurrection happened. St John takes delight in describing the way the linen cloths and the napkin were when he entered the tomb behind Peter. When he saw them, "he saw and believed" (20:8). Up to that they had not understood the scripture. "that he must rise from the dead" (20:9).

21 Dogm. Const. *Lumen gentium* 3.
22 Dogm. Const. *Lumen gentium* 58.

He gives great importance to the empty tomb and makes it very clear that the napkin was not with the linen cloths but in a place by itself.

Like Jesus' passion and death, his resurrection is closely linked to the foundation of the Church and the full authority with which our Lord expressly endowed it. Only after the resurrection does Jesus hand the Apostles the power to forgive sins: "If you forgive the sins of any, they are forgiven; if you retain the sins of any, they are retained" (20:23). And, also after his resurrection Jesus confirms Peter in primacy of jurisdiction over the whole Church (21:15-17).

First, however, our Lord wants to hear Peter's triple confession, to test his love and atonement for his three previous denials. Peter learns the lesson and, deeply repentant, confesses his weakness — and also his sincere love for our Lord. Only then does Jesus hand over the power and authority he had earlier promised Peter: "After his resurrection, Jesus conferred upon Simon Peter alone the jurisdiction of supreme shepherd and rule over his whole fold with the words, 'Feed my lambs ... Feed my sheep'."[23]

From this moment onwards, all those who, by God's grace, are converted and enter the Church, will find in Peter and his successors the security and strength that is the endowment of Christ's vicar on earth. From union with this head the whole body derives its cohesion, its vigour and its growth. The Fathers of the Church have pointed to the symbolism in the miraculous draught of fish after the resurrection: the sea is the world; the boat, the Church; the fishermen, the apostles; the net, doctrinal unity in the preaching of the Gospel; and the fish, the elect. By giving the exact number of fish caught (153 large fish) St John points to the multitude of faithful people whom the Church will comprise, thus ending his Gospel on a note of optimism and hope, the same note as is struck by the Synoptics.

THE ACTS OF THE APOSTLES

The earliest tradition of the Church and internal analysis of the text both concur in attributing this inspired book of the New Testament

---

23 Vatican I, Dogm. Const. *Pastor Aeternus*, DZ 1822; cf. Dogm Const. *Lumen gentium* 18.

to St Luke, the human author of the third Gospel. This tradition is to be found in St Irenaeus, Tertullian, Clement of Alexandria, Origen, the Muratori fragment, St Jerome and Eusebius of Caesarea, among others.

The continuity between St Luke's Gospel and the *Acts* is easy to recognize. Often there is a coincidence of style, vocabulary and even doctrinal theme. Even more convincing is the argument that the second part of *Acts*, which covers the journeys of St Paul, contain a "diary" written by one of his companions in the first person plural. The diary stops at certain points and the first person disappears, whenever its author was not present. From St Paul's Letters we know who his companions were and that only St Luke could write the "we" when he was the eyewitness of the events recounted.

As regards the date and place of composition of the book the following information can be deduced: the *Acts* finish with St Paul's imprisonment in Rome (61-63). Since St Luke wrote his Gospel first, perhaps towards the end of 62, *Acts* must have been written between 62 and 64. The latter year was when Nero's persecution began, but there is no reference to the persecution in *Acts*; in fact, St Luke's last episode shows St Paul in prison in Rome, the capital of the Empire, and Paul free to preach the Gospel without interference. And even though he on occasion predicts that he will suffer, no reference is made to his martyrdom. From this we may conclude that *Acts* was written in Rome shortly before the July 64 fire after which Nero began his persecution of Christians. This could explain the rather rushed conclusion we can notice at the end of the book.

Purpose St Luke, an educated man, by profession a physician, meticulous and orderly, sets out in *Acts*, under the inspiration of the Holy Spirit, to prove the truth of the Apostles' teaching and show how rapidly it spread; the Church's expansion, among the Gentiles particularly, was marked by miracles; the content of his book covers a large part of the history of the origins of Christianity, bearing out what our Lord had foretold: "You shall receive power when the Holy Spirit has come upon you; and you shall be my witnesses in Jerusalem and all Judea and Samaria and to the ends of the earth" (Acts 1:8).

And so the Christian faith spread out from Jerusalem, where on the day of Pentecost some three thousand people were converted and baptized (2:41). From that point onwards, with the help of the Holy Spirit, an expansion began which would continue until it covered the entire world. Many of those first Christians were hellenist Jews before their conversion (6:1), who after the martyrdom of Stephen were persecuted and expelled from Israel (8:3-4). Their outlook, open to other lands and cultures, enabled them to put down roots, first in Samaria and border countries and then in more distant regions. Thus, for example, we know that by the time of Paul's conversion, Christianity had already reached Damascus, where the disciples included Ananias (9:10). This first expansion is attested to by St Luke before he relates the miracles worked by St Peter at Lydda and Joppa: "The church throughout all Judea and Galilee and Samaria had peace and was built up; and walking in the fear of the Lord and in the comfort of the Holy Spirit it was multiplied" (9:31).

A second important step in the spread of the Church stemmed from the arrival of persecuted Christians, after the martyrdom of Stephen, in Phoenicia, Cyprus and Antioch (11:19). There the Gospel was preached at every opportunity. It was in Antioch that "the disciples were for the first time called Christians" (11:26). From that point onwards Antioch became the second focus from which the faith spread. Already there was frequent contact between Antioch and Jerusalem (11:27ff), St Luke making it clear that Jerusalem enjoyed pre-eminence. After each of his three apostolic journeys St Paul made his way back to Jerusalem, and was imprisoned there on the last occasion.

The third significant stage in the spread of the Church resulted from St Paul being brought to Rome, where he remained under arrest pending trial. Even though he was in chains for love of Jesus Christ, his vigorous apostolate continued unabated.

We can see, therefore, that *Acts*, rather than a detailed and complete account of the origins of the Church is a trustworthy and specific report of the extraordinary aid which the Holy Spirit gave the Church from its inception.

The teaching contained in Acts Just as the four Gospels tell of the incarnation of the Son of God and his work of salvation, the *Acts of the Apostles* is a kind of fifth Gospel containing the only account we possess of the coming of the Holy Spirit and his action in support of the Church during the first thirty years of its existence.

Here is a very brief summary of the teaching which the book contains:

1. *Jesus Christ* After receiving the Holy Spirit at Pentecost, the disciples openly preach that Jesus is the Messiah. St Peter specifically ends his address on the very morning of Pentecost with this statement: "Let all the house of Israel therefore know assuredly that God has made him both Lord and Christ, this Jesus whom you crucified"

(2:36). Thus, the messianic character of everything Jesus did is made perfectly clear, both the prophecies that spoke of him in advance and the miracles which marked his life. Of these, the greatest, the definitive, miracle is his own resurrection (2:24-32), which decisively proves his divinity. St Paul also, as soon as he is converted, preaches that Jesus is the Son of God (9:20; 13:33). It is Jesus who sent the Holy Spirit and who forgives sins, because he is the Author of life (3:15); he it is who saves all men, for as the "suffering servant" undergoing his passion and death he redeems all mankind (8:32-33); and, because he is God, his name is all powerful (4:10-12) and he, before all others, must be obeyed (4:19). Just as in the Old Testament the name of God is invoked, now the name of Jesus must be invoked with the same faith, for in him all authority and virtue resides. To him the Apostles have recourse in all their trials, and in his name they preach and baptize those whom they convert. Finally, it will be a privilege for them to suffer persecution for confessing his name — and even to give their very lives for the Lord.

2. *The Holy Spirit* The Spirit promised by the prophet Joel (Joel 2:28-32) is the very Spirit who on Pentecost comes down on the Apostles and fills them with his grace; among them is the Virgin Mary, the mother of Jesus (2:3-4). The *Acts* show that the Apostles saw the Holy Spirit as a person distinct from the Father and the Son, though he shares in the same divine nature. Hence to lie to the Holy Spirit, as Ananias and Sapphira did, is the same as lying to God himself (5:3).[24] Even the Apostles' preaching is the work of the Holy Spirit, for it is really he who speaks through the mouth of the disciples (4:8; 11:28). The Holy Spirit also gives instructions to Philip (8:29) and to St Peter (10:19). The most important decisions of the Church, as for example those taken at the Council of Jerusalem, are decisions of the Holy Spirit and of the Apostles (15:28).[25] Apostolic activity begins at his express command (13:2-4). He guides the Apostles, or restrains them (16:6); he appoints the bishops (20:28) and it is he who works the miracles (10:46; 19:6). Therefore, those who are not aware of his existence, even though they may believe in the Father and in the Son, cannot yet be considered true disciples of his (19:2-6).

24 The punishment this married couple received was a lesson for the early Christians — and for all Christians — about the respect due to the Church and the Apostles and ultimately the Holy Spirit, who governs the Church.

25 The Apostles took this decision under the influence of the Holy Spirit, which guarantees that their decisions on matters of faith and morals are infallible. The very wording used in Acts 5:28, at the start of the Church, is that still used by the Church in its dogmatic conciliar decisions (cf. Dogm. Const. *Lumen gentium* 18 and 25).

The *Acts* speak of a real presence of the Holy Spirit, a permanent not a passing presence — such as charisms — in the soul of every Christian as soon as he is baptized (2:38; 5:32). He transforms and sanctifies those in whom he dwells. His interior presence, vital and profound, spreads throughout the world through the sacraments which the Church administers. Confirmation is one of these sacraments (Acts 8:15-17).

3. *The Church* The life of grace, the new life which the Holy Spirit brought at Pentecost, created and shaped the first Christian community, that is, the Church. From the very start it was clear that only in the Church, the mystical body of Christ, can salvation be found, because only the Church has the means necessary for attaining salvation — grace and the sacraments, with the gifts of the Holy Spirit. But the Church is open to everyone — not only the heirs of the promise, the Jews, but also the Gentiles: open to everyone provided they believe that Jesus is the Son of God, the promised Messiah, and accept his teaching. Our Lord himself expressly desired that all men should be saved through his Church. As Vatican II puts it "Those cannot be saved, who knowing that the Catholic Church was founded through Jesus Christ, by God, as something necessary, still refuse to enter it, or to remain in it. Although in ways known to himself God can lead those who, through no fault of their own, are ignorant of the Gospel to that faith without which it is impossible to please him (Heb 11:6)."[26]

As soon as the Apostles admitted Gentiles into the Church, dispensing them from circumcision and the Mosaic law, the split between Church and Synagogue became explicit, for it became obvious that the Church was the new Israel, the new chosen people (15:14), and not, as some thought, simply a sect of Judaism. This teaching was confirmed by the Council of Jerusalem (15:1ff), which explicitly stated that no Christian, not even those of Jewish background, was obliged to keep the Mosaic law; this teaching had been upheld by Stephen, the first martyr, and the Holy Spirit had charged Peter and Paul to preach it from the very beginning.

4. *The life of the first Christians* The *Acts* tell us a great deal about the lifestyle of the first Christian community. As St Luke describes it early on in the book, "they devoted themselves to the apostles' teaching and fellowship, to the breaking of bread and the prayers" (2:42) — spiritual resources for the spiritual goal which God gave them by calling them to the faith. The four pillars on which their

26 Vatican II, Decree *Ad gentes* 7.

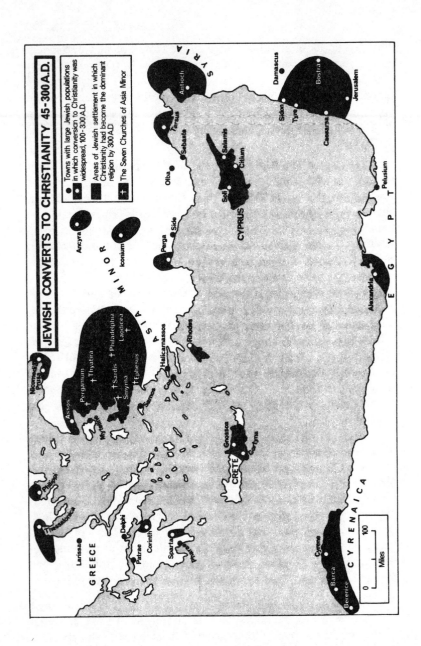

Map 10

perseverance was built are the same today: *faithfulness* to the Apostles' teaching; *unity* among all those who practise the same faith, being of one heart and soul (4:31); active sharing in the *Eucharist;* and *constant prayer*, which keeps us united to God. The early Christians prayed unceasingly when Peter was imprisoned by Herod (12:5); Peter and Paul pray before they work miracles (9:40; 28:8); Paul and Silas pray in the prison at Philippi, at midnight, after being beaten with rods, and all the other prisoners can hear them (16:25). Prayer is a kind of background music preceding and accompanying all apostolic activity.

Even the sharing of property practised among the first Christians was simply a logical result of their perfect unity of spirit. They all felt concern for each other and gave the Apostles whatever they could to alleviate the situation of the poorer members of the community (2:44-45). This property-sharing was something which grew up spontaneously: it was never something laid down by Church authority: as St Peter tells Ananias, he was free to do whatever he wanted with his property.

We can also notice a certain basic hierarchical organization in the Church of the *Acts*. It is to the apostles that the people give the proceedings of the sale of their surplus property, regarding them as God's representatives (4:35). When they are baptized they are conscious of submitting both to the authority of Peter, who exercised primacy of jurisdiction in the whole Church, and to that of the other Apostles (10:44-48).

This should not lead us to think that the early Christians were a closed group of people isolated from others and uninvolved in the life of society. Under the influence of the Holy Spirit they bore witness to Jesus "in Jerusalem and in all Judea and Samaria and to the end of the earth" (1:8). They were extraordinarily zealous in their apostolate: this was something which came from their spirit of prayer and their union with God. They really did act as a leaven in a world hostile to Jesus and to the Gospel. Within very few years, after the fall of Jerusalem in the year 70, they would turn society around, thanks to their docility to the action of the Holy Spirit. Thanks to their effort — even to the point of shedding their blood for Jesus Christ — they brought the seed of the Christian faith to the known world, thereby setting an example for Christians of all eras.

The Letters of St Paul

The *Letters of St Paul*, which complemented his preaching, were written to instruct and exhort new Christians, and sometimes to take them to task or to clarify some difficult points of doctrine.

St Paul is the New Testament writer about whom most is known. A good two-thirds of the *Acts of the Apostles* has to do with his life and, together with the *Letters*, they show us, in detail, his early background, his conversion and then his amazing apostolate among the Gentiles.

We learn, for example, that St Paul was born in Tarsus of Cilicia of Jewish parents who were zealous and faithful followers of the Law (Acts 23:6). His early education was in Hebrew, but he also learned Greek in Tarsus and became familiar with hellenic culture. The very fact that he is sometimes called Saul and sometimes Paul reflects this mixed cultural background and the two sides of his personality. His religious training was rounded off in Jerusalem, where he was taught by Gamaliel (Act 22:3), an upright and religious man, and he became a thorough Pharisee (Acts 23:6).

St Paul was also passionately in love with the things of God. His commitment was total: God meant everything to him; therefore he served him unconditionally and with total loyalty. His vision of Jesus on the road to Damascus (Acts 9:1ff) radically changed his life. His conversion was not something emotional or psychic; it came about due to a very special grace from God, which as he puts it, 'made me his own' (Phil 3:12). From that moment on all his zeal for God and for his neighbour was expressed in a life of complete self-giving to him who had called him and whom he loved with his whole soul. Effort, privation, suffering and even mortal danger could not separate him from 'the love of God in Christ Jesus our Lord' (Rom 8:35-39). This love was to lead him to total identification with the passion and cross of his Master (2 Cor 4:10-11; Phil 3:10), to the extent of dying to himself, so that he could say, 'I have been crucified with Christ; it is no longer I who live, but Christ who lives in me' (Gal 2:19-20). This identification with Christ was the source of his zeal

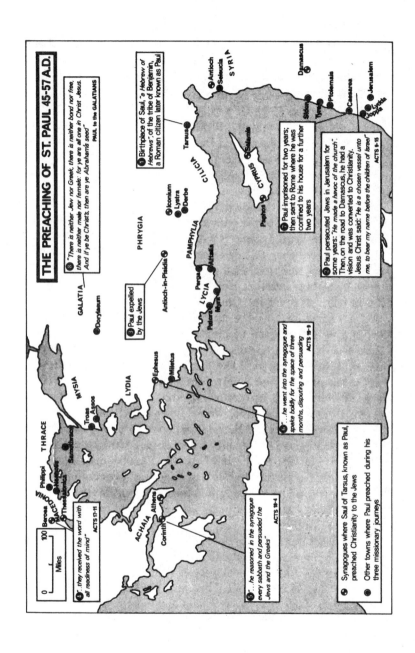

THE PREACHING OF ST. PAUL 45-57 A.D.

① Birthplace of Saul, "a Hebrew of Hebrews", of the tribe of Benjamin, a Roman citizen later known as Paul

⑥ "There is neither Jew nor Greek, there is neither bond nor free, there is neither male nor female: for ye are all one in Christ Jesus. And if ye be Christ's, then are ye Abraham's seed".
PAUL to the GALATIANS

② Paul imprisoned for two years; then sent to Rome where he was confined to his house for a further two years

③ Paul persecuted Jews in Jerusalem for some years: "He made a havoc of the church". Then, on the road to Damascus, he had a vision and was converted to Christianity. Jesus Christ said: "He is a chosen vessel unto me, to bear my name before the children of Israel"
ACTS 9-15

④ Paul expelled by the Jews

⑤ "...he went into the synagogue and spake boldly for the space of three months, disputing and persuading"
ACTS 19-8

⑥ "...he reasoned in the synagogue every sabbath and persuaded the Jews and the Greeks"
ACTS 18-4

④ "...they received the word with all readiness of mind"
ACTS 17-11

⊕ Synagogues where Saul of Tarsus, known as Paul, preached Christianity to the Jews

● Other towns where Paul preached during his three missionary journeys

Map 11

to bring everyone the teaching of Jesus, and of his self-denial and 'anxiety for all the churches' (2 Cor 11:28).

St Paul made three great missionary journeys. The first (45-49) took place after the Holy Spirit chose him for this mission, along with Barnabas (Acts 13:2). He went to preach to the Gentiles, covering Cyprus, Perga in Pamphylia, Pisidian Antioch and three cities in Lycaonia — Iconium, Lystra and Derbe. Despite the many difficulties he met, mostly due to resistance from the Jews to whom he preached in the first instance, he established Christian communities of Gentile converts in all those places.

On his return from this journey, the Council of Jerusalem was held (Acts 15:1ff) to sort out the question posed by Judaising Christians about whether Gentile converts to Christianity should be obliged to keep the Mosaic law. The agreement arrived at, ratified by Peter, James and John, confirmed Paul and Barnabas in their ministry. There was no longer any question of its being necessary to practise the old Law in order to enter the Church.

Accompanied by Silas, the Apostle set out on his second journey (50-52) after the Council of Jerusalem. From Antioch he crossed Cilicia and visited in Lycaonia the Church he had previously founded there. In Lystra he was joined by Timothy. He went through Phrygia and Galatia and, despite illness, preached the Gospel wherever he went. The Holy Spirit led him to Troas and from there into Europe, passing through Macedonia, where he founded the churches of Philippi, Thessalonica and Berea. Due to strenuous opposition from Jews, he then moved to Corinth, where he preached for a year and a half. There he met Aquila and Priscilla, a Jewish married couple who had been expelled from Rome by Claudius' persecution. While in Corinth, and before returning to Antioch, St Paul wrote two letters to the *Thessalonians* (these are regarded as the first canonical books of the New Testament).

He began his third journey (53-58) in Antioch. He crossed Phrygia and Galatia and reached Ephesus, where he wrote *Galatians* and *1 Corinthians*. After his sudden departure from Ephesus (Acts 19:23ff) we find him in Macedonia with Titus, who gives him disturbing news of the church of Corinth: this provokes him to write his second letter to the *Corinthians*. At the end of the winter of 57 he arrives in Corinth, the last stage of his third journey. There he writes the letter to the *Romans*.

Then, due to accusations made by the Jews, he was imprisoned in Jerusalem and led under arrest to Caesarea. After failing to obtain freedom (he spent two years in captivity) and after interrogations by two procurators, Felix and Festus, he appealed to Caesar, as was his right as a Roman citizen. Towards the end of the year 60 he started out for Rome, under guard, and spent another two years in captivity of sorts: he was able to preach the Gospel with his accustomed vigour. During this first Roman captivity (61-63) he wrote the letters to the *Ephesians, Philippians, Colossians* and to *Philemon* (these are known as the Captivity Letters).

From what St Luke tells us in *Acts*, it is quite possible that after these two years he was free to make the journey to Spain which he had been looking forward to for so long; this would have taken place in the same year, 63. On his return it is also probable that he made a last journey east (according to *1 Timothy* and the letter to *Titus*, both written in Macedonia). From *2 Timothy* we learn that he is once more in prison in Rome; and the very earliest tradition is that it was in Rome in 67 that he suffered that martyrdom for which God had long been preparing him.

As far as the Letters are concerned, this seems to have been the chronological order in which they were written:

1. During his first journey (50-52) he wrote *1 and 2 Thessalonians*.
2. During his second journey (53-58): *1 and 2 Corinthians, Galatians* and *Romans*.
3. During his first captivity in Rome (61-63): *Ephesians, Philippians, Colossians* and *Philemon*.
4. Towards the end of his life (65-67): the pastoral letters to *Timothy* and *Titus*. The letter to the *Hebrews* will be discussed separately.

Although the Letters appear in the Bible in a difference sequence (first *Romans*, and *1 and 2 Thessalonians* at the end, before *Hebrews*), we are going to deal with them in a different order, as follows:

— pre-captivity letters
— captivity letters
— pastoral letters.

PRE-CAPTIVITY LETTERS

1 and 2 Thessalonians

St Paul first came to Thessalonica — modern Salonika — around the year 50 (early on in the course of his second apostolic journey). It was one of the most important cities in the Roman province of

Macedonia. Its very busy port, its strategic position on the main highway between Rome and its provinces in the East, and its position on the route from Thrace to Acadia meant that many people, mainly Greeks, gravitated to Thessalonica in search of employment; it had a sizeable Jewish community, with its own synagogue.

Zealous as ever, St Paul spoke in this synagogue on three consecutive sabbaths, explaining that Jesus was the true Messiah, in whom the Old Testament prophecies found their fulfilment. Only some of these Jews accepted the Gospel, but many Greek proselytes became Christians as well as "not a few of the leading women" (Acts 16:25-17:4).

The Apostle was immediately persecuted and had to flee the city by night, leaving his catechetical work unfinished. As soon as he reached Athens he sent Timothy back to Thessalonica, and Timothy soon returned with good reports. By this time Paul was already in Corinth and from there, happy to hear of the Thessalonians' firmness in the faith and of their affectionate regard for himself (despite what detractors were saying about him), he wrote to them to console them and clarify some points of doctrine; two points, particularly — the lot of those who die before the Parousia* (the second coming of the Lord) and the disruption caused by those who refused to work and constituted a burden on the Christian community in that city.

1 Thessalonians   After thanking God for the steadfast faith of the Thessalonians, St Paul vigorously defends the supernatural character of his mission. Contrary to what some people were alleging out of greed and vanity, he had brought them the Gospel "not only in word, but also in power and in the Holy Spirit and with full conviction" (1:5): "we speak, not to please men, but to please God who tests our hearts" (2:4).[1] A proof of this is the fact that during the time he spent among them he worked with his own hands, to avoid being a burden on them (2:9-10). Therefore, he insists on the mutual love they should have for one another — and everyone's responsibility to pull his weight, to do his daily work and obey those whom God has placed over him. Finally he touches on the Parousia and on what happens to those who have already died when the Parousia comes. The Thessalonians were in no doubt about the resurrection of the dead, nor did they think that the Parousia was imminent; but they

1 St Paul never tried to derive any personal advantage from his preaching, was never deceitful in his teaching or ever tried to impose it on people. "From the very beginning of the Church the disciples of Christ strove to convert men to confess Christ as Lord, not however by applying coercion or the use of techniques unworthy of the Gospel but, above all, by the power of the God" (Vatican II, Decree *Dignitatis humanae* 11).

wanted to know what the position of the dead would be, for they thought that those who were still alive at the time of the Parousia would have some kind of privileged position. St Paul sets their minds at rest by assuring them that everyone — the dead and the living — will share in the Lord's triumphant cortege because "we who are alive, who are left until the coming of the Lord, shall not precede those who have fallen asleep" (4:15).

2 Thessalonians The Thessalonians were very happy with the first letter, but they began to ask themselves further questions, which left them uneasy. St Paul had not told them anything about when the Parousia would happen, and some of them, who were perhaps naturally nervous or impulsive types, were making out that the Parousia was in fact imminent. This sort of thinking made them disinterested in things around them.

This is the new theme of Paul's second letter, written some months later, a letter which is a logical extension of the first. A maritime city like Thessalonica, with a sizeable proportion of unemployed and idle people, was just the sort of place where gossip, intrigue and false rumours thrived. And naturally, among recent converts to Christianity, there were some people who felt disinclined to do a solid day's work — and more inclined to speculate about the future and discuss predictions than to take St Paul's teaching seriously and follow the example of his hardworking and orderly life.

In this letter, the Apostle, after encouraging them to remain steadfast in the faith, goes into more detail about "the day of the coming of the Lord".[2] He tells them that it is not around the corner, for first two main things must happen — the great rebellion and the advent of Antichrist. These have not happened yet, so why should they make the mistake of thinking that the Parousia is imminent? We do not know who or what this Antichrist is, or what power restrains him: St Paul reveals nothing about this. All he does is warn them not to be impressionable and not to be alarmed by mere rumours, because this could undermine their perseverance in the faith. "If any one will not work, let him not eat" (3:10), he tells them; they should follow the example he himself has given them. This shows that it is wrong to say St Paul thought that the Lord's coming, the end of the world, was imminent, and that he spread this false idea among

2 The "day of the coming of the Lord" — the Parousia — refers to Christ's second coming, when his triumph over death will be revealed and he will be glorified in his saints, raising the dead to life and presenting them to the Father. This day will bring to an end, forever, the earthly stage of the kingdom of God (cf. 1 Thess 4:14-17; 1 Cor 15:22-28).

the early Christians. What these letters do contain is an echo of Jesus' prophecy about the destruction of Jerusalem (Lk 17 and Mt 24) and of the persecutions the Church will experience until the end of time.

1 and 2 Corinthians

In St Paul's time, Corinth was the capital of the province of Achaia and the seat of the Roman proconsul. Julius Caesar built it (44 B.C.) on the ruins of a Greek city of the same name. It had two ports in the isthmus where it was sited — one in the Aegean Sea and one on the Gulf of Lepanto. Its excellent geographical position soon made it a prominent centre of commerce, with a much higher standard of living than its neighbours. But it was also a loose-living city, rendering religious cult to the goddess Venus, a serious threat for those — Jews or Christians — who worshipped the true God.

St Paul established a Christian community at Corinth during his second missionary journey (50-52). He preached the Gospel there for a year and a half, aided by Silas and Timothy. Due to his remarkable zeal, quite a number of people were converted to the true faith, some of them Jews. Very soon many Jews in the city became openly hostile to the Apostle's preaching, but since they had little social influence they failed to obstruct his work. This may explain why the proconsul Gallio refused to listen to the charges they brought against Paul (Acts 18:12ff).

After he left Corinth, the city had a series of apostolic visitors. Apollos, a brilliant preacher (Acts 18:24-26), arrived about a year after Paul left. He made many additional converts and confirmed the Corinthians in their faith. It is likely that around this time St Peter paid a short visit to Corinth. Up to that point, the Corinthian church was at peace and there was no sign of any doctrinal difficulties.

Almost two years later, some Christian Jews from Palestine arrived in the city, people who had previously been very apostolic but had now clearly gone off the rails of sound teaching. St Paul does not hesitate to call them "false apostles" (2 Cor 11:13), even though they boasted of being colleagues of the Twelve. They tried to undermine St Paul's work. They were over-tolerant of Christians fraternizing with pagans, failing to warn them of the risks involved. They became very influential, with the result that the Corinthians began to take things easy.

Paul heard about this soon afterwards (he was in Ephesus at the time; the year was 57). Three influential Corinthians brought him a letter in which they and others asked for guidance on matters they found problematic. They probably filled out the information given in the letter, asking him to go quickly to Corinth.

1 Corinthians St Paul preferred to postpone going to Corinth in order to give everyone more time for reflexion and repentance; this is why he wrote his first letter, shortly before Easter 57. It is not a doctrinal treatise like the Letter to the *Romans* : it is more like an acknowledgment of their letter, but availing of it to answer about the things which were worrying them. He begins by taking to task Christians who had been unfaithful, but does this with great tenderness and charity, presumably to win over people who were confused in their minds by the preaching of the false apostles.

From a doctrinal point of view the letter centres on these points:

1. The need to reject false human philosophy and pretentiousness, to embrace Christ's cross, the source of all wisdom. God chose to confound the wisdom of the world by choosing for servants humble people, poor and uneducated. Thanks to their humility they responded to grace and spread the Gospel far and wide, showing that God was working through them. "For the divine work which the Holy Spirit has raised them up to fulfil transcends all human energies and human wisdom."[3]

2. Their obligation to avoid every kind of greed; and an invitation to perfect continence — the excellence of virginity. He outlines the duties of married couples and of widows. It should be stressed that St Paul does not despise the body: he regards it as the temple of the Holy Spirit, which is why he stresses the importance of Christian purity. As Vatican II has put it: "It is not lawful for man to despise his bodily life. On the contrary, he must regard his body as good and honourable, since God has created it and will raise it up on the last day. However, wounded by sin, man feels rebellious stirrings in his body. Therefore, human dignity demands that man glorify God in his body and forbid it to serve the evil inclinations of his heart."[4]

Hence the excellence of virginity. Everyone must faithfully follow the calling he has received from God, but "perfect continence embraced on behalf of the kingdom of heaven has always been held in particular honour by the Church, as being a sign of charity and

3 Vatican II, Decr. *Presbyterorum ordinis* 15.

4 Vatican II, *Gaudium et spes* 14.

stimulus towards charity, and an exceptional source of spiritual fruitfulness in the world."[5]

3. Criteria about attendance at pagan rites (this is not permitted) and about eating food offered to idols.

4. Criteria about how agapes should be celebrated.

5. Confession of faith in the real presence of Jesus Christ in the Eucharist, which Christians should approach with a clear conscience, because it is the Body and the Blood of the Lord that they are receiving.

The Apostle speaks very explicitly about the real presence of Jesus in the Eucharist (1 Cor 11:26-29), reflecting the faith of the first Christians: the Eucharist is not a mere commemoration but the very sacrifice of Calvary, offered now in an unbloody manner through the priestly ministry. Priests, "acting in the person of Christ and proclaiming his ministry, unite the votive offerings of the faithful to the sacrifice of Christ their head, and in the sacrifice of the Mass they make present again and apply, until the coming of the Lord (cf. 1 Cor 11:26), the unique sacrifice of the New Testament, that namely of Christ offering himself once and for all a spotless victim to the Father (cf. Heb 9:11-28)".[6]

6. Mentioning various gifts, he recommends in chapter 13, as the most excellent of all, charity. Faith and hope, being theological virtues, have to do mainly with the Christian's life here and now, preparing him for his definitive meeting with God in heaven. But they disappear once a person sees and possesses God, whereas charity, the first among the virtues, lasts forever: in heaven it attains its perfection, in that uninterrupted embrace which unites the soul to God forever.

7. Finally, he reaffirms faith in the resurrection of the dead. Thus, for example, in chapter 15 St Paul deals with the last and most important subject of controversy at Corinth — the resurrection of the bodies of the dead, a basic article of Catholic faith. For "we believe that the souls of all those who die in the grace of Christ — whether they must still make expiation in the fire of purgatory, or whether from the moment they leave their bodies they are received by Jesus into paradise like the good thief — go to form that people of God which succeeds death, death which will be totally destroyed on the day of the resurrection when these souls are reunited with their bodies."[7]

5 Vatican II, *Lumen gentium* 42.

6 Vatican II, *Lumen gentium* 28.   7 Paul VI, Creed of the People of God, 6.

Paul's letter was well received at Corinth; it convinced many waverers and some of those who had rebelled against his authority; but a minority, allied to the Judaizers, remained unconvinced. Titus brought him a report on the reaction to his letter (Paul was probably in Philippi at the time). He was very pleased (2 Cor 7) to know that he could count on the fidelity of the Corinthians and he set about winning over the remaining objectors.

In the meantime, however, the false apostles had been intriguing, twisting what Paul had said in the first letter. They accused him of being all talk, irresponsible, and ambitious, pointing out that he had not made his promised visit to Corinth. There was every chance, therefore, that the church at Corinth would begin to stray again.

2 Corinthians To deal with this situation, as a preliminary to his visit, the Apostle wrote a second letter, very shortly after the first, probably towards the end of 57 or at the beginning of 58. In it he first apologizes for not being able to visit them, but he feels confident that he has behaved throughout as a minister of Christ.

The Corinthians must have been very disappointed to learn that Paul was postponing his visit and was heading for Macedonia (1 Cor 16:5-7). Now he tells them that in doing so he had not acted capriciously or like a "worldly man", suiting himself: he felt he did the best thing in the circumstances: his "yes" follows the example of Jesus, who is always straightforward (2 Cor 1:17-18). He calls on his own conscience to witness that he has never acted in a worldly way but always with holiness and godly sincerity (2 Cor 1:12). In fact he does not live his own life, does not follow his personal preference, for "while we live we are always being given up to death for Jesus' sake, so that the life of Jesus may be manifested in our mortal flesh" (2 Cor 4:11). Paul identifies himself with Christ, and suffers along with Christ over the rejection of his teachings by the recalcitrant members of the Corinthian church. Yet his suffering is nothing compared with what Christ had to suffer on our behalf; and his love for the people at Corinth is such that he leaves until the end of his letter the harsh words he has to speak in fidelity to the teaching of Christ.

St Paul did not want his own personality to obtrude. Self-praise is deeply repugnant to him, yet he has to praise himself in order to expose the false apostles. He vigorously defends the apostolic ministry God has given him; he simply cannot allow the truths of faith to be diluted, and therefore he gives a short summary of what Christian commitment entails, exhorting them "not to accept the grace of God in vain" (2 Cor 6:1) — that constant stream of graces which God gives everyone to enable him fulfil his obligations in the Church and in the world. Although the Apostle seems to be referring to those who are still rebellious, his teaching can apply to anyone who is lukewarm or apathetic.

Finally, St Paul justifies his attitude by showing what it means to be chosen by the Lord for the work of evangelization; but he speaks in all humility, because he recognizes that "we have this treasure in earthen vessels to show that the transcendent power belongs to God and not to us" (4:7).

Probably no other letter of St Paul gives us such insight into his personality. Warmhearted, extremely understanding and affectionate, he also has great courage and decisiveness. This explains his prudence and patience in biding his time when he is under personal attack, and his intervention with the full force of his apostolic authority when God's honour and the community's good are at stake. This, in fact, is the principle on which these two letters are based — the unity of the Church and the communion of saints (which always go together and which form the framework of Christian holiness).

Galatians

At the beginning of this third apostolic journey, around the year 53 (Acts 18:23), St Paul passed through Galatia to visit the Christian communities he had established in the area (Acts 13:14ff), which he had also visited during his second journey (Acts 16:1-5). The communities in question were in the southern part of Galatia — Pisidian Antioch, Iconium, Derbe and Lystra. The Galatians had responded very well to Paul's apostolate and the churches were flourishing.

However, on this last journey St Paul was very surprised to find that the Galatian Christians — most of whom came from a Gentile background — had been led astray by "false brethren", Judaizers, who made out that Christians should conform to the Mosaic law and, therefore, should be circumcised.

Perhaps because he was short of time, the Apostle was unable to go into the matter in detail; at any rate, when he reached Ephesus (53-54) he wrote the Galatians a letter refuting the errors involved, in which he goes into the whole question of the relationship between the Gospel and the Mosaic law, between the Old Covenant and the New. He tries to get them to see that the key point is this: accepting Mosaic doctrine would mean in practice renouncing the justification won for us by Christ — and therefore denying the value of the redemption; it would imply renouncing freedom, because they would be submitting to the yoke of the Law, which is slavery; it would mean rejecting the grace and salvation which faith in Jesus Christ brings with it. The universality of the Church would be destroyed and Christ's doctrine irreparably damaged.

The Judaizers, for their part, were arguing that God himself had instituted the law of Moses, which Christ had come not "to abolish but to fulfill" (Mt 5:17). They even went as far as to invoke the authority of the Twelve against Paul, ignoring (because they did not want to obey them) the decisions of the Council of Jerusalem which had gone into this whole question and with whose teaching St Paul was in line (Acts 15:28-29).

With characteristic energy and zeal, Paul defends his apostolic authority and denounces the error of the Judaizers, into which many of the Galatians had fallen. He ends by telling them in no uncertain terms: "if you receive circumcision, Christ will be of no advantage to you" (5:2).

However, the content of the letter — which is reminiscent of *Romans* — ranges much more widely than this. For example, it makes the following points:

1. While recognizing St Peter's pre-eminent position as visible head of the Church, the letter stresses that the Church is one and universal, a community entered into through Baptism, one in teaching and government, under the infallible and absolute authority of the Apostles (1:9; 2:9; etc.).

2. Transition from a state of sin or alienation from God to a state of grace happens only through faith in Christ, who by dying redeemed us from all sin — original sin and personal sin. Faith makes us truly children of God — who share in God's own life — and heirs of heaven, in keeping with God's promises.

3. This faith in Jesus Christ is the only faith by which we can be saved; through it we attain the grace of forgiveness and the true freedom proper to the children of God. Therefore, as the Apostle says, anyone who submits to the observances of the Mosaic law falls back into the slavery of the Law and denies the redemption wrought by Christ.

4. Christians, whether of Jewish or Gentile background, are the true children of Abraham, according to the spirit, because through faith in Christ they have been justified and incorporated — through Baptism — into his Church, the new people of God.

5. Jesus Christ, true God and true man, died on the cross as the representative of all mankind, to make satisfaction for all sin — not only sins against the Mosaic law but also those against the natural law.

6. Following in Christ's footsteps, Christians also must die to the old Law if they want to live for God (2:19): this is the death of the old man brought about through Baptism, which enables us to live a new life, the life of grace, so we can "walk by the Spirit" (5:24) and not under the Law (5:18).

7. Only in this way will Christians attain the true freedom of the sons of God — which requires that we mortify our vices and the concupiscence of the flesh to become "a new creation" (6:15) and reproduce in ourselves the life of Christ, of whom we are both a member and a temple.

8. This new life, the life of grace, makes Christians yield the fruit of the Spirit (5:22-23). The Law no longer has any power; what matters is faith in Jesus Christ, which works through love (5:6).

Romans

Written by St Paul from Corinth around the year 58, this is the most didactic of all his letters and the most doctrinally profound. It is also very beautifully written, from a stylistic point of view. It contains a summary (naturally, an incomplete one) of Christian teaching, starting with the Old Covenant and an outline of God's plans for man's salvation after the fall of our first parents.

The letter is explicitly addressed to the Christians at Rome, whom St Paul plans to visit on his way to Spain (15:25). He writes to preach the Gospel of God (1:1), for that is the mission to which God has called him; in particular he writes to the Christians at Rome "whose faith is proclaimed in all the world"; most of them are Gentile converts and they are being told by Jews resident in Rome that salvation comes through the law of Moses, whereas they had been taught that it was based on faith in Jesus Christ, and that it was not necesary to keep the Mosaic law. St Paul feels that they need a more theological induction into that Christian teaching which they have already accepted and this he now gives them, at the same time announcing his forthcoming visit.

There are two parts to the letter — a dogmatic part, centering on the question of justification (1:18-11:34), and a moral part, which spells out the duties and obligations of Christians (12-15).

On the matter of justification (that is, salvation) St Paul starts with the fact that all men, and not just Gentiles, are sinners (3:23) and as such are deprived of God's grace. Pagans were abandoned by God because of their idolatry, which led them into ever more serious sin, exchanging natural sexual relations for unnatural ones. They reached this sorry state because they drowned the voice of their own conscience, foolishly refusing to listen to the law God had engraved on their hearts (1:18-32). They were unable to make their way from experience of created things to the maker and creator of those things. The Jews, for their part, also cut themselves off from God (2:17ff) in spite of the gifts and privileges they received: they had the law of Moses, which prepared the ground for the coming of the Saviour; this law told them God's will, and they expounded this law to others; however, most of the Jews, even though they knew the law, did not practise it — and far from freeing them from God's judgment this made them even more blameworthy in the sight of their own conscience.[8]

To escape from this situation and attain salvation, the only route, for Gentiles as for Jews, is, St Paul states, faith in Jesus Christ: our Lord by his passion and death has made expiation for us (5:25) so that through faith in him (4:5) all of us can be justified. St Paul uses the example of Abraham to illustrate his teaching. Abraham was justified by faith, not by works (circumcision did not yet exist) and "in hope he believed against hope" (4:18). He believed in God's promise that he would be the father of many nations. God did not grant him this inheritance as a reward for fidelity to the articles of

---

8 In Rom 1:26-33 St Paul lists a series of vices which follow on logically from people refusing to give God glory by recognizing him as the beginning and end of all things. "What revelation shows us agrees with experience. Examining his heart, man finds that he too is inclined towards evil and is immersed in a whole series of ills which cannot come from his God Creator. By often refusing to recognize God as his beginning, man has disrupted also his proper relationship to his own ultimate goal and at the same time has become out of harmony with himself, with others, and with all created things" (Vatican II, *Gaudium et spes* 13).

214 THE LETTERS OF ST PAUL

a contract (the Law), but in view of the faith with which he accepted that God's promise would come true. St Paul wants to emphasize that the Old Law was orientated towards a higher and more perfect law, which Jesus Christ, the Messiah, would inaugurate through his redeeming death.

In this letter the concepts of *justice* and *justification* refer to the cancellation of a previous state of injustice or sin. The justification which Jesus Christ merits for us is the same thing as forgiveness of sins: all the sins of mankind are totally forgiven; it is not just as if God turned a blind eye to them. This is what is called *objective redemption* (5:15), meaning that Jesus has overcome sin (6:6). Along with this should come *subjective or personal redemption* whereby Jesus' merits are applied to the individual to free him from the stain of original sin and regain his lost friendship with God. Justification is attained through faith and baptism (intimately linked to one another), which allows us to die to the 'old man' and be reborn to a new life in Jesus Christ. This is what Baptism is about: the Christian is immersed in water and there the "old man" is buried along with all his sins so he can die with Christ. United with Christ, we are reborn to a new life, the life of Grace, which makes us true sons of God. Thus, "by Baptism, men are plunged into the paschal mystery of Christ: they die with him, are buried with him, and rise with him; they receive the spirit of adoption as sons, 'by virtue of which we cry: Abba, Father'" (Rom 8:15).[9]

This new life of grace is what makes us truly to be God's children and allows us to share in the intimacy of the three divine Persons (8:11). We do not just seem to be, we in fact are his children, for "it is the Spirit himself bearing witness with our spirit that we are children of God, and if children, then heirs, heirs of God and fellow heirs with Christ, provided we suffer with him in order that we may also be glorifed with him" (8:16-17).

This fact of being sons of God means that we should seek to Christianize our whole life. In this letter, the Christian life is expressed in mainly two ideas — holiness (sanctity) and sanctification, which parallel, on the level of personal application, the concepts of justice and justification.[10] Holiness means striving to identify oneself with Jesus Christ and to direct towards God everything which previously

9 Vatican II, *Sacrosanctum Concilium* 6.

10 "Justification", the Council of Trent teaches, "is not only forgiveness of sins but also sanctification and renewal of the inner man by free acceptance of grace and gifts, which changes man from unjust to just, from enemy to friend, making him heir to eternal life" (Dz. 799).

had been under the law of sin and therefore had become profane, cut off from God (6:19, 22; 15:16).

The sin of our first parents (Gen 3:17) also affects the whole of creation. Creation is in disarray and it can be put in order again to the extent that every man is converted and directs everything he does to God's glory. As St Paul put it, "the whole creation has been groaning in travail together until now" (Rom 8:22) but it will be set "free from its bondage of decay" (v. 21) by those who are and behave as sons of God.

The Apostle also reveals that the Jewish people will be converted (11:25-26). When this will happen is a mystery of faith and of hope, for God keeps his promises and his rejection of Israel was neither absolute nor permanent. But we do know that first the Gospel must be preached to the whole world, "until the full number of the Gentiles come in [to the Church] and so all Israel will be saved."

In the second part of the letter, St Paul draws out the consequences of these principles. The Christian, a citizen of the world, should be known for the virtues of humility and simplicity as befits someone who realizes that everything he has he has received from God (12:3). Also, he should give an example of charity towards everyone, without any trace of hypocrisy, being understanding and forgiving, never vengeful; he should readily obey lawful authority, because that is God's will (13:1); he should avoid passing judgment on his neighbour, unless he has a special obligation to do so (14:10); rather, he should put up with the failings of the weak (15:1), thereby imitating Christ. St Paul ends the letter by recommending to the Christians of Rome (and indirectly to us) "to live in such harmony with one another, in accord with Christ Jesus, that together you may with one voice glorify the God and Father of our Lord Jesus Christ" (15:6).

THE CAPTIVITY LETTERS

Under this heading are included the four letters written by St Paul during his first imprisonment in Rome (61-63 A.D.) to the churches of Ephesus, Colossae (Asia Minor) and Philippi (Macedonia) and the letter to Philemon (a Christian at Colossae).

The letters show considerable homogeneity. Most non-Catholic critics argue against Pauline authorship (especially for *Ephesians* and

Colossians), whereas almost all Catholic scholars support it. The earliest Christian tradition says that they were written by Paul and this is supported by internal evidence. The text also supports Rome as the place of composition: cf. the references to the spread of the Gospel among the praetorian guard and even in Caesar's household (Phil 1:13; 4:22); St Paul's hope and even certainty about being set free soon (Phil 1:25; 2:23; Philem 22); also, the relative freedom enjoyed by the Apostle at the time suggests that he was in Rome, a prisoner for Christ as the end of *Colossians* shows (4:18).

As far as the teaching contained in these letters is concerned, it all concerns the problems which have arisen in these young churches. Over-emphasis on Mosaic practices linked with the special importance of angels, and the need for a certain basic pastoral organizational structure, lead St Paul to centre his argumentation on Jesus Christ, the one and only mediator, to whom even the angels are subject; within his Christology he develops his teaching on the Church. The Church is Christ's mystical body. Christ, the Head of this body, gives it life; it is he who makes all the faithful living members of this body. Through incorporation into this body we appropriate the grace of redemption. Whatever form pastoral organization takes, it must be compatible with this theology of the Church.

Ephesians

Towards the end of his second apostolic journey (in the year 52) St Paul stayed for a while in Ephesus (Acts 18:19ff), one of the great cities of Asia Minor, where he preached and founded the church to which this letter is addressed. Shortly after this, a distinguished personality, Apollos, appeared in Ephesus; he received instruction from Aquila and his wife Priscilla, two disciples of Paul (cf. Acts 18:24-26) and he, in his turn, prepared the ground for Paul's preaching (54-56). Paul's visit was not without incident (cf. Acts 19-20): he was forced to leave the city because of an uproar caused by Demetrius the silversmith.

Paul did not forget the Ephesians, however, and, from Rome, he wrote them this letter. Some scholars think that this was really a circular letter, addressed to all the churches — on the grounds that there are no personal references in it, nor does it have the opening greeting and the sign-off which are so characteristic of the Apostle's letters. Without the heading (which is not included in some codexes), this theory makes sense. However, the more common opinion, among ancient and modern scholars alike, is that the letter was addressed in the first instance to the Ephesians — not just because of the title it bears but because this is confirmed by St Irenaeus, the Muratori fragment, Clement of Alexandria, Tertullian and others.

St Paul's main purpose in writing seems to be to explore the great mystery of the redemption, of which Christ himself is the cornerstone (2:20), the foundation of the entire spiritual building into whom all Christians should be built. The letter therefore divides into two main parts:

a) *Dogmatic section* (1:2-3:21): here St Paul shows that the benefits of the redemption are available to everyone: everyone is predestined from before the creation of the world to become sons of God; both Jews and Gentiles are called, without distinction, to be one in Christ Jesus, to make up one body, the new people of God, the Church. This union of all in Christ is the express will of God the Father; it is merited through the redemption wrought by the Son and brought to fulfilment in people's souls through the action of the Holy Spirit. To proclaim this mystery to the Gentiles God chose Paul. A direct implication of this teaching is that Christians should have an open, universal, ecumenical outlook. "If the Church is to be in a position to offer all men the mystery of salvation and the life brought by God, then it must implant itself among all these groups [people who do not know the Gospel message] in the same way as Christ by his incarnation committed himself to the particular social and cultural circumstances of the men among whom he lived."[11]

b) *Ethical section* (4:1-6:9): in the second part of the letter the Apostle exhorts all Christians to live one and the same faith, to be consistent with their faith; that is, he encourages them to practise solidarity, to seek always what unites and avoid anything which gets in the way of the peace and love which should flow from this solidarity, this unity, which is one of the characteristics of the true Church. He specifically reminds them of duties involved in marriage and family life — teaching which still applies today: referring to Christian married couples Vatican II says that "in virtue of the sacrament of Matrimony by which they signify and share (cf. Eph 5:32) the mystery of the unity and faithful love between Christ and his Church, they help

11 Vatican II, Decree *Ad gentes* 10.

one another to attain holiness in their married life and in the rearing of their children. Hence by reason of their state in life and of their position they have their)wn gifts in the people of God."[12]

Philippians

In Philippi, a city north of the Aegean Sea called after Philip of Macedon, the father of Alexander the Great (360 B.C.), St Paul founded the first Christian church in Europe around the year 51, during his second apostolic journey. He lived in Philippi for some years and had special affection for the Philippians, which they reciprocated. He suffered imprisonment and the lash on their account, as St Luke records in Acts 16:11-40, and the Philippians for their part sent Epaphroditus to Rome to look after Paul when he was imprisoned there for the Lord. The Apostle, typically, was very appreciative of this affection. However, Epaphroditus, who was a great help at first, soon became seriously ill, and once he was on the way to recovery St Paul decided to send him back home.

When he left, Epaphroditus carried with him a letter from Paul to the Philippians, a letter written during his imprisonment in 61-63. This letter is not didactic or apologetic in purpose: Paul simply expresses his gratitude to the Father of all consolation and to the Philippians for the kindness and attention they showed him and for never being a source of worry to him but rather of consolation.

The letter, which overflows with joy, is an intimate conversation of a father and his children. Full of tenderness, it encourages and exhorts the Philippians to be ever better athletes of Christ until they reach their final goal — holiness.

St Paul uses a simile taken from the games, which enjoyed great popularity during this period. He compares the virtues a Christian has to live, with athletic competitions: just as an athlete does not look behind but has his eyes always on the goal, so a Christian should forget himself, his past life, and trust in God's grace: but, like a good athlete, he should never feel satisfied until he has reached his goal.

In the course of this very familial letter, St Paul writes one of the most profound passages on Christology, when he proposes Christ as the model of humility and self-denial:

12 Vatican II, Dogm Const. *Lumen gentium* 11.

though he was in the form of God, [he] did not count equality with God as a thing to be grasped, but emptied himself, taking the form of a servant, being born in the likeness of men. And being found in human form he humbled himself and became obedient unto death, even death on a cross (Phil 2:6-8).

According to the general opinion of the Fathers, the expression "the form of God" means that Jesus is by nature divine; he is true God, the living image of the Father (Col 1:15; Heb 1:3), consubstantial and co-eternal with him. Despite this he, as it were, emptied himself and took on human nature, becoming like us in all things but sin.

Colossians

From the relative freedom he enjoyed during his Roman imprisonment, St Paul wrote this letter to the Colossians some time in 61-63. Colossae was a city in Phrygia, about 200 kilometres (125 miles) from Ephesus, very close to Laodicea. Although this church, composed of Christians mostly of Gentile background, was not founded by St Paul himself — it was founded by a disciple of his, Epaphras (1:7) — Paul was well informed about how it was faring.

In fact, a visit by Epaphras to Rome was what occasioned the letter, because he reported to the Apostle about erroneous doctrines which had recently made their way into the church at Colossae, threatening both faith and morals. False teachers were introducing a series of outdated Mosaic practices — such as observance of the law of the sabbath, identification of certain foods as unclean, and an exaggerated emphasis on the role of angels as intermediaries between God and men, which threatened to undermine the true doctrine of Christ as the only mediator. Christians hold that Christ's mediation, his redemption, is something infinite: no one's personal suffering can add anything to it. However, any Christian, since he is a member of Christ's mystical body, can unite himself to our Lord's sufferings which are on-going in the Church: "you suffer as needs be to contribute through your suffering to the sufferings of Christ, who has suffered in our head and who suffers in his members, that is, in yourselves" (St Augustine).

St Paul uses the occasion to instruct the Colossians and to restate for them the truth about the absolute supremacy of Jesus Christ, as beginning and end of all creation. He is the true creator, conserver and redeemer, for he is the Son of God. That is to say:

> He is the image of the invisible God, the first-born of all creation; for in him all things were created, in heaven and on earth, visible and invisible, whether thrones or dominions or principalities or authorities — all things were created through him and in him all things hold together. He is the head of the body, the Church; he is the beginning, the first-born from the dead, that in everything he ought to be pre-eminent (Col 1:15-18).

This text speaks of the activity of the Son prior to his appearance on earth. Paul particularly stresses the pre-existence of the Word, thanks to which all things were created by him; and this pre-existence is based on the fact that he is God, co-eternal with the Father. The "beloved Son" of Col 1:13 is now described as "the first-born of all creation" — an expression which, given the context, must be taken in a comparative sense: that is, he is *before* all creation or, which is the same thing, he exists from all eternity.

It is very far from Paul's thinking, therefore, to present the Son of God as the first among creatures — an error into which Arius fell through misinterpreting this text. St Paul, on the contrary, describes Jesus Christ as the Creator in the widest and fullest sense of that word, which is proper to God alone. Thus, he calls him "the image of the invisible God", to underline his complete identity of nature with God, concluding that "in him the whole fullness of deity dwells bodily" (Col 2:9); divinity and humanity are united in Jesus Christ in his own person, which is divine, in the same kind of way as the soul is the form of the body and with the body constitutes one single principle of operation. Through his sacrifice on the Cross, Jesus has become the universal mediator reconciling all men to God. Thereby he becomes the supreme Head of the Church, which is rightly called the Body of Christ. From effective union with the Head the Christian receives the new life which should imbue all his actions; this requires us, since we have a share in the life of the risen Christ, to die to the old man, that is, to reject worldly living, which is something for people who do not know Christ. Therefore, the Colossians should not focus on matters of food or on things merely external to man, but on the very heart of man's personality: thereby they will learn the way to upright living. Hence the programme which God inspires St Paul to outline:

> Now put them all away: anger, wrath, malice, slander, and foul talk from your mouth. Put on, then, as God's chosen ones, holy and beloved,

compassion, kindness, lowliness, meekness and patience, forbearing one
another [...], forgiving each other (Col 3:8-13)

The Apostle describes the way they should practise charity in their
dealings with others: their conversation — the test of true fraternity
— should be seasoned with salt, that is, with prudence and refinement,
which will advise them what to say to each person at any particular
time (cf. Col 4:6).

Philemon

Philemon was a wealthy Colossian; a personal friend of Paul, who
converted him to the faith. He had a slave called Onesimus, who
stole from him and then ran away to escape punishment. Later he
in turn met Paul and became a Christian.

After Onesimus had been in Rome a short time, Paul asked him
to go back to Colossae, to his master, bringing with him a letter from
the Apostle. This short letter is a fine example of the art of letter-
writing, full of sensitivity and refined charity. St Paul makes no
demands in it; he simply makes a humble appeal to Philemon.

The letter, which has been decribed as the *magna carta* of Christian
freedom, touches on a subject of special importance in ancient times
— that of slavery.

St Paul does not directly denounce slavery — then the basic structure
of labour relations — but he does establish the groundwork for its
abolition. By stressing the dignity of the human person, he shows
that slaves' real master is Christ, even if they render service to Christ
through obedience to their masters: as he puts it elsewhere, they
should act not as "men-pleasers, but as servants of Christ, doing the
will of God from the heart" (Eph 6:6). This is a direct consequence
of the freedom which Christ won for us, which makes us his sons
and therefore brothers of those who share our faith — on a level of
equality with other Christians, without any distinction of race or
colour or class or condition. Centuries later, when this teaching
imbued the civil law, slavery would become a thing of the past.

PASTORAL LETTERS

1 and 2 Timothy and Titus

St Paul's two letters to Timothy and his letter to Titus have been described from earliest times as "pastoral letters' because they are written to pastors of the churches of Ephesus and Crete respectively. They contain a series of rules and recommendations for the good government of those young communities, whose members mostly were of Gentile background.

Around the year 66, St Paul wrote from Macedonia his first letter to Timothy and the letter to Titus. Worried about the damage being done by false teachers, he wanted to do what he could to help these two pastors carry out their serious responsibility.

Sometime later, during his imprisonment in Rome, he wrote the second letter to Timothy. He senses that his end is approaching and feels the need for Timothy's help. It is not, therefore, his first imprisonment (61-63), from which he obtained release and probably was able to make his planned journey to Spain (cf. Rom 15:24-28), going on later to the East — which would have been in 65. His second captivity would have been shortly before his martyrdom in the year 67. This letter, therefore, is his last and can be regarded as his spiritual testament.

Some critics have questioned the Pauline authorship of these pastoral letters (an attribution confirmed by tradition and by the Magisterium of the Church) on the grounds of their literary style and doctrinal content, arguing also that the Church's organization evidenced in the letters is much more advanced than that to be seen in other letters of the Apostle. They also point out that the frequent references to "sound doctrine" (1 Tim 1:10; 2 Tim 1:13) or the advice he gives about guarding "the truth that has been entrusted to you" (1 Tim 6:20; 2 Tim 1:14) do not seem to fit in with Paul's style.

These objections disappear if one bears in mind that the differences of style — the style is simpler and less rich than that of other letters — fit in with St Paul's being already an old man, as can be deduced from internal textual evidence. The new teaching which these critics see in the letters — the Apostle puts special emphasis on good works — can also be explained by the practical or pastoral character these letters have. If he makes much of the need for "sound doctrine" and for guarding the deposit of faith, it is because he realizes that his end is near and he wants to put Timothy and Titus on their guard against erroneous and very dangerous new doctrines which threaten to make "shipwreck of their faith" (1 Tim 1:19). There is no sign here of Gnostic teachings which would appear much later on, in the second century. It is, rather, a matter of "a morbid craving for controversy and for disputes about words" (1 Tim 6:4), favoured by certain Judaizing Christians, the result of influences emanating from hellenized Judaism and syncretism, which Paul had to deal with years before, as he says himself in his letter to the Colossians.

The teaching he gives in these letters is rich and abundant, though he does focus particularly on practical or pastoral aspects. He was evidently very concerned about matters internal to those young communities. One of the basic points that needs attention is precisely the way the hierarchy should be organized. Far from implying — as some suggest — that church structures have reached an advanced stage (which would be the case in a later period) these letters reflect an organization-structure which is only incipient, in which, for example, the designation "bishops" and "elder" are not yet defined and even sometimes seem to mean the same thing (Tit 1:5-7) — as was the case years earlier (cf. Acts 20:17-18). But the fact that the descriptions are not distinguished does not imply that there was confusion about the role of or about the levels in the hierarchy, for both Timothy and Titus were in fact bishops and acted as bishops: it is they who ordain the elders or presbyters (1 Tim 5:19-22; Tit 1:5-7). What initially had to do with the specific mission of the Apostles was little by little being passed over to those they chose to be their successors. This was done by means of episcopal ordination and consecration. For example, St Paul will say to Timothy: "what you have heard from me before many witnesses entrust to faithful men" (2 Tim 2:2). The mission which Timothy received — on the day of his episcopal ordination — was one of passing on everything to do with the deposit of faith, which was the charge St Paul himself received from the Lord. This passage indicates the critical importance of the role oral tradition played in the instruction of the faithful.

The letters to Timothy and Titus reflect precisely the period of transition when the Apostles' authority — the episcopacy established by our Lord — was being passed on to immediate successors of the Apostles. Very soon after this — in the second century — the term "bishop" would become the established way to describe one who held the fulness of the priesthood — governing the college of presbyters and the other members of the faithful in a particular community, thus clearly differentiating the three levels in the hierarchy, bishops, priests and deacons.

224 THE LETTERS OF ST PAUL

These three letters also bring out the central points of Christian dogma — faith and hope in Christ, the mediator between God and man; the redemption and God's desire that all men be saved; the Church as God's household and the pillar and ground of truth: one, holy, universal, that is to say, catholic in the sense that everyone is called to belong to it, irrespective of race, language or nation. The consequence of this is that while it is on earth the Church is composed of all kinds of people — unfaithful as well as faithful. In this one piece of material (Rom 9:21), some are saints or at least on the way to becoming saints, and others are not, because their infidelity prevents grace from acting in their souls: St Paul in this way says it is wrong to think that the Church has room only for saints and sinless people; no one should be scandalized when he sees evidence of Christians' human shortcomings.

Hence the need to pray for everyone, living and dead; hence, also, the necessary part played by good example if any effective apostolate is to be done, and the dangers inherent in the active life if interior life and the pursuit of virtue are neglected. Everything St Paul recommends echoes what our Lord taught his disciples and what the Magisterium of the Church also teaches today.

HEBREWS

The *Letter to the Hebrews* appears in the New Testament after the thirteen Pauline letters and before the seven catholic letters. Early tradition, in the main, attributed this text to St Paul, but the western Church did not accept its Pauline authorship until the fourth century; and even in the east some (including Clement of Alexandria and Origen) had reservations about whether its literary style coincided with Paul's. Internal examination of the text does show that it is in many ways different from the rest of St Paul's writings. For example, it is more elegant, more eloquent, it does not carry the usual greeting and introduction, and it does not quote Scripture in the way Paul does. Its doctrine is Pauline but the way it is expounded makes it difficult to attribute its direct authorship to Paul.

The letter's canonicity is not in doubt; it was included in the canon by the Council of Trent (8 April 1546) among the other writings of St Paul, although the Council chose not to state categorically that it was written by Paul. The Pontifical Biblical Communion in a decree issued on 24 April 1914, reaffirmed its canonicity. It answered the question: "Has the Apostle Paul to be regarded as the author of this letter in the sense that not only must one hold that he conceived it and expressed it under the inspiration of the Holy Spirit, but that he gave it the form in which it has come down to us?" Its reply was: "No, not unless the Church decides so in the future".[13] This is probably why there is no direct reference to St Paul as author of this letter in recent liturgical books. However, St Paul can be regarded as the indirect author of *Hebrews*. Researchers are free to explore this matter. Some scholars think it may have been written by Barnabas or Silas, disciples of St Paul; others suggest Apollos, an Alexandrian Jew noted for his eloquence (cf. Acts 18 24:28), in view of the way it quotes the Old Testament and its beautiful style and language. In any event, this is a secondary question which has nothing to do with matters of faith.

Date and purpose   We have no definite information about where and when *Hebrews* was written, or to whom it was addressed. Probably the author wrote it in Italy (cf. "Those who come from Italy send you greetings" — 13:24), although this could mean it was written in a place where Christians from Italy were living.

The date of composition can be deduced with a certain degree of probability from the reference it contains to the temple of Jerusalem and the worship offered there — implying that the temple is operational. Since it warns Christians against the temptation of returning to the ancient Levitical form of worship, it would seem to have been written before 70, the year the Temple was razed. On the other hand, the letter is aware of Paul's captivity letters, which it uses. Therefore, *Hebrews* must be later than the year 63, and very probably was written towards 67 in view of its urgent call for perfect faith, "all the more as you see the Day drawing near" (10:25).

It was obviously written to people whom the author knew to be steeped in the Old Testament, people who were in all probability converts from Judaism, and who may previously have even been priests or Levites. After becoming Christians, because of the difficult circumstances of the time, they had to abandon Jerusalem, the holy city, to seek refuge in some coastal city, possibly Caesarea or Antioch. In their exile they look back with nostalgia on the splendour of the cult they played a part in prior to their conversion. They feel deceived and are tempted to give up their new faith, in which they are not

13 EB 418; Dz 2178.

yet well grounded. In addition to this they are discontented by the persecution they suffer because of their faith. Obviously, they are in need of help and in particular of clear doctrine to bolster their faith and enable them to cope with temptation to infidelity.

Content The basic teaching of *Hebrews* centres on showing the superiority of the Christian religion over Judaism. The argument develops in three stages:

1. Jesus Christ, the incarnate Son of God, the King of the universe, "reflects the glory of God and bears the very stamp of his nature" (1:3) and is superior to the angels (1:4-2).

2. Christ is also superior to Moses, "as the builder of a house has more honour than the house" (3:3).

3. Moreover, Jesus, the Son of God, is the great high priest who has passed through the heavens (4:14); his priesthood is of the order of Melchizedek, superior to the priesthood of Aaron, from which the Levitical priesthood derived.

These Christological principles lead on to conclusions to do with the redemption, which stem from the Word's taking on our human nature in order to save it.[14] These conclusions are, in summary:

1. With Christ, and through the redemption he has brought, we are released from the slavery to the devil which sin and death imply.

2. What makes Christ's death meritorious is his obedience (5:8; 10:9); through it those who were under the yoke of sin are redeemed (9:12 and 15).

3. In other letters the emphasis was laid mainly on the power of Christ's resurrection as the source of his glorification; here the stress is put on his entry into the heavenly sanctuary (9:11-12), where he is seated at the right hand of God the Father. Christ's sacrifice — which is a once-for-all sacrifice — is distinguished from the sacrifices offered by the priests of the Old Law, for which they entered the earthly sanctuary once every year.

4. Hence, when man approaches Christ in a spirit of faith, he is in fact approaching the mediator of the new Covenant. Through union with Christ the individual attains salvation or sanctification: he acquires grace which he should preserve, for it is the principle of

14 "The Fathers of the Church constantly proclaim that what was not assumed by Christ was not healed. Now Christ took a complete human nature just as it is found in us poor unfortunates, but one that was without sin" (Vatican II, Decree *Ad gentes* 3).

life, the cause of the soul's salvation and the ultimate goal of human existence.

Towards the end of the letter, the sacred author asks: How does man attain this principle of life? A person can become a friend of God, with the help of grace, only by the act of faith, for "without faith it is impossible to please him. For whoever would draw near to God must believe that he exists and that he rewards those who seek him" (11:6). The Council of Trent in fact quotes this verse when it defines that 'faith is the beginning of man's salvation, it is the foundation and the root of all justification"

But theological faith is closely linked to hope. The letter says that 'faith is the assurance of things hoped for, the conviction of things not seen' (11:1).

This text does not so much give a theological or essential definition of faith as a descriptive definition, which stresses one of the main effects of faith in the soul of the believer — the assurance, the guarantee, that one will attain what one hopes for. It does not explicitly say what the material object of faith is (the truths revealed by God) or the formal motive of the act of faith (the authority of God revealing). The First Vatican Council defined the act of faith as "a supernatural virtue by which, with the inspiration and help of God's grace, we believe that what he has revealed is true — not because its intrinsic truth is seen by the natural light of reason, but because of the authority of God who reveals it, of God who can neither deceive nor be deceived."[15]

Final salvation, to which faith leads us, can only happen after death, when man sees God face to face, to the degree his charity allows — in other words, to the extent that he has put his faith into practice. This is indicated in chapter 11, which gives an impressive account of the saints of the Old Testament, who were men of heroic faith, confident of the day when the divine promises would be fulfilled. Through the suffering, difficulties and obstacles they experienced in this life — and which they accepted with unshakeable faith — they eventually attained the reward which God had promised them.

---

15 Vatican I, Dogm. Const. *De fide catholica* (Dz 1789).

The Catholic Letters

After the thirteen letters of St Paul and the letter to the *Hebrews* come seven other letters (one by St James, two by St Peter, three by St John and one by St Jude) which since the time of Origen, Eusebius and St Jerome have been known as the 'catholic' letters, letters to the Church at large, not directed to a particular church or individual: the second and third letters of St John, even though they are addressed to a private individual are regarded as appendixes to his first letter and are also included in the 'catholic letters' category.

St James

This letter, which was accepted as canonical from the second century onwards, is attributed to St James, the son of Clophas and of Mary, the Blessed Virgin's sister or cousin. To distinguish him from the other St James, the son of Zebedee (cf. Mt 10:2-4), this James is called "the less" and, also, "the brother (= cousin) of the Lord" (Mt 13:55) From the *Acts* we know that he enjoyed great authority in the church of Jerusalem (Acts 15:13-19). St Paul describes him as one of the pillars of the Church (Gal 2:9) and gives him a prominent place among those to whom our Lord appeared after his resurrection.

St James the Apostle was, then, bishop of Jerusalem until his death in the year 62. He wrote his letter around the year 60. In it he shows himself to be steeped in the Old Testament and in the teachings of Jesus deriving from the Sermon on the Mount; and he passes these on in a document of high literary quality. As he himself says, he is writing to "the twelve tribes of the Dispersion" (1:1), that is, to Christians of Jewish origin scattered throughout the Greco-Roman world. He seeks to encourage them to bear persecution bravely and to practise the Christian virtues, especially patience in the face of trial (1:1-12) and control of the tongue (1:26; 3:1-18); for, as we well know, prudence in speech prevents many sins, whereas uncontrolled talk can lead to further lack of self-control and even to speaking badly about one's neighbour behind his back, thereby committing sins against charity and even against justice.

St James also gives great importance to care for the poor and humble, advising Christians not to give preference to people who are well-to-do or have a high social position — the reason being that Jesus Christ was no respecter of persons, and Christians should imitate him. Our Lord loves both poor and rich, educated and uneducated: he gave up his life for everyone. We should not grade people according to their position, much less according to external appearances (Jas 2:1ff), for a person's quality is something that derives from his union with God: the more humble and understanding he is, the more honour he deserves.

The apostle energetically criticizes the rich (5:1ff), that is, ambitious and greedy people, who not only do not use their wealth properly but defraud labourers of their wages. They make wealth their main objective; they show no pity to their poor neighbour and do not even give him what justice demands. People like this seem to be very fortunate and privileged, but in God's eyes and in their own conscience they are the ones to be pitied. St James' denunciation in 5:1ff is very direct and hard-hitting.

All this ties in with the central message of the letter: "faith, by itself, if it has no works, is dead" (2:17), for "a man is justified by works and not by faith alone" (2:24). Ever since the time of Luther, who discredited this letter because it did not fit in with his doctrine of faith without works, many people have tried to make out that it is at odds with St Paul's teaching "that a man is not justified by works of the law but through faith" (Gal 2:16; Rom 3:20). But the contradiction is only apparent, because from the context it is clear that St James (who knew *Galatians*) is talking about the "good works" which Jesus recommended in the Sermon on the Mount, for "not every one who says to me, 'Lord, Lord', shall enter the kingdom of heaven, but he who does the will of my Father" (Mt 7:21). St Paul, on the contrary, is referring to the Old Covenant, which he regarded as superseded, and he is taking issue with these Judaizers who made out that Christians had to keep the observances of the Mosaic law if they were to attain salvation.

St Paul and St James, then, are at one. Paul shows this when he speaks of "faith working through love" (Gal 5:6); and in *Romans* he is even more specific when he says that God "will render to every man according to his works" (Rom 2:6). Faith it is that brings us to know God and love him. Therefore, knowledge of the truth should never be a cerebral thing: it should be something practical, something that helps us love God and our neighbour as ourselves: which implies a daily effort to do God's will and keep his commandments.

Finally, the letter contains a very interesting passage about the sacrament of the anointing of the sick (5:14-15), as indicated by the Council of Trent.[1] St James here promulgates a sacrament instituted by Jesus. As Vatican II puts it: "By the sacred anointing of the sick and the prayer of priests the whole Church commends those who are ill to the suffering and glorified Lord that he may raise them up and save them. And indeed she exhorts them to contribute to the good of the people of God by freely uniting themselves to the passion and death of Christ."[2] Thus, as a result of anointing and prayer the sick person will be saved — and will be healed, if that is God's will; and any sins he has committed will be forgiven.

1 and 2 St Peter

The canon of Scripture contains two letters attributed to St Peter. The first he wrote from Babylon (= Rome) (5:13), very probably around 63-64, given that it contains no references to the persecution unleashed by Nero after July 64. The letter is addressed to the Christians of Asia Minor (Pontius, Galatia, Cappadocia, Bythnia) (1:1) — Gentiles evangelized mainly by St Paul. It is written in correct, even elegant, Greek — the Greek of Silvanus (5:12), who is the same person as the Silas who was St Paul's companion (Acts 15:22).

In this exhortatory letter, St Peter seeks to console and strengthen the faith of Christians who are experiencing difficult times; this is quite in keeping with his role as head of the Church. This message, a very practical one, is a faithful reflexion of the catechesis of apostolic times. Rich in content, it is written in a simple style, full of energy and supernatural warmth, as one would expect of preaching during those early days. The teaching in the letter may be summarized as follows:

1. St Peter calls for a *more holy Christian life*, as befits "obedient children" (1:14), who have been ransomed with the precious blood of Christ (1:16). This is what God, who is the "holy" one (1:16),

1   Cf. Council of Trent, canons on extreme unction (1-4), (Dz 926-9).
2   Vatican II, Dogm. Const. *Lumen gentium* 11.

expects of them; and he will judge them according to the degree of holiness they have attained.

2. This holiness is tested by the quality of that *brotherly love* which people born to the life of grace should have. They should be constantly growing in this love, realizing that they are "living stones" (2:5), built on Christ, who is the cornerstone, becoming a spiritual temple and a holy priesthood (2:6 and 9). This union with Jesus Christ "gives them a share in his priestly office, to offer spiritual worship for the glory of the Father and the salvation of man. Hence, the laity, dedicated as they are to Christ and anointed by the Holy Spirit, are marvellously called and prepared so that even richer fruits of the Spirit may be produced in them."[3]

3. Only by living in this way can they persevere in the midst of tribulations, taking Christ as their model who, though he was just, died for the unjust. "If you are reproached for the name of Christ, you are blessed" (4:14) on account of your upright conduct and exemplary union with the Lord. Trials will have the effect of showing forth their patience: instead of being irritated by the evil done them they should return good for evil and show understanding and sweetness to their persecutors. They should be the first to obey those in positions of lawful authority, thereby "by doing right, putting to silence the ignorance of foolish men" (2:13-15). They should be good citizens "for the Lord's sake" — for, by obeying their governors they are indirectly obeying God, who is the source of all authority — provided of course that the orders they are given do not conflict with God's law (cf. Rom 13:1-7).

The second letter is also written by Simon Peter (1:1), the witness of our Lord's transfiguration (1:16-18), the author of the first letter (3:1), although probably he used, as before, the services of a secretary, who gave the letter its final form. This letter is addressed to the same people as the first and it was written from Rome, a year before Peter's martyrdom. In it he seeks to warn Christians to keep away from the heresies and errors of the Simonites and the Nicolaitans, forerunners of that Gnosticism which wrought such havoc among Christians in the following century. He directly refutes the error of those who try to downplay the importance of the judgment of God, those who deny the Second Coming, making out that the world will continue indefinitely. Those who are born of God and have become "partakers of the divine nature" (1:4), should believe whatever the Son of God

3 Vatican II, Dogm. Const. *Lumen gentium* 34.

has revealed, what they have heard spoken by the "voice from heaven" (1:16), paying attention to this "as to a lamp shining in a dark place, until the day dawns and the morning star rises in your hearts" (1:19). Finally, the head of the Apostles invites them to practise truly Christian lives, and not "be carried away with the error of lawless men and lose your own stability" (3:17).

He also recommends patience: the Lord will not be slow to keep his promises. Christians should realize that with God there is no time: to him everything is a continuous present; what to us seems delay is really nothing other than a sign of the patience and mercy of God, who wants all men to be saved and to come to the knowledge of the truth (1 Tim 2:4). But we should not fall asleep or act presumptuously: repentance and conversion should be a daily experience for us, for we do not know when God will call us to account.

1-3 St John

Three letters are attributed to St John. The first, written from Ephesus towards the end of the first century, carries no opening greeting and no sign-off but John's authorship is apparent from the content. He who has heard, seen, looked upon and touched with his own hands the word of life (1:1) bears witness so that all may know what was revealed from the beginning. The letter has very much the same tone as the fourth Gospel and it has been described as a kind of introduction to the Gospel. The writer seeks to show, in this letter also, the divinity of Jesus Christ and to confront the heresies which were beginning to make inroads among the Christians of the time. Therefore, it contains the same type of doctrine as is found in John's Gospel. Starting out from the Word who is life, truth and love, as befits one who exists for all eternity, one who gives existence to all things, it draws the logical conclusion: that is, it spells out the consequences this has for those whom grace has made children of God, even though they be still sinners.[4]

4 By Baptism we have been justified, sanctified, called to full communion with God. But anyone who believes that during his earthly life he can stay free from sin would be mistaken. All of us are sinners — with the exception of the Blessed Virgin, who by a singular grace of God was "conceived without any stain of sin, in anticipation of the merits of Christ Jesus, the Saviour of the human race" (Pius IX, Bull *Ineffabilis*, 8 December 1854). Everyone else, even the just, was born in sin, and no one can say that he is free of sin in this life. If he dared to do so he would be contradicting God, who has explicitly said that all men are sinners (cf. Ps 13:3; Prov 20:9; Eccles 7:20).

In essence the letter deals with the love of God and of the brethren which are the hallmark of the Christian. For "if anyone says 'I love God', and hates his brother, he is a liar; for he who does not love his brother whom he has seen, cannot love God whom he has not seen. And this commandment we have from him, that he who loves God should love his brother also" (4:20-21). As we have seen in many places, the commandment of fraternal love is an old commandment: God always wanted us to love others and he made this a basic commandment for the people of the Old Alliance (Lev 19:18). But it is also a "new" commandment because it finds its fullest meaning in Christ's life and teaching (Jn 15:12-13). Through fidelity to this commandment, Jesus said, "all men will know that you are my disciples" (Jn 13:35). Therefore, "he who hates his brother is in the darkness" (1 Jn 2:9).

St Jerome tells us that when John was a very old man his only message was "little children, love one another." And when his disciples asked him why he was always saying the same thing he always replied, "My children, this is what the Lord commands; if we do this, nothing else is necessary." The reason for this is that there is no other way to conquer the world, which is God's enemy. St John sums up in this way the things which separate us from God: "the lust of the flesh" — disordered love of pleasure, surrender to the sensual part of our nature; "the lust of the eyes", that is, disordered love of things, which leads to envy etc; and "the pride of life", which is the root of the more internal vices of pride, ambition and vanity. All this comes from the world insofar as it is at odds with the will of God.

St John's second letter is addressed to "the elect lady and her children" — a symbolic reference to a church, which we cannot identify, which is under threat from false teaching. While expressing his joy at its perseverance in the faith, St John exhorts the Christians of that church to practise charity and fraternal love as the best weapons for combatting heresy.

The third letter, which is very short, is addressed to Gaius, a Christian in a church of Asia Minor, for whom the Apostle has special affection. He praises Gaius' faith and charity, but upbraids Diotrephes for refusing hospitality to pilgrims.

St Jude

Jude, surnamed Thaddeus, was one of the Apostles, "the brother of James" (1:1) and therefore one of the "brothers of the Lord" (Mt 13:55; Mk 6:3). His short letter was accepted as canonical from the very beginning, although some people cast doubt on its inspiration on the grounds that it quotes the apocryphal book of Enoch and the "Assumption of Moses." But just as St Paul twice quotes Greek poets in his letters, so Jude cites these works, which were held in high regard in his time, to illustrate a point of doctrine. That is the opinion of Clement of Alexandria, Origen, Tertullian, St Athanasius and St Cyril of Jerusalem, to mention a few. This letter was formally included in the canon by the Council of Trent.

Jude sent this letter, written between 62 and 66 (the years St James and St Peter, respectively, died) to "those who are called, beloved in God the Father" (1:1), that is, to Christian converts from Judaism who at this time were scattered throughout the Roman empire. It is probable that he avails of the death of St James to use his authority to warn these Christians to be on their guard against false teachers who attempt to subvert their faith. He speaks in the same language as we find in the preceding letters, especially the second letter of St Peter. The two letters are so alike that some scholars claim that Jude derives from *2 Peter*. But St Jude's does seem to be earlier than St Peter's; what is said in summary form in *Jude* seems to be amplified in *2 Peter*, with some of the passages clarified.

Essentially, what the letter says is this:

1. God the Father (1b) is the source of grace and authority. From him comes salvation for all men (1:5).

2. In the present economy of salvation, Jesus Christ, who is our Lord and Master (4b), speaks through the Apostles (17).

3. It is the Holy Spirit who maintains us in the love of God (20); in him we find hope of attaining eternal life (21).

4. The Christian has received a divine vocation, which derives from God's love. He is destined to live by faith, keeping to the teaching he has received from the Apostles, provided he is motivated by charity. That charity will give him apostolic zeal. But if he neglects charity and seeks disordered pleasure (12, 16) his faith will founder (4, 8) and he will be punished (14-15).

The Apocalypse or Book of Revelation

The last book in the biblical canon of the New Testament is the book of the *Apocalypse* (= *Revelation*), written by St John towards the end of the reign of Emperor Domitian (95 A.D.), when he was in exile on the island of Patmos. St John's authorship is affirmed by St Justin, St Irenaeus, Clement of Alexandria, Tertullian and the Muratori fragment, — really by the entire tradition of the Church from the second century forward. The doctrine contained in this book and that in the fourth Gospel run parallel to each other, but naturally the two books differ in language and style because they belong to different genres. To give just one example: St John is the only inspired New Testament writer to call our Lord the *Logos*, a description which we find both in the *Apocalypse* and in the fourth Gospel. Also both books have a pronounced preference for contrasts: such as light and darkness, truth and lies, life and death, the Lamb and the Beast, Jerusalem and Babylon, the archangel Michael and the Dragon, etc.

Its genre and purpose   The last book of the Bible belongs to the genre of apocalyptic literature, a variant of prophetical literature differing from the latter in that prophecy takes, as its point of departure, human events, judging them in the light of the Covenant, whereas an apocalypse is a revelation which God communicates to man by projecting a vision of the future, although sometimes it does make reference to present, historical events insofar as they help to announce future events.

However, the aim of the *Apocalypse* — the most difficult book of the Bible to interpret — is eminently practical. It contains a series of warnings addressed to people of all epochs, for it views from an eternal perspective the dangers, internal and external, which affect the Church in all epochs.

As far as external perils are concerned, the book uses as its starting-point the persecutions the early Christians suffered from the time of Nero onwards, particularly those experienced in Rome and in Asia Minor, which were the places where Christianity had put down its deepest roots. Internally, the danger came from heresies, which were beginning to develop, and from defections which were beginning to undermine the unity of the Church, a situation not helped by those who had lost the fervour of their first charity (2:3-7). Many Christians thought that, after the destruction of the Temple of Jerusalem (in the year 70), after which Judaism was no longer a threat of any kind, the Church would enter into an era of peace and tranquillity; instead, they had to cope with new and very violent persecutions: more obstacles — and more formidable ones — seemed to face them. Inevitably they asked: When will our Lord show himself and come to the rescue of his own and establish his kingdom once and for all? In the *Apocalypse* St John — inspired by God — tries to answer this question. The first thing which God has given him to "see" is that the Redeemer is indeed triumphant and that the faithful are victors with him. But he also points out that the Church will be persecuted throughout its pilgrim way on earth, and the faithful will suffer the same lot, if they stay united to the Lamb. The powers of darkness will make war unceasingly against the Spouse of Christ, and will try to undermine the faith of believers. But they should not be dismayed: the Church will always triumph over its persecutors, and in union with the Church the faithful who stay true to the end will also achieve victory.

St John, therefore, identifies the prime enemy of the Church in his own time as the Roman empire (= the beast), the tool of the Dragon (= Satan). Because it has prostituted itself (Babylon = Rome) it cannot win. It will be completely overthrown and the Church is sure to triumph.

This prophecy is as it were the hub of the Apocalypse. Around it St John gradually unfolds the plan God has for the future of his Church. To do this he uses images very like those used by the prophets of old (Ezechiel, Daniel, Zechariah) to predict these persecutions, all these predictions being only an echo of what Jesus himself foretold: "In the world you have tribulation, but be of good cheer, I have overcome the world" (Jn 16:33; Lk 18:7ff). Then, as now, all that the faithful need do to obtain victory like their Master, is to persevere until the end. As our Lord promises: "Be faithful unto death, and I will give you the crown of life" (Rev 2:10ff), for "behold, I am coming soon, bringing my recompense, to repay everyone for what he has done" (22:12)

Symbolism and realism In a series of elaborate and beautiful images St John goes on to develop in successive cycles the subject with which he opens his book. To understand his meaning correctly it is important to realize that apocalyptic literature goes in for a great deal of symbolism — concrete material things being used to convey spiritual realities beyond the grasp of man's mind. Among the symbols St John uses are these:

— *colours:* white is the symbol of victory and of purity
scarlet, of luxury and extravagance
red, of violence
black, of death
green, of decomposition

— *numbers:* seven is the symbol of completeness or fullness
six, of imperfection (7-1)
twelve, of Israel, old and new
four, of the created world (the four elements: air, earth, fire, water; the four parts: sky, earth, sea, abyss; the four points of the compass)
one thousand, a figure used to represent a long period or something vast

— *things:* a lampstand symbolizes a particular church
seven burning lamps or seven eyes, the seven spirits of God
the seven heads of the Beast are the seven hills (of Rome) or else seven kings
the stars represent the angels
linen, being white, symbolizes the good work done by the faithful

Although Jesus Christ, because he was God, knew the entire course Church history would take, he never wanted to speak very explicitly about future events. This is why, like the prophets, he chose apocalyptic language — then in frequent use — when he predicted the destruction of Jerusalem and the perils his disciples and their whole generation would experience. Thus, for example, he had warned:

> For as the lightning comes from the east and shines as far as the west, so will be the coming of the Son of man. . . . Immediately after the tribulations of these days the sun will be darkened and the moon will not give its light, and the stars will fall from heaven, and the powers of heaven will be shaken; then will appear the sign of the Son of man in heaven (Mt 24:27-30).

Our Lord is referring here not only to the end of the world nor to this being the result of some sort of cosmic cataclysm, though that could be a legitimate thesis. He is simply (cf. *Daniel* and *Ezechiel*) telling us to be on guard against unfaithfulness: he uses the event of the fall of Jerusalem in the year 70 as a vivid illustration.

A message of suffering and hope   As a revelation of the course Church history will take the *Apocalypse* seems to divide into three parts: an introduction (1:1-8), an epilogue or conclusion (22:6-21) and a series of teachings (1:9-22:5) which in turn can be divided into three parts:

1. In a vision in which he sees the Redeemer (1:9-3:22) John is charged with writing to the seven churches of Asia Minor. The content of these letters stresses the danger resulting from incipient heresy, opposition from the Jews (the synagogue of Satan) and some Christians' lack of zeal and true charity. It should be pointed out that John writes to only seven churches but the figure seven symbolizes totality, completeness, and therefore in fact he is addressing the entire Church on behalf of "him who is and who was and is to come"; Jesus is lord of time, because he is eternal — which is reminiscent of the revelation God gave to Moses when Moses asked him what his name was: "I am who I am" (Ex 3:14).

2. In the central part of the book St John has a series of visions, in this order:

— transported to heaven, he sees God's throne and court (chap. 4). Here Jesus will be enthroned as Redeemer, symbolized by a slain Lamb.

— the Lamb opens the seven seals, letting loose all the evils which will plague the world (6-8:1).

— then comes the vision of the seven trumpets, which are sounded to announce a series of divine punishments (8:2-11:18).

— St John also sees the seven signs of the incarnation of the Son of God, the incarnations of the dragon, and, finally, the visitation of God's judgment (11:19-14:20).

— another portent is the seven bowls of God's wrath against Rome (15-16), with the announcement of the judgment which will be meted out to Rome, of the destruction of Rome and the consequences which will follow it (17:1-19:21).

— finally, we are given the prophecy of the millenium and of the battle against Gog and Magog (20:1-10).

Over the centuries, many interpretations have been offered of the "thousand years", but most have made the mistake of identifying it with a particular time when the world will come to an end. St John refers to the power of the dragon (Satan) being controlled by a superior power (Jesus Christ, who will vanquish the devil by dying on the cross) for a thousand years (a symbolic number indicating the time that must pass between the beginning of Christianity and the end of the world). Before the world comes to an end Satan will be let loose for a while (the reign of the Antichrist) and then he will be destroyed for all eternity.

3. This central part of the book closes with the last judgment (20:11), the new Jerusalem and the glory the saints will enjoy in heaven. We should remember that this glory, in which the bodies of the saints will share on the day of the final resurrection, involves also the renewal of all creation ("a new heaven and a new earth"), because thanks to the redemption all created things will share in the incorruptibility of glorified bodies (cf. Acts 3:20-21): this is the new Jerusalem, of which the Church during its sojourn on earth is the type and figure.

To sum up, we can say that the message of *Revelation* is a message full of hope, albeit in the midst of tests which those who remain firm in the faith will always undergo. It is a message which applies to all men of all periods, because all will be besieged by a series of external perils and particularly internal hazards, hazards whose source lies in the after-effects of original sin — ambition, pride, greed, sensuality, indolence etc. However, Jesus Christ will always stay with his Church, and therefore the Church's ultimate victory is assured, which is why the *Apocalypse*, the "eternal good news" (it has been called "the eternal Gospel") is to be proclaimed to those who dwell on earth, to every nation and tribe and tongue and people" (Rev 14:6).

The entire theology of the book of *Revelation* consists in an inspired poem about the Son of God. The sacrificed and risen Lamb is the focus of the struggle between the city of God and the city of Satan: to him will go both heaven and earth. *Revelation* is the final synthesis of the ideals and aspirations of the New Testament, and the prophecy of the new or last times, that is to say, of the messianic era, the definitive era ushered in by the incarnation of the Word.

This was the hope which inspired St John's life and which he passed on — as he expressly states in the last verse of the book. These echo the original source from which the revelation comes, to him who bears witness to everything that has been revealed and who says: "Surely I am coming soon." For St John this is what really matters, as he logically expresses in his final prayer: "Come, Lord Jesus!", which is, a sort of last golden clasp on the *Apocalypse* and on the entire revelation begun with the books of the Old Testament. It is a prayer which should be frequently on our lips, to have the Lord fill our lives, our actions, sufferings and joys, until that day comes when — by his good grace — we see him face to face in heaven.

Appendix 1   Glossary

Alliance: see *Covenant*

Angels: entirely spiritual creatures, members of the court of heaven, messengers and intermediaries between God and man. Angels sometimes are sent by God with the mission of executing some punishment (cf. Ex 12:23; 2 Kings 19:35); others are sent to guard nations and individuals (cf. Ex 23:20; Dan 10:13). God sent Raphael (= God heals) to accompany Tobias on his journey, appearing to him in the form of a man. Michael (= who is like God) is the great prince who defends God's faithful (cf. Dan 12:1). Gabriel (= God's strength) told Daniel the way God would restore the fortunes of Israel from the time of the return from exile to the coming of the Messiah (Dan 9:21; 8:15); it is also he who is sent to announce to the Virgin Mary that Jesus Christ will be born of her by the work of the Holy Spirit.

There are myriad angels (cf. Gen 32:1ff; Heb 2:3; Dan 7:10); in the Bible they are divided into a series of hierarchies — seraphim, cherubim, thrones, principalities and powers.

Baal: the name common to all the Phoenician gods, which means simply 'Lord'. In the plural it is used to refer to idols. Baal and Astarte were the two Canaanite gods in this period (Judg 2:13). Baal was the masculine divine principle and Astarte (= *Istar* in Assyrian and *Asherah* in the Bible) Baal's consort, the goddess of love and fertility.

Canon, biblical: this is the Church's official list of inspired books; by including a text in its canon the Church is defining that it is inspired by God and is free from error. However, it is theoretically possible that some text exists which *is* inspired but is not in the canon. Inspiration is the work of God, canonicity the work of God and of the Church, to which he has entrusted the deposit of faith.

Christ: this word comes from the Hebrew *masîah* (= anointed). It was applied as a name to those who received sacred anointing, priests and kings alike, when they were being given the mission of guiding or governing Israel on God's behalf (Ex 28:41; 1 Sam 2:35). However, from the second century B.C. this title was used exclusively to designate the Messiah, the anointed *par excellence*.

Circumcision: practised also by other ancient people, this was made the sign of the covenant between God and Abraham (cf. Gen 17:10ff), establishing a sacred bond between God and the chosen people: circumcision will remind all future generations that they belong to the people of Israel, and of the obligations which flow from that fact. However, as time went by circumcision became a mere external rite, forever being denounced by the prophets, who called for circumcision of the heart (Jer 4:4; Ezek 44:7) — sincerity in all one's actions, and obedience to God's laws. With the coming of Jesus Christ circumcision was abolished and its place taken by the sacrament of Baptism, in which all its spiritual implications survive in a supernatural form (cf. Acts 15:9-29; Col 2:11, 2 Pet 3:21).

Covenant: the pact (from the Hebrew *berith*) made by God in fulfilment of the promise he made our first parents (Gen 3:15); really a bilateral contract, perpetual and inviolable, sworn by God himself. The Covenant emerges at three points in history: a) the Covenant with Abraham (patriarchal period) when God undertakes to form a people (Gen 15) of the line of Abraham, a people whom he will greatly bless; b) with Israel, in the Sinai wilderness, made through Moses (Ex 19-23), which makes Israel God's very own people; c) with David (2 Sam 7), from whose tribe will arise the kingdom of Judah and the Messiah. Finally, Jesus Christ seals with his blood a New and definitive Covenant in place of the provisional or Old Covenant.

Day of atonement: on this day (cf. Lev 16) sins and effects of legal uncleanness were blotted out. No one was allowed to enter the "holiest place" — except the high priest, once a year, on the day of atonement (now *Yom Kippur*). The rite he performed symbolized the definitive atonement for sin, to be effected by Jesus Christ's sacrifice on the cross.

Day of Yahweh: this is the name given in the Bible to the long-awaited but indefinite point at which God will dramatically intervene in favour of his people. The prophets described this day as the day of judgment, when the just would be rewarded and sinners punished (cf. Amos 5:18; 8:9). In the New Testament this day is referred to as a *parousia*, when the Lord will make his appearance (cf. Luke 17:22-37). With an eye to this day the faithful are recommended to be watchful and to have good works to show (cf Mt 24:37ff).

Decalogue: the ten commandments (Ex 20:2-17) given directly by God to Moses, precepts exclusively religious and moral in character, valid for all men of all times. The decalogue is the principal law of the Covenant, summarizing the basic principles of the natural law. The Gospel incorporated and perfected the decalogue, so that these commandments form part of the Church's endowment (cf. Mt 5:17-47). The so-called "code" of the Covenant (cf. Ex 21:1ff) was structured like a set of civil laws and was promulgated by Moses in God's name. Compared with the commandments — the moral law — it was on a lower level and conplemented them. Some of these laws were perfected by the Gospel (cf. Mt 5:21-47), while others were abrogated.

Devil: see *Satan*

Diaspora: a Greek word meaning dispersion. The Jews of the Diaspora were those who stayed in foreign lands after the exile, or who were imprisoned later and led captive into foreign territories. These Jews organised themselves into small communities and were treated as far as civil law went as if they were Romans: their religion was respected and recognized by the law. They enjoyed the exclusion from military service and were treated very favourably by the Caesars. They had synagogues in most important cities: from the second century B.C. there were a number of synagogues in Rome. Jews of the Diaspora translated the Bible into Greek (the Septuagint version) and were of assistance in the spread of the Church in that they allowed the Apostles to preach in their synagogues. One of the main concentrations of the Diaspora was in Alexandria, where as early as the fourth century B.C. it is reckoned there lived some 120,000 Jews.

El Shaddai: God uses this name to show himself as the Almighty. The word is an emphatic plural of *sad* (= powerful), which comes from sādad (= to act with force), indicating God's omnipotence. God sees us; nothing is hidden from him. Our lives should be such that all we do can bear God's inspection.

Gehenna: received its name from the valley of Hinnom, on the south of Jerusalem. In another period this valley was profaned by sacrifices to the God Moloch (cf. Lev 18:21). There was always a fire smouldering in Gehenna, which was used as the city dump — which was why the name Gehenna was given to hell, symbolizing the unquenchable fire into which the damned are sent (cf. Mt 5:22-29; 10:28).

Hell: see *Gehenna, Sheol*

High places: these (cf.1 Sam 2:12) were shrines close to towns; in the earlier period, according to the Canaanite custom, sacrifices were offered to the god Baal at the high places (cf. Jud 6:25). Later, this was replaced by the worship of Yahweh and the high places were tolerated for quite some time (cf. 1 Kings 3:4), until eventually they were banned by the law (2 Kings 23:8) which confirmed that there should be only one shrine/sanctuary/Temple (Deut 12:2).

Inspiration: inspiration is a gift or charism given by God to man, not for his own sanctification but for the good of the Church. In the Bible context it means a divine grace or supernatural influence by which God enlightens the mind of the hagiographer or sacred writer and assists his will to enable him to write down faithfully and without error whatever God communicates to him. The net effect of this is that God is truly the principal author of the book, because whatever the human author affirms is something affirmed by the Holy Spirit himself (cf. Dogm. Const. *Dei Verbum* 11).

Jews: in 2 Kings 16:6 the sons of Israel or the Israelites are described in the Bible as "Jews" for the first time. When the northern kingdom collapses and its ten tribes are deported, only the tribe of Judah (and part of the tribes of Simeon and Benjamin) remains. Later, when the southern kingdom falls and after the Babylonian exile, only a remnant of the tribe of Judah return to their fatherland. From this point onwards the name Judea refers to the main part of Palestine, and the Israelites are described as Jews.

Judaism: Judaism was founded by a decree of Artaxerxes (Ezra 7:12-26). Apparently formulated by an influential Jew in Artaxerxes' court, the decree permitted Jews living in exile in Babylon to re-establish themselves in Judea. The decree also accented the Mosaic law as the civil law of Judea, from this point onwards obligatory on all inhabitants of Israel (cf. Esd 6:12ff). By recognizing the Mosaic law Artaxerxes gave the Jews rights such as they had never dreamed of obtaining.

Levirate marriage: The law (Deut 25:5-10) allowed a childless widow to marry her husband's brother and closest relative to produce an heir of the first husband. If the relative did not exercise this right he was regarded as behaving dishonourably and the moral duty passed to the next nearest relative. It was regarded as a great disgrace not to have descendants (cf. 2 Sam 14:7).

Messiah: see *Christ.*

Parousia: a Greek word meaning "coming" or "presence", used in the Greco-Roman period to offer to the ceremonial visit of an important personality. In the New Testament the word also means "presence" (1 Cor 2:12) and "coming" (1 Cor 15:23), though not always necessarily referring to the physical coming of the Lord at the end of time. For example, some passages refer to the Parousia as a special presence, through which our Lord will manifest his power when he comes to establish his messianic kingdom (the Church). Some of those who heard Jesus speak knew that they would see him come (Mt 16:28) — as happened when Jerusalem fell and the Temple was destroyed (Mt 24:3ff; Lk 21:7ff). This particular parousia is connected with the "day of Yahweh" the prophets speak of (Is 2:12; 13:6), in that it was one of the Lord's dramatic interventions in history and in the lives of individuals. The final Parousia, however, is connected with the last coming of the Lord, at which point the earthly phase of the kingdom of God will be brought to a close, with the resurrection of the dead, the Last Judgment and the handing over of the elect to God the Father (1 Cor 15:22-28; 50-57).

Passover: the most solemn feast of the chosen people (cf. Ex 12:1-11). Its name comes from the Hebrew *Pasaj* (= passing over, passing by without stopping) and commemorates Yahweh passing over his people. While Egyptians were lamenting the death of their firstborn, God "passed over" the homes of the Israelites whose lintels had been smeared with the blood of the lamb, without causing any harm. The Jewish pasch thus was a figure of the Christian pasch, which brings about our true liberation, not from the yoke of Egyptian slavery but from sin and from the yoke of Satan. The Jewish paschal lamb is a figure of Christ, the Lamb of God (Jn 1:29), who saved us from sin and death by his death on the cross.

Pharisees: these were laymen opposed to the priestly aristocracy of the Saduccees. In Jesus' time they constituted a Jewish sect. Devoted to the study of the Torah (Law) and the traditions of the fathers (Mishnah) they were held in high regard by the people. Despite the soundness of their teaching (Mt 23:3) they were over-rigid in their interpretation of the law, especially regarding the sabbath, legal impurity and tithes — points on which they were continually in dispute with Christ. Our Lord's severe condemnation of them referred not to their teaching but to their pride and hypocrisy (cf. Lk 1:37-44), which the Baptist had earlier criticized (Mt 3:7). But some of the Pharisees were fine people — for example Gamaliel, Saul before his conversion, Nicodemus, Joseph of Arimathea.

Publicans: Roman provinces were taxed to provide Rome with revenue. Palestine was in this position during the period of the Roman empire. The collection of tribute was rented out to private individuals in the various localities (*publicani*), people who were therefore hated on account of the huge sums of money they controlled and because they were collaborators of the Romans. They were often regarded in the same way as sinners (Mt 9:10) and having any contact with them was a cause of scandal. However, some of them were quite decent people, such as Zacchaeus (Lk 19:2) and Levi (Mt 10:3).

Remnant of Israel: prior to the exile, the Prophets spoke of two kinds of remnant — the *historical* remnant, made up of that part of the chosen people which had survived punishment, and the *eschatological* remnant, consisting of those who would attain salvation (cf. Mic 5:6ff; Is 4:4; Jer 23:3). After the exile the notion of the "faithful remnant" appears — the people who were regarded as heirs of the promises (Is 49:3). From this remnant would emerge the Servant of Yahweh.

In the New Testament the faithful remnant is that part of the chosen people who have believed in Jesus Christ (Rom 11:5): they are the true Israel, thanks to whom the infidelity of Israel according to the flesh will not prevent God from fulfilling his promises (Rom 9:1-7).

Saduccees: one of the main sects in Israel into which Judaism appears to have been divided at the beginning of our era. The declared enemies of the Pharisees, the Saduccees drew their support mainly from the aristocracy and the higher ranks of the clergy. They were tolerant of hellenism and of foreign culture in general, and therefore they had less aversion than the Pharisees to Roman domination. Although they believed in the existence of God, they had not very strong convictions and they fell into serious doctrinal error. They denied, for example, the existence of angels (Acts 23:8), the resurrection of the body, and therefore, very probably, the immortality of the soul.

Samaritans: around the year 710 B.C., after the collapse of the northern kingdom (Israel), the whole region was planted with non-Israelite farmers, shepherds, etc. Initially the religion of these people was pagan (cf 2 Kings 17:29) but later on it became mixed with the worship of Yahweh. Later still they gave up their idolatrous practices and worshipped only Yahweh, like the Jews. However, these Samaritans soon developed marked differences from the Jews, for the only sacred books they recognized were the Pentateuch: they refused to accept the other books on the grounds that they were inventions of the Jews after their return from exile. Another point of friction with the Jews had to do with where worship of Yahweh should be carried out. The Samaritans maintained that the proper place was Mount Garizim, following the practice of the patriarchs, whereas the Jews regarded the temple of Jerusalem as the only valid site (cf Jn 4:20). So the worst insult one could offer a Jew would be to call him a Samaritan (cf. Jn 8:48)

Sanhedrin: there was a tradition that the Sanhedrin was founded by Moses (Num 11:16-17; 24-25). However, except for the coincidence in the number, there was no connexion between the assembly of the seventy elders and the Sanhedrin. There is documentary evidence of the existence of the Sanhedrin in the time of Antiochus IV (233-187). Its members belonged to the priestly aristocracy. This institution was very important during the Seleucid and Roman periods. Under the Romans the Sanhedrin enjoyed very considerable autonomy due to the fact that the Romans had litle desire to get involved in internal Jewish affairs — which they found difficult to fathom. This tribunal was mainly concerned with religious affairs, but it also controlled the administration of justice within its area — short of applying the death penalty. As we have said, it had seventy members, in addition to the High Priest, in three categories — high priests, scribes and elders (cf. Mt 27:41 and par.).

Satan: the name comes from the Hebrew *has-satán* (= the enemy); he is the leader of the fallen angels who rebelled against God's designs. In Greek he is known as the *devil* (= the accuser). Jesus says of him that "he was a murderer from the beginning, and has nothing to do with the truth, because there is no truth in him" (Jn 8:44). As the father of lies he is the open enemy of God and of those who are faithful to God. He can taunt people, but unless he is given permission he cannot read man's conscience or exercise any internal force on man's will. When man is tempted by Satan and commits sin, he does so of his own free will.

Septuagint: the Greek translation of the Bible made over a period by Hebrew scholars (the "Septuagint," taking its name from the Latin word for "seventy") is by far the most important ancient version of the original text. In the fourth century B.C. Greek language and culture began to spread around the whole Mediterranean area; Jews of the Diaspora living in Alexandria (Egypt) produced this version in the course of the third and second centuries B.C.

Servant of Yahweh: prophetic revelation reached one of its highpoints — a disconcerting one — in the songs we find in *Isaiah* (42:1-9). These four songs speak of God's election of the Servant of Yahweh, whom he endows with the spirit of prophecy. The Servant of Yahweh — who is distinct from Israel, which is also given the title of servant — is consecrated by God for a mission of peace which involves instructing and judging all men. But in the third and fourth songs the Servant's ignominious death is foretold, a death in expiation of the sins of all, a death to which he voluntarily gives himself up and through which he will be rehabilitated in glory. This image contrasts with others in the Old Testament depicting the Messiah-King as powerful and victorious. Not surprisingly the Messiah's humble appearance and his passion and death, so clearly foretold in these texts, were a scandal to the Jews, who were expecting a completely different sort of messiah.

Scribe: a description used from the time of the Babylonian captivity onwards and especially from the time of Ezra for a Jew well-versed in the Law of Yahweh — later given the honorary title of doctor of the Law (cf. Lk 10:25). In the absence of prophets, these learned men devoted themselves professionally to the interpretation of Sacred Scripture, effectively forming a body of experts or doctors. They were also given the title of *Rab* (= Master) or *Rabban* (my master or our master). From the beginning they enjoyed the unconditional respect of the ordinary law-abiding Jew (cf 2 Mac 6:18ff; Sir 39:1ff); but centuries later many scribes, through a spirit of intolerance and exaggerated attention to detail actually broke the Law themselves, causing Christ to censure them severely.

Sheol: although its etymology is unclear, Sheol was for the Hebrews the place where the dead found rest when they descended into the depths of the earth (Gen 37:35; Is 14:9). It was "the land of gloom and deep darkness" (Job 10:21; 17:3), where both the good and the bad dwelt (Ps 89:48; Ezek 32:17-33), though with different expectations, for one the reward of the just, for the other the punishment to be meted out to the impious, according to their works, as explained in the wisdom books.

After his death and resurrection Jesus descended into Sheol (1 Pet 3:19), to the bosom of Abraham or the dwelling-place of the just, where they were awaiting their redemption.

"Sign of the times": in biblical language this expression is used to show that the messianic times have arrived. It is therefore a misuse of the phrase to use it, in a religious sense, to refer to events in some particular period which have no connexion with salvation history: trends, cultural fashions, general aspirations of people, etc. The Church, which accepts as divine revelation only what it has received from the Apostles judges every person's problems in the light of that revelation, pointing out what is compatible with God's plans and what is not. It will often have to take issue with what most people regard as good or ideal or progressive.

"Son of man": this is the term God almost always uses to refer to Ezekiel, to underline the infinite distance that exists between God and man. Jesus will apply it to himself in a messianic sense, the sense in which the name was used from Daniel onwards to refer to the coming of the Messiah (Dan 7:13).

Synagogue: from the Greek *sinagogé* meaning assembly, meeting. Originally the synagogue was the place where Jews living outside Palestine gathered for prayer and religious instruction. Synagogues probably first originated in meetings organized by Jews during the Babylonian captivity to keep alive faith in Yahweh and fidelity to the Covenant of Sinai. But later on this institution spread further afield, the word being used to designate both the assembly and the building which used as a house of prayer. The latter was usually rectangular in shape, and originally had no ornamentation of any kind. In a small sanctuary, behind a curtain, the sacred ark was kept, containing the scrolls of Scripture; and in the centre of the room there was a kind of pulpit for the lector and commentator. The seats between the ark and the pulpit were considered as positions of honour, on which Pharisees typically had their eye (cf. Mt 23:6). "Moses' seat" (Mt 23:2) was a special ornamented seat for the leader of the community. Women followed the synagogue ceremonies from a gallery or from either side of the body of the building; and children were given religious instruction in a building alongside. After the destruction of the Temple in the year 70, Judaism retreated to the synagogues, the very survival of Israel in some way depending on this institution.

Tent of Meeting (tabernacle of the Covenant): prior to the building of the First Temple of Jerusalem, the Tent of Meeting was the dwelling-place of God, where he communicated with Moses and the people of Israel during the years the Hebrews spent in the wilderness. It was like a huge portable temple made from acacia wood, overlaid with gold (cf. Ex 25:10-12). The inside of this Tabernacle was divided into two parts by a veil; the inner chamber was the "most holy place" or "holy of holies," where the ark of the Covenant containing the tablets of the Law and the manna were kept.

Yahweh = (He is): God's personal name which he revealed to Moses (Ex 3:13-15) and which is the one most used in the Bible (6,823 times), it is called the "tetragram" after its four consonants. It is an archaic form of the second person singular of the Hebrew verb "to be" — *qal* — which God himself translates as "I am who I am." In the book of *Revelation* our Lord is cast as he who is, was and is to come (Rev 1:4; 11:7) — that is, the eternally present Lord of time, who shapes all the events of history and guides and protects his people in keeping with his promises. This name expresses being *par excellence*, self-subsistent being, absolutely one and simple, to whom our entire life should be directed.

Particularly after the exile in the sixth century B.C. the Jews avoided pronouncing the tetragram, out of respect for God's infinite majesty, but they continued to use the more generic name, Adonai (= my Lord). When the Massoretes (sixth to tenth century A.D.) specified the vowel points, some people pronounced the tetragram with the vowels of *Adonai*, which gave rise to the erroneous reading of *Jehovah* for *Yahweh*.

Zealots: originally this Greek term was used to designate those Jews who were zealous observers of the Law and enemies of foreign domination (cf. 1 Mac 2:50). Later, the same word was used for a revolutionary political faction whose main feature was open resistance to the Romans (cf Acts 5:37). They played an important part in the revolt of 66-70 under the leadership of Eleazar who, after a brave effort to defend the Temple, took refuge in the fortress of Masada until the spring of 73. Flavius Josephus tells us that the Zealots were also known as *sicarii*, because they used carry a little *sicca* (= a dagger). Barnabas probably had been in one of these groups (cf. Lk 23:19). Many exegetes also think that Simon the apostle had been a Zealot; but although he is described as a Zealot in Lk 6:15 and Acts 1:13) it is not certain that he belonged to this revolutionary grouping.

Appendix 2   Chronology of the Bible

This chronology deals with events whose importance is a function of their direct connexion with the History of Salvation. The dates given, particularly the earlier dates, are inexact but approximate. A good biblical dictionary will provide more detailed information.

OLD TESTAMENT

The Patriarchs

Abraham	1850	Election and promise. Moves from Ur of the Chaldees.
Isaac		God renews his promise.
Jacob		The angel changes his name to that of "Israel" (= powerful with God).
Joseph	1700	His brothers sell him into slavery. He brings them to Egypt. The Hebrew people develop.

The Exodus

Moses	1250	God calls Moses. The institution of the Passover. The liberation of the Hebrew people. The Covenant of Sinai.

The entry into the promised land.

Joshua	1200	The passage of the Jordan. The division and conquest of the country.

The Judges

Deborah and Barak	1125	The Canaanites are defeated.

Samuel	1040	Judge and prophet. The shrine at Shiloh.

The establishment of the monarchy

Saul	1030	The theocratic authority of the king. Victory over the Ammonites and Philistines.
David	1010	Takes Jerusalem, Unites the twelve tribes. Jerusalem, the political and religious capital of Israel. Nathan's prophecy promising the Messiah, the son of David.
Solomon	970	Building of the Temple. Marriage with the daughter of Pharaoh. Religious crisis and discontent in the north.

Political and religious schism

The assembly at Sichem	931	Division of the kingdom. Samaria separates from Judah. Jeroboam I reigns in the north (Samaria) and Rehoboam in the south (Judah).

Activity of the prophets

Elijah	874	Ahab marries Jezebel, daughter of the king of Tyre. The cult of Baal begins in the north. Elijah's reaction. The covenant on Mount Carmel.
	870	Jehoshaphat acts against idolatry. Alliance with Ahab.
Elisha	850	Continues the work of Elijah.
Amos and Hosea	750	Prophesy in the northern kingdom and predict terrible punishment if the people do not turn to God.
Elijah and Micah	740	They do the same in the south.

	721	The northern kingdom falls and Samaria is taken by Shalmaneser V and its population deported.
	700	Hezekiah's building works. He conducts the brook Gihon into Jerusalem.
Zephaniah	630	In 622 the book of the Law is discovered. Josiah's religious reforms.
Nahum	612	Prophesies the fall of Nineveh.
Daniel	605	Is deported and then educated at the court of Nebuchadnezzar in Babylon.
Jeremiah	605	Warns Judah of imminent punishment The prophecy about the seventy weeks.

The exile

	598	Nebuchadnezzar II besieges Jerusalem. King Jehoiachim surrenders and is succeeded by his uncle Zedekiah.
Ezekiel	597	First deportation and the end of the kingdom of Judah. Ezekiel is deported and predicts the ruin of Jerusalem.
	589	Rebellion of Zedekiah.
	587	The final destruction of the Temple, and the second deportation to Babylon. Ezekiel in exile become the prophet of hope for the exiles, consoling them and instructing them in the faith.

The return

Persian domination (539-533)	539	Cyrus II, king of Persia, conquers Babylonia.
	538	He signs an edict allowing the Jews to return to their country.
Zerubbabel	520	The start of building of the Second Temple. Samaritan opposition. The activity of Haggai and Zechariah, prophets.

Ezra	458	His mission.
Nehemiah	445	The building of the walls of Jerusalem.

Greek domination
(333-63)   333   Alexander the Great conquers Syria and destroys the Persian empire. When he dies, in 323, his empire is divided: the Ptolemies rule in Egypt and the Seleucids in Syria. Judea comes under the Ptolemies until 197, when the Seleucids take over (197-142).

Antiochus IV
Ephiphanes   167   The period of persecutions begins and hellenization threatens the Jews.
The decrees abolishing Jewish customs.
The Temple is given over to the worship of Jupiter.
Jewish rebellion quickly follows. The deeds of the Maccabees.

145   The beginning of the Pharisee sect. The Qumran community.

John Hyrcanus   134   High priest and ethnarch.
Favours hellenism. Nationalistic messianic hopes grow.

Roman domination
(63 B.C. - 135 A.D.)   Pompey conquers Jerusalem.
Strong religious nationalism.

Herod the
Great   37   Builds the Antonia fortress, his palace in the upper part of Jerusalem, and in the year 20 B.C. starts the reconstruction of the Temple.

NEW TESTAMENT

Reference must be made to the mistake of Dionysius Exiguus (sixth century) who, placing Herod's death in the year 754 after the foundation of Rome, used this to fix the year of Christ's birth (1 A.D. = 754). But we know that Herod died in Jericho in April 750 (= 4 B.C.), and from the massacre of the holy innocents (Mt 2:16) we know that Jesus must have been born almost two years before Herod's death which therefore means he was born around 7-6 B.C., a date which agrees with the edict of Caesar Augustus announcing the census carried out by Quirinius (Lk 2:2)

	7-6 B.C.	**Birth of Jesus**
Herod	4 B.C.	Death of Herod. His body is transferred to Herodion.
	6	Procurators govern Judea and Samaria.
Tiberius	14	Elected emperor of Rome (14-37)
	15	Annas is deposed.
Caiaphas	18	Appointed High Priest (18-36).
Pontius Pilate	26	Appointed procurator (26-36).
	27	**John the Baptist's preaching.** Baptism of Jesus
	28	**Jesus begins his public ministry.**
	29	The beheading of John the Baptist
	30	In April (Nisan), the death and resurrection of our Lord. **Pentecost** (50 days after the resurrection)
	33-34	Death of Stephen. Conversion of Saul The Gospel is preached in Samaria and Antioch.
Herod Agrippa I	44	Orders the beheading of James the Greater, brother of John, and the imprisonment of Peter. Peter is set free by an angel.
	45-49	First apostolic journey of Paul and Barnabas.
	48-49	Council of Jerusalem.
Claudius	49	The Jews are expelled from Rome.
	50-52	Second apostolic journey of Paul.
	53-58	Third apostolic journey of Paul.
Nero	54	Elected emperor of Rome (54-68).
	62	Martyrdom of James the Less in Jerusalem.
	64	Burning of Rome. Persecution of the Christians.
	64-65	Martyrdom of Peter in Rome.
	66	Jewish rebellion.
	67	Martyrdom of Paul in Rome.
Vespasian	69	Elected emperor.
	70	Titus besieges and takes Jerusalem. Destruction of the Temple. Development of the Church.
Domitian	95	Persecutes the Christians and exiles John to Patmos.
	98-100	Death of St John in Ephesus.

Index

The Navarre Bible: New Testament

FACULTY OF THEOLOGY, UNIVERSITY OF NAVARRE

This twelve-volume series consists of: Revised Standard Version Catholic edition with New Vulgate Latin and Commentaries and Introductions by the editor. The commentaries provide explanations of the doctrinal and practical meaning of the scriptural text, drawing on a rich variety of sources, Church documents, the exegesis of Fathers and Doctors, and the works of prominent spiritual writers, particularly Blessed J. Escrivá, who initiated the Navarre Bible project.

'We heartily and strongly recommend this splendid volume [St Mark]. It is just what so many have been waiting for' Wm. G. Most, *Homiletic & Pastoral Review*.

'This [Acts] is a superb volume for adult Bible study as well as college and university work; most helpful, enlightening and fascinating' David Liptak, *Catholic Transcript*.

'What I find most useful in this edition is its attitude to Scripture. The Gospels are presented unambiguously as the inspired Word of God and, with the help of commentaries, we are introduced to two thousand years of contemplative Christian reading and living of the sacred word. This edition is both prayerful and, in the true sense of the word, scholarly' Andrew Byrne, *Osservatore Romano*.

'It has appeal for the specialist as well as general readership, as much of the commentary consists of a selection of the most interesting observations from two thousand years of scholarship' *Catholic Weekly*, N.S.W.

'It is refreshing to come across a non-technical commentary which ... seeks to expound the Word of God according to the accumulated wisdom of the Church. Most people desiring to understand Scriptures are looking for something that will deepen their reverence for the Word of God, help them apply it to their daily lives, and move them to prayer' *Faith Magazine*.

The Navarre Bible: single volumes (pbks)

St Matthew	*Thess. & Pastoral Epistles*
St Mark	*Captivity Epistles*
St Luke	*Corinthians*
St John	*Hebrews*
Acts of the Apostles	*Catholic Epistles*
Romans & Galatians	*Revelation*